TIMOTHY PICKERING
AND AMERICAN DIPLOMACY
1795–1800

INTERNATIONAL RELATIONS SERIES

Timothy Pickering

AND

AMERICAN DIPLOMACY

1795 – 1800

BY

GERARD H. CLARFIELD

UNIVERSITY OF MISSOURI PRESS

COLUMBIA · MISSOURI

Frontispiece portrait is from the collection of
Arthur T. Lyman. Used by permission.
Photograph by Harding-Glidden Inc.

Standard Book Number 8262–8414–0
Library of Congress Card Number 69–13333
Printed in the United States of America

FOR JULIE

PREFACE

$\mathcal{T}$ IMOTHY PICKERING, who served as Secretary of State to both George Washington and John Adams, has in general been over-looked by historians of the Federalist period. Most have probably ignored him, together with the Secretary of the Treasury, Oliver Wolcott, Jr., and James McHenry, the Secretary of War, because it has been assumed, as Gilbert Chinard wrote many years ago, that all three "were Hamilton's creatures and devoted to their chief." In 1957, however, Stephen Kurtz, in his fine study *The Presidency of John Adams*, added a corrective to this view by pointing out that, although McHenry and Wolcott were more or less unquestioning supporters of Hamilton, Pickering was not.

In fact, Timothy Pickering was very much his own man. A chronicle of his relationship with Alexander Hamilton, for example, would show that, while the former Secretary of the Treasury did attempt to influence him, the task was difficult and the results were never certain. There are, of course, examples of close coopera-tion between the two, and sometimes Hamilton's influence did prove telling. But then too, Pickering often acted independently and in ways sometimes quite disturbing to the New Yorker. Moreover, and perhaps most revealingly, Hamilton always treated Pickering with deference, clearly feared the Secretary's explosive temper, and was usually careful to avoid disagreement with him. It is simply far too unsafe a generalization, then, to write the vigorous Pickering off as a mere pawn of Alexander Hamilton.

Neither under Washington, who relied primarily upon Hamilton, nor under Adams, who quickly came to distrust his Cabinet, was Pickering allowed a major role in policy formulation. But he was an aggressive man, and, through the day-by-day conduct of affairs, was able to use his position as Secretary of State for a real impact on the course of American diplomacy. That impact was significant, first, because of the overdeveloped sense of independence that was one of the more remarkable aspects of his personality and, second, because he disagreed with the policy of nonentanglement in European politics pursued by both Washington and Adams.

A deep inner need to be independent made it next to impossible for Pickering to act as a subordinate to any man. He chafed at authority and served even the great Washington with some reluctance. John Adams, it is clear, never had his complete support. This need to be independent, so strongly felt, led Pickering to a quite remarkable understanding of his role as a Cabinet officer. He maintained that he was not simply an administrative assistant to the President, but an independent member of the Government. He concluded from this that, if there was even a chance that the Chief Executive might act in a way injurious to the national interest, it was his duty to obstruct the presidential policy. Thus, in order to influence the course of events, he sometimes withheld important information from Washington. John Adams fared even worse. Not only did the Secretary on occasion keep information from him, he frequently lobbied in the Senate against the President's policies and appointments. Indeed, throughout the more than three years of his official relationship with Adams, Pickering followed a generally obstructionist course.

Pickering's independence alone, however, does not fully explain his tempestuous career in the Cabinet. More important was his refusal to accept the principle of political nonentanglement upon which America's foreign policy was in large part based. A deep concern for the security of New England's commerce, an antipathy for the ideology of the French Revolution, and a real sympathy for Britain in her struggle against France, ultimately led the Secretary to the conviction that, so long as the wars of the French Revolution continued, America could be truly secure only in an alliance with England. Although this position was not clearly stated until mid-1798, the twin objectives of Pickering's diplomacy from 1795 onward were to maximize differences between France and the United States while simultaneously eliminating frictions with Great Britain. In his judgment, close rapport with England offered many advantages. It would at once end the threat of British harassment of American commerce, throw the weight of the United States into the scales against the French Revolution, afford British naval protection for American shipping threatened by French cruisers, and lastly, disarm the opponents of government at home. The risk of involvement in European affairs, especially after the spring of 1798, seemed to Pickering worth taking.

John Adams, at least as determined and courageous a man as his Secretary of State, insisted, in contradiction to Pickering, upon maintaining a policy of noninvolvement. Although in 1798, during the crisis with France, Adams favored informal cooperation between the United States and England, he would accept nothing more. A trained diplomatist, he refused to allow either commercial considerations or personal emotion to obscure his understanding of national interest. Above all, he would not be enticed into a needless and dangerous involvement in Europe's power struggle. When, in late 1798, Adams reopened negotiations with France, he and Pickering openly split. A bitter hostility came to characterize their relations, and finally Adams removed Pickering from office.

I am very grateful to the many archivists and librarians throughout the country who were so helpful to me while I was engaged in doing the research for this book. I wish to thank especially the staffs at the Massachusetts Historical Society, the Essex Institute, the Manuscript Division of The Library of Congress, the New York Historical Society, the Pierpont Morgan Library, the New York City Public Library, the Columbia University Library, the University of California Library at Berkeley, and the Sacramento State College Library.

The kindness and cooperation I received everywhere was most gratifying.

To those who helped me in the difficult task of writing I also offer my thanks. Armin Rappaport read the manuscript in its earliest form, made many useful suggestions, and was at all times ready with kind encouragement. Richard E. Fauber and Richard Lower were always available whenever an idea needed talking out, and they, too, often made useful suggestions. Ernie Isaacs was sometimes nothing short of inspirational, and his presence made a tangible difference to me as a historian. Finally, I thank my wife Julie, who read and criticized a good deal of my work, especially in the earlier more difficult phases of the writing. Her criticisms were always helpful and to the point.

G.H.C.

Sacramento, California
July, 1968

CONTENTS

1

BEGINNINGS

IMOTHY PICKERING'S STATURE among the men who shaped events in the early period of the Republic has been dwarfed by the giants among whom he moved. His significance in the formation of the young nation's foreign policies emerges, however, in any study of international relations during the troubled Federalist era, for they bear the stamp of his personality. As Secretary of State during the administrations of Washington and Adams and, later, as a member of the United States Senate and of the House of Representatives, he served his country for over forty crucial years.

The second of two sons and the eighth of Deacon Timothy Pickering's nine children, he was born in Salem, Massachusetts, on July 17, 1745. His family was one of long residence in the community. Indeed, the first Pickering to settle in Salem was five generations removed from the younger Timothy and, according to town records, was living there in 1637.[1]

Pickering's father, the Deacon, was a man of firm and in many ways unusual convictions. As a lay leader of orthodoxy, an abolitionist, and a prohibitionist, he held virtually unchallenged the position

---

[1] Octavius Pickering and Charles W. Upham, *The Life of Timothy Pickering*, I, 3.

of town controversialist. His almost unceasing public criticism of the many influential members of the commercial community who profited from their trade in slaves, molasses, and rum, assured this standing. Both assertive and combative, the elder Pickering always welcomed a good fight and the more public it became the better he seemed to enjoy it.[2]

Some of his contemporaries viewed Deacon Pickering as a hypocrite more intent upon attracting notice to himself than upon achieving social reform. John Adams, for one, sensed sham beneath the Deacon's reforming zeal:

> This man famous for his writings in newspapers concerning church order and government, they tell me is very rich; his appearance is perfectly plain, like a farmer; his smooth combed locks flow behind him like Deacon Cushing's though not so gray; has a quick eye like————: he has an hypocritical demure on his face like Deacon Foster; his mouth makes a semicircle when he puts on that devout face.[3]

Years later, an embittered Adams, writing to his cousin William Cunningham, referred again to the elder Pickering in scathing terms:

> If ever you should see the Salem newspapers, published forty or fifty years ago, you will find them abounding with the writings of the good Deacon, in vindication of rights and prerogatives of the first church of Salem. He became so emboldened by the noise he made, that he wrote and published several letters to the King, subscribed with his name. One part of the public was amused, another diverted, and a third fatigued with his ostentatious vanity for some years.[4]

Although others doubted the Deacon's sincerity, his son saw only strength and great moral purpose in his father's life. "All his actions," he once wrote, "showed that he deemed virtue alone entitled to respect."[5] The younger Pickering would one day demonstrate the

---

[2] James Duncan Phillips, *Salem in the Eighteenth Century*, 266–68.

[3] John Adams, *The Diary and Autobiography of John Adams*, Lyman Butterfield, ed., III, 320–21.

[4] John Adams to William Cunningham, November 25, 1808, *Correspondence Between the Honorable John Adams Late President of the United States and the Late William Cunningham Esq.*, 54–58.

[5] Pickering and Upham, *Timothy Pickering*, I, 6.

same uncompromising, crusading spirit and the same disconcerting belief in his own innate morality.

Self-righteousness, a penchant for reform, and public combativeness were not all that Pickering inherited from his father. A strict Calvinist, the elder Pickering reared his children in the formal Protestant tradition, emphasizing as virtues hard work, frugality, honesty, and order; life he saw as a struggle for purity. Although the son later rejected the orthodoxy of an earlier day, the Calvinist ethic remained an underlying and fundamental principle. Within the private world of the younger Timothy Pickering, there was little room for relativism. People as well as ideas were judged as either good or evil. Man was in a constant conflict with evil, and righteousness was a difficult quality to achieve.

The era into which Pickering was born was one of both passion and reason. It spawned two great political revolutions and simultaneously emphasized a rationalistic philosophy that stressed the importance of social order and cohesion. Pickering, in this sense very much a man of the age, reflected this paradox. While lending support to a revolution, he was throughout his life a passionate defender of social and political order. The emphasis he placed upon order was a product of a peculiar class consciousness that he shared with many men of the eighteenth century. Each person had a place in society commensurate with his economic position and intellectual capacities. Acceptance of class inequality did not conflict with revolutionary ideas, for Pickering was no social revolutionary. Throughout his life he insisted that democracy, with its tendency to blur and destroy class distinctions, threatened that fundamental social stability upon which political order was founded. Recognition of class structure and of its role in the maintenance of social stability was one source of Pickering's fundamentally antidemocratic sentiments.

If an appreciation of the virtues of stability and order was crucial to Pickering's political convictions, a recognition of the importance of commerce was the key to his political ambitions. Salem in the eighteenth century was a bustling commercial town. Trade was its life and the merchants its elite. Politically, socially, and economically, the great trading families, the Pickmans and the Ornes, the Cabots and the Gardners, and later the Crowninshields and the Derbys, ruled.

Commerce, Pickering understood, was the key to power, and power lay with the elite. Prestige and position fell only to those who associated themselves with that group. Although his father had spent a lifetime combating the immoralities of Salem's leadership, Pickering joined those with whom his father had contended and dedicated himself throughout his political career to the advancement of the interests of New England's commerce.[6]

It is not altogether surprising that Pickering emerged as a major public spokesman for New England's commercial interests. Political ambition was an irresistible and driving force within him. Moreover, his commercial orientation was practically dictated by family connections and environment. John Gardner and George Williams, members of two of Salem's most important commercial families, were both brothers-in-law to Pickering. His own father-in-law, Captain Benjamin White, was a ship's master whose home port was Boston. Then too, there were other relatives who, if they were not merchants themselves, shared the commercial orientation of the section and became leading political figures in the period. One brother-in-law, Paine Wingate, served in later years as representative to the Confederation Congress and as United States Senator from New Hampshire; another, Nathaniel Peaslee Sargeant, became Chief Justice of the Massachusetts Supreme Court.[7]

As the son of a prosperous farmer and town leader, Pickering enjoyed many advantages unusual in his time. One of these was an education at Harvard College. In 1763, having spent four years within ivied walls, he returned to Salem, a youth of eighteen, ready to assume his responsibilities as a Pickering. Aided by his family's importance in the town and by his ambitions, he began immediately to carve his own place.[8]

Like most young men, he made false starts. In 1766 he completed work toward a Master's degree at Harvard, probably in preparation for the life of a clergyman — it was fairly general practice among prospective clergymen of the time to take such a degree. But religion as a vocation apparently held few attractions; two years later he was

---

[6] Samuel E. Morison, *Maritime History of Massachusetts*, 167.
[7] Pickering and Upham, *Timothy Pickering*, IV, 393–95.
[8] Phillips, *Salem*, 130.

admitted to the Massachusetts bar and, like so many other public figures of his generation, became a lawyer. The law, however, proved little more interesting to him than had religion, and he never became a practicing attorney.[9]

Even in his early years Pickering showed a deep interest in public administration, military affairs, and politics. It was here that he would discover his place. A position as clerk in the office of John Higginson, register of deeds for Essex County, marked the beginning of Pickering's long administrative career. Simultaneously, his interest in military affairs led him to seek a commission in the Salem Militia. In 1766 he was appointed a lieutenant in the Fourth Company of Foot; in 1769 he was promoted to the rank of captain.[10]

From the very first he demonstrated a serious interest in the establishment of a disciplined militia. The holiday atmosphere that surrounded training days he found appalling, while the lack of military bearing displayed by officers and men alike proved almost more than his orderly mind could tolerate. In 1769 the young officer took up his pen and, under the pseudonym "A Military Citizen," published two articles in the *Essex Gazette*, demanding reform.[11] These articles are significant not only as a manifestation of his intolerance for the democratic — one might almost say anarchical — nature of the militia, they also mark the beginning of a long career of public controversy. Soon, Timothy Pickering, Jr., like his father before him, became known throughout Essex County for the effectiveness of his "Pickeronian pen."

The New Englander emerged as a young man of promise in Salem's affairs at a time when relations between England and the Colonies had begun to deteriorate. By the late sixties the imperial question and local political conflicts had divided the people of Salem. In the beginning Pickering chose the Tory side. Several factors help to explain this choice. In the first place, his rise to military prominence had been supported by Salem's Tory Colonel of Militia William Browne and by the Royal Governors, Francis Bernard and Thomas Hutchinson; in the second, he owed his position in the Registry of

---

[9] Pickering and Upham, *Timothy Pickering*, I, 31.
[10] Pickering and Upham, *Timothy Pickering*, I, 14, 16.
[11] Pickering and Upham, *Timothy Pickering*, I, 16.

Deeds to another Tory, John Higginson. Important too was Pickering's personal distaste for any sort of social disorder. The Stamp Act protests, highlighted by undisciplined mob violence, and agitation in the Colonies over the Townshend duties, naturally tended to drive the conservative young man into the Tory camp. Finally, parental influence may have played a role. Deacon Pickering was a Tory and remained one until his death in 1778.

Despite these influences, in the autumn of 1770 Pickering developed second thoughts about his Tory affiliations and moved over into the Whig coalition.[12] By this time Salem was dominantly Whig and it had become clear that the town's affairs were to be controlled by that faction. Pickering's decision to change sides was in all likelihood based upon consideration of the local political situation and probably had little or no relation to imperial affairs. By the time he switched allegiances, after all, the conflict between the Colonies and England had quieted to a murmur. Most men believed that relations had been stabilized and that the Empire would remain intact. Moreover, it is clear from later developments that Pickering was no vigorous opponent of the imperial system. He was, for example, one of the last to accept the inevitability of armed conflict.

Once Pickering had made his decision, the doors to political advancement in the province opened wide. In 1772 he was elected Selectman of Salem and Town Clerk. Upon Mr. Higginson's death in 1774 he was elected Register of Deeds for Essex County. His appointments as Justice of the Peace, Justice of the Inferior Court of Common Pleas for the county, and Justice of the Maritime Court for

---

[12] Pickering and Upham, *Timothy Pickering*, I, 23–30. At the time that he decided to take the Whig position, he denied that he had ever fully espoused the Tory cause. However, in his personal defense, which was published in the *Essex Gazette* in October, 1770, and which is largely reprinted in the biography, he is clearly squirming. He denies that he "entirely adopted" the political opinions of the Tories, but he admits that for years past he had vigorously disapproved radical violence and that he had been angered by those who allowed themselves to be intimidated by radical mobs. He admits further that on occasion he had said that he himself would rather "perish" than be so intimidated. His closest associates "for three or four years past" had been Tories, while in the past a considerable part of his "conversation turned upon the wicked, selfish motives of some popular leaders, in their opposition to government." Perhaps Pickering is correct in stating that he never "entirely adopted" Tory views. But then, how many Tories had?

the counties of Suffolk, Essex, and Middlesex, followed in quick succession. Not long after, he became a representative from Salem to the Massachusetts General Court.

Like many other conservative men who had joined the Whig faction for local political reasons, Pickering became inextricably entangled on the Whig side of the pre-Revolution turmoil. In 1774 he was elected one of the members of Salem's first Committee of Correspondence. In the following year he became one of thirty members of the Committee of Safety, Inspection, and Correspondence.[13] Throughout the whole period, however, he remained cautious and used his position as a Whig to check the more violent among his colleagues.

Pickering made his conservative position unmistakably clear after the closure of the Port of Boston in 1774. Governor Gage, seeking to divide the colonists, had proposed that Salem replace Boston as the principal entrepôt for New England. The Tory element in Salem rose to the bait by addressing the Governor and "commending to him the trade and welfare of the port of Salem." Timothy Pickering penned the reply of the town's Whigs. Moderate and conciliatory, it nonetheless rejected the proffered advantage:

> By shutting up the Port of Boston some imagine that the course of trade might be turned hither, and to our benefit; but Nature, in the formation of our harbour, forbids our becoming rivals in commerce to that convenient mart. And were it otherwise, we must be dead to every idea of justice — lost to all feelings of humanity — could we indulge one thought to seize on wealth and raise our fortunes on the ruin of our suffering neighbors.

The petition contained no harsh words, issued no threats:

> A happy union with Great Britain is the wish of all the colonies. 'Tis their unspeakable grief that it has in any degree been interrupted. We earnestly desire to repair the breach. We ardently pray that harmony may be restored. And for these ends, every measure compatible with the dignity and safety of British subjects we shall gladly adopt. . . . We assure your excellency we shall make it our constant endeavor to pre-

---

[13] Pickering and Upham, *Timothy Pickering*, I, 34–35.

serve the peace and promote the welfare of the province; and
hereby we shall best advance the interest of our sovereign.[14]

It was only a short time after his election as Colonel of the First
Essex Regiment that he was thrown into the midst of the revolutionary movement and given one more opportunity to demonstrate
his essential conservatism. April 19, 1775, dawned a fine spring day.
Pickering was already at his office at the Registry of Deeds when,
between eight and nine o'clock in the morning, a messenger arrived with news that a force of British regulars had met and fired
upon American militiamen at Lexington. The threatened violence
had finally erupted. The news traveled quickly throughout the
town, and a special meeting was held to decide on a course of action.

At the meeting Pickering argued strongly for restraint. The
British force, he said, would retreat from Lexington; they would
have too great a head start for troops from Salem to catch up with
them. They would soon be in Boston, where attackers would be at
great disadvantage. Others, either more eager for action or concerned lest other towns accuse Salem of shirking her duty, urged
the mobilization of the militia. Pickering objected, but was overruled. Very unwillingly he marched at the head of his regiment
on the road for Boston. At Danvers he halted, ostensibly to wait
for news of the expected British retreat. The men in the ranks,
including "some prominent citizens," grew restive and demanded
a resumption of the march. After still another conference Pickering
agreed. Too late he and his men arrived on the heights overlooking
the road from Cambridge to Charleston. The British force, which
had not stopped at Lexington but had gone on to Concord, was
now ahead of him and unassailable, safely supported by British
artillery. Had Pickering been more of a warrior or more anxious
for conflict, the British column might well have been cut off.[15]

On the following day the Colonel of the Essex Militia attended
a meeting of officers outside Boston. There the energetic Joseph
Warren and others wished to plan strategy for a siege. Pickering
objected. A political settlement upon agreeable terms, he argued,

---

[14] Phillips, *Salem*, 323–26.
[15] Phillips, *Salem*, 72; Arthur B. Tourtellot, *Lexington and Concord*, 201–2.

was still practical. With all the zeal at his command he urged his fellow officers to restrain themselves from military action. Using every argument he could muster, he tried to convince them that a military victory was impossible. With the forces at their disposal, he contended, they could not possibly take Boston; sensible men would return to their homes.[16] On the next day he and the men of the Essex Militia did just that.

The war finally caught up with Pickering; indeed, it caught up with him in full force. While others served, there were few who invested as much time as he or spent so freely of their energies. It was not long after his marriage to Miss Rebecca White that the military phase of his career began in earnest. From December, 1776, until 1785 he served as a colonel of militia, then as The Adjutant General of the Army, next as a member of the Board of War, and finally, from 1780 to 1785, as Quartermaster General of the Army.

In many ways Pickering's wartime experience was disillusioning to him. Quickly enough he came to accept and believe in the Colonies' rationale for rebellion. Thus, for him as for so many others, the Revolution became a struggle not only against an oppressive Ministry but also against the contagion of British corruption. At first Pickering was filled with the provincial's pride in the moral superiority of the Colonies over the mother country. He believed not only in the justice of the American cause, but also in the idea that out of the war would emerge a new, ethically superior civilization, an example for all mankind. His early experience in the Army created doubts. Yet even as he began to realize that his was indeed "a wicked generation," he clung to his hopes for the future. Americans were fighting in "a just cause, on which the happiness, not of innocent Americans only, but of the thousands of poor, oppressed people in every kingdom in Europe, depends." [17]

During the first year of the fighting the Essex militiaman's convictions began to wither. Pennsylvanians, for example, proved "abomi-

---

[16] Pickering to Wingate, April 26, 1775, Timothy Pickering Papers (Massachusetts Historical Society), XVII, 13; Tourtellot, *Lexington and Concord,* 222.

[17] Pickering to Rebecca Pickering, August 29, 1777, in Pickering and Upham, *Timothy Pickering,* I, 152–53.

nable extortioners," demanding "solid coin" in payment for provisions even for the "poor wounded men." Certainly, Pickering came to believe, if the outcome of the war were dependent upon "the goodness" or "the *moral Virtue*" of Americans, there was no chance of victory. Yet, a spark of faith remained in "*the justice of our cause.*" He continued with the conviction that for "the sake of the righteous in the land, . . . God will in the end grant . . . victory." [18]

With each passing month, Pickering learned more fully of the degeneracy of colonial society. Everywhere, it seemed, were to be found those who were willing to corrupt or to be corrupted. In politics the evidences were far too common. "Modes of defrauding the public have taken place which I hoped had been unknown on this side of the Atlantic. And when I view the general depravity of manners, I sometimes almost think Europe does not exceed us in crimes." [19]

When corruption did not rob the innocent, petty politics often did. In Pennsylvania, for example, a purely political squabble between commissioners, appointed by Congress to purchase provisions for the Army, and state authorities blocked purchasing. The Army went hungry while the politicians deadlocked, and a harassed member of the Board of War appealed to the heavens:

> Would to God we had some great, some patriot Pitt, to rescue us from impending danger, and conduct us to victory and glory, by a wise arrangement and vigorous execution of public measures! But where shall the man be found? [20]

Toward the end of the fighting Pickering was ready to admit that American society was generally corrupt. Only the Regular Army remained a repository of virtue. While others had speculated and profited during the conflict, the men of the Continental line had done their duty and had suffered the greatest privations. But how did these virtuous men fare at the hands of the people? They

---

[18] Pickering to John Pickering, September 25, 1777, Pickering Papers, V, 51–52.

[19] Pickering to Rebecca Pickering, January 8, 1778, in Pickering and Upham, *Timothy Pickering*, I, 201.

[20] Pickering to Alexander Scammell, February 17, 1778, Pickering Papers, XXXIII, 178A.

were dispensed with in the most cavalier fashion. While the nation enjoyed the fruits of a postwar boom, the men of the Army were left destitute, with no real hope of receiving even the back pay owed to them. Worse still, while the Army was kept in being, pending the arrival of a definitive treaty of peace, supplies ran short. In the midst of a nation indulging in "a luxury" unknown before the conflict, those who had won it were "left to endure an increase of misery." [21]

Pickering emerged from the war a cynic, confirmed in his conservatism and convinced both of his own righteousness and of his belief that virtue was a commodity in short supply among his countrymen. He was deeply confused by his war experiences. He remained convinced of the justice of the American cause, yet there was much wickedness among his countrymen. Numbers of speculators had made fortunes from the war, while those who had done the fighting were denied even their wages. The ambitious Pickering was bitterly determined, now that the war was all but over, to succeed in trade. Salem beckoned, his friends and relatives urged him to return, but he refused, for in Salem he would always be a second son, doomed to "peddle in trade" or to "starve in public office." [22]

Philadelphia seemed the sensible place to settle. Here he, his wife "Becky," and the boys could make a home. Here too he could, as a commission merchant, profit by his connections in New England. Thus, although he remained a New Englander in spirit, he severed the ties with Salem to remain in Philadelphia, where he joined in partnership with Samuel Hodgdon, a former colleague of his in the Quartermaster's Department. The firm of "Pickering and Hodgdon" never prospered. Commercial dislocations precipitated by the disruption of the old imperial system may have been a factor, or perhaps the new firm could not extend the credit necessary for success in such an endeavor. In any case, in less than two years the business had closed its doors.[23]

---

[21] Pickering to John Pickering, September 22, 1782, Pickering Papers, XXXIV, 38A.

[22] Pickering to Samuel Hodgdon, April 6, 1782, in Pickering and Upham, *Timothy Pickering*, I, 456.

[23] Pickering and Upham, *Timothy Pickering*, II, 175.

In 1784, while still serving as Quartermaster General, Pickering learned that Benjamin Lincoln, the Secretary of War, had resigned. He immediately sought the appointment. He wrote to Elbridge Gerry, the head of the Massachusetts delegation in Congress, pressing his plea. Gerry promised his support but warned Pickering that there were other candidates and that the competition would be sharp. For over a year Pickering, together with his partner Hodgdon and other friends, lobbied for his appointment. In the end, Congress appointed General Henry Knox to replace Lincoln.[24] In the same year Congress voted to eliminate the position of Quartermaster General of the Army, and Pickering's only regular source of income was taken from him.

In the period that followed, Pickering came close to desperation. Denied political position by the Congress and financially pressed by the failure of his mercantile venture, he turned to the wilderness. A man of stubborn pride and vigorous determination, he was ready to carve from nature a position of authority and importance in a new society. With his remaining funds he purchased from the State of Pennsylvania some ten thousand acres of land along the great bend of the Susquehanna River near the New York state line in what was then called the Wyoming Valley.

Pickering's move into the valley seems, in one sense at least, out of character. That a mind trained to frugality and caution should have undertaken a speculative venture is difficult to understand. But Pickering was an ambitious man, hard pressed by both economic and political misfortune. Evidently, he hoped in a new territory to become a leader, an aristocrat. He would keep, he thought, enough land to maintain position as one of the most important men in this new country, but he would, as settlers arrived, dispose of enough of his land at a price sufficient to yield a profit on the venture. Too, Pickering entered the valley not only as a land speculator, but also as an important official of the State of Pennsylvania. In Luzerne County he was to serve as Prothonotary, Register of Deeds, Judge of the Orphans Court, Justice of the Court of General Quarter Sessions, and Recorder.[25]

---

[24] Pickering and Upham, *Timothy Pickering*, I, 494–501.
[25] Pickering and Upham, *Timothy Pickering*, II, 193–95.

Before becoming involved in this new venture Pickering took precautions to assure its success. He realized that an active problem in the Wyoming area was the clearing of titles to land. Land companies chartered in Connecticut had for some time been selling titles to land that was either being sold simultaneously by the State of Pennsylvania or to which there were rival claims founded upon grants made earlier by the Penn family. Pickering received assurances from powerful friends that the Pennsylvania legislature would enact a law guaranteeing the legitimacy of claims made by settlers who had come from Connecticut to the area before 1782. On this point he was insistent; he would not move into the valley or make any effort at establishing county government there unless the state legislature "would quiet" the Connecticut settlers "in their possessions."[26] Only then could there be a chance for social stability and orderly elections; only then would Pickering himself be secure in his holdings.

In early 1787 Timothy Pickering journeyed to the Wyoming Valley and began organizing Luzerne County. At first, matters went well. The Pennsylvania legislature, despite the protests of many Pennsylvania claimants, passed a "quieting act" guaranteeing the legitimacy of all Connecticut claims made prior to 1782. The county was organized and peaceful elections were held. The expatriate New Englander felt confident enough to bring his wife and five sons — one an infant — to live with him in Wilkes Barre.[27]

By the summer, however, the promises of the spring had faded as rumors spread that the Pennsylvania legislature intended to repeal the "quieting act." Moreover, there were many young and determined settlers who had come from Connecticut after 1782 and who were ready to resist eviction from their lands. In such an atmosphere it took little effort by representatives of the Connecticut land companies with claims in the area to stir up trouble. The valley was once again in turmoil and Pickering, as Pennsylvania's chief representative in the area, was a walking target. Violence surged so close about his household that Pickering was once forced to flee

---

[26] Pickering to Henry Pickering, December 31, 1818, Pickering Papers, XXXVIII, 238A.

[27] Pickering and Upham, *Timothy Pickering*, II, 287.

to Philadelphia. On another occasion he was kidnapped by a group of Connecticut claimants who hoped that they could thereby force his intercession in favor of the leader of their faction, whom Pickering had helped arrest and who was jailed in Philadelphia. Characteristically, Pickering was righteously intolerant of the Connecticut demands and, when kidnapped, proved even more stubborn than his abductors. After three weeks of wandering through the wilderness of back-country Pennsylvania the captors turned their captive loose, begging that he overlook their little indiscretion. Perhaps three weeks of Pickering's moralizing on the virtues of law and order had made these lawbreakers repent. It is more likely, however, that his preaching became intolerable and, unable to endure any more and unwilling to risk murder, they allowed him his freedom.[28]

In 1789 the Pennsylvania legislature ended any chance of establishing order in the valley by repealing the "quieting law." A long time was to pass before peace would come, and in the meantime the insecurity of land titles, coupled with the violence in the area, discouraged settlers. Pickering was trapped, unable to dispose profitably of any significant portions of the land he held.[29]

By the spring of 1790 he was looking anxiously for a way out of his predicament. When he heard that William Duer had resigned as Assistant Secretary of the Treasury, he wrote to his acquaintance of Revolutionary days, Alexander Hamilton, asking to be considered for the post. His letter reflected the desperation he felt. He was without funds and in debt. The Wyoming experiment had been characterized, he wrote, by "a train of disasters and a ruinous expense."[30] In his efforts to secure the office, Pickering even enlisted the aid of his brother-in-law Paine Wingate, at the time a senator from New Hampshire, hoping that Wingate could influence Hamilton.[31]

In the end Pickering did not get the position. But influence was at work for him, and a few months later Wingate wrote to inform him that the office of Postmaster General of the United States would

---

[28] Pickering to Henry Pickering, December 31, 1818, Pickering Papers, XXXVIII, 244A–258A.
[29] Pickering to Henry Pickering, December 31, 1818, Pickering Papers, XXXVIII, 258A–259A.
[30] Pickering to Hamilton, April 6, 1790, Pickering Papers, XXV, 88.
[31] Pickering and Upham, *Timothy Pickering*, II, 442.

soon be open and that he might have it if he was interested.[32] Pickering leapt at the opportunity and wrote immediately to President Washington in quest of the position. The President's reply was almost, but not exactly what, the New Englander had hoped. The post he wanted had not yet opened; it would, however, soon be vacant, and Washington virtually promised it to him.[33]

In the interim Pickering was employed on two occasions as a representative of the United States Government to Northeastern Indian tribes. The Northwestern tribes were contesting American sovereignty west of the mountains, in the area between the Canadian border and the Ohio River. Diplomacy required that these tribes be isolated and especially that the Six Nations of the Northeast not join with them in a war against the white man. On two occasions, once in the autumn of 1790 and again in the summer of 1791, Pickering was sent on special missions to the Northeastern Indians. On both occasions his diplomacy proved successful.

Following his return from this second mission Pickering was appointed Postmaster General of the United States. A mature forty-six when he assumed office, he brought to his tasks not only "independence, combativeness and courage," but also a firm and inflexible conservatism tested by the experience of years. He presided over the Post Office Department with admirable efficiency. The same zeal and care for detail with which he handled his position as Quartermaster General of the Continental Army were applied to this new position. Yet, although Pickering's tenure witnessed real growth in both the size of the department and the problems of administration, he introduced no qualitative changes to facilitate this expansion. Even though suggestions came from several directions for the improvement of the department, Pickering maintained intact the bureaucratic establishment he had inherited. This adherence to established routine was indicative of the intellectual characteristics of the man; a conscientious administrator, he lacked not only imagination but the ability to appreciate the insights of others as well.

The years as Postmaster General were pleasant. Philadelphia, the

---

[32] Wingate to Pickering, August 2, 1790, Pickering Papers, XIX, 192.
[33] Pickering and Upham, *Timothy Pickering*, II, 458–60.

most important city in the new nation, was once again home, and
the transplanted Yankee had few bases for complaints. His life became gratifyingly arranged around his work. The postal department
became a barony that he ruled with single-minded dedication to
efficiency, regularity, and order.

Life as Postmaster General, however, was not altogether placid.
As one complication, relations with the Northwestern tribes continued to be badly deranged, and Pickering, perhaps because of his
earlier diplomatic successes, remained involved in negotiations. In
1791 and again in 1792 American forces suffered military defeats
in engagements with the Northwestern Indians. In the spring of
1793, while Anthony Wayne trained his forces for a third thrust
against them, Washington tried diplomacy. Pickering was one of
three envoys chosen for the arduous journey into the Northwest. At
Niagara, under the watchful eyes of the British general John G.
Simcoe, he and his colleagues failed to find peace; the five-month
trek had been in vain.[34]

In the autumn of 1793 Pickering returned from Niagara in time
to witness one of the worst epidemics of yellow fever in Philadelphia's history. It is a testimonial to his and his wife's physical
strength that they survived, despite the fact that they both fell
ill and, in the best medical practice of the time, were bled and purged
by their friend the well-known physician Benjamin Rush. The
tragedy of the epidemic did, however, touch their family. Six-year-
old Edward Pickering died either of the fever, or of the bleeding,
or perhaps of a combination of the two.[35] By early November,
1793, the epidemic had abated and affairs in Philadelphia returned
to normal.

Pickering had arrived at the outskirts of national prominence almost by chance and at a moment of great political and administrative difficulty. The internal heat that developed within the Cabinet
during the first Washington Administration was more than any
government could reasonably have been expected to withstand. Inevitably, forces working from within turned the Administration's

---

[34] Pickering and Upham, *Timothy Pickering*, III, 43–47.
[35] Pickering and Upham, *Timothy Pickering*, III, 58–63.

cracks into fissures and its fabric to ruin. Late in 1793, frustrated by years of futile opposition to the policies of Alexander Hamilton, Thomas Jefferson resigned his position as Secretary of State and returned to Monticello. Next, Hamilton informed the President that he could no longer afford the luxury of retaining the important but impecunious post of Secretary of the Treasury.[36] The Secretary of War, Henry Knox, also wished to resign.[37]

The President was reluctant to surrender the services of either Hamilton or Knox. Positions in the national government, even Cabinet posts, were not easily filled. Salaries were worse than poor. Moreover, power and influence were diffused among the various states, so that men of ability who were willing to serve in political office gravitated, not to Philadelphia, but toward the centers of local power at the state level.

Washington was fortunate to have the younger Oliver Wolcott available as successor to Hamilton. Filling the post of Secretary of War, however, would be more difficult. Having prevailed upon Knox to remain temporarily in office, the President sought a replacement. First, Charles C. Pinckney, the influential South Carolinian, refused the post.[38] Then, his friend Colonel Edward Carrington, would not even consider the office. The President carried on a desultory search until, in December, 1794, Knox resigned.[39] Washington acted almost immediately by promoting Timothy Pickering to the vacancy in his Cabinet.

Certainly the addition of the proud-spirited and provincial New Englander did nothing to improve the quality of the Cabinet. On the other hand, Pickering was unquestionably a capable administrator. He had managed the postal department efficiently and economically. Morever, his service on the Board of War and the five years he had grappled with the enormous problems that confronted the Quartermaster General of the Continental Army could not be ig-

---

[36] Hamilton to Washington, December 1, 1794, *The Works of Alexander Hamilton*, H. C. Lodge, ed., X, 79.

[37] North Calahan, *Henry Knox, General Washington's General*, 310–13.

[38] Washington to C. C. Pinckney, January 22, 1794, *Writings of George Washington*, J. C. Fitzpatrick, ed., XXXIII, 248–49.

[39] Washington to Knox, December 30, 1794, Washington, *Writings*, XXXIV, 76.

nored. He was familiar with the administrative intricacies of his new office, and he had already proven himself capable of handling problems of this nature. Perhaps most importantly, he was available. At best a man of little more than ordinary intellect, Pickering had arrived at a position of national prominence almost by default.

2

THE FIRST ENCOUNTER

ICKERING JOINED THE CABINET at a moment when the nation was about to plunge into the most vigorous foreign policy controversy of a decade marked by controversy. The issue that sharpened the already bitter differences between Republicans and Federalists was ratification of the recently negotiated Treaty of 1794 between England and the United States. At stake was America's future as a trading nation in a world violently torn by the conflict between England and France.

The Treaty of 1794 was the result of urgent negotiations on the part of the American envoy extraordinary to England, John Jay, and Britain's Foreign Secretary, William Wyndham, Lord Grenville. Before Jay had been sent to London, the two nations seemed on the verge of open conflict. For a multiplicity of reasons, some dating back to the Revolution, war seemed unavoidable.[1] The Jay Treaty promised to avert conflict that had seemed inevitable. The cost to America, however, was very great. The treaty not only failed

---

[1] Samuel Flagg Bemis, *Jay's Treaty: A Study in Commerce and Diplomacy*, 265, 269–73.

to provide solutions for many of the irritating issues over which Americans had become aroused during the preceding decade, but it also involved an American surrender of the principle of "freedom of the seas." This was the liberal American interpretation of neutral rights that had been first clearly stated in the Model Treaty of 1776, some of the principles of which were incorporated into the Franco-American agreement of 1778 and which was fundamental to the entire structure of American neutrality.

On several points the Jay Treaty narrowly limited America's rights as a neutral. It defined *contraband* to include not only provisions but naval stores, a group of commodities the United States had always contended was noncontraband and which was not listed as contraband in the treaty between France and America.[2] Nowhere in the agreement was there any definition of a legal blockade. The United States had long urged such a definition and had previously held that, to be legal, a blockade had to be geographically limited in its application. Worst of all, Jay had been forced to submit to the British contention that free ships did not mean that the goods they carried were "free" — safe from seizure. Goods of belligerent nations found on neutral ships, therefore, were not protected from capture by virtue of the carrier's neutral identity. Thus, according to the proposed treaty, French products being carried in American bottoms were subject to confiscation by British cruisers.[3] Because the Franco-American Treaty adhered to the principle that "free ships make free goods," French cruisers were denied the reciprocal right to seize British goods on American vessels. Ratification of the Jay Treaty meant the institutionalization of an inequality in the relationships of the United States, a major neutral carrier, with the two belligerents. This inequality, it was clear, would inevitably cause trouble with the French, who would not long allow the disadvantages of their situation to go unchallenged.

The Jay Treaty was not a direct violation of any of the stipulations of the Franco-American Treaty of 1778. It was, however, an overt

---

[2] Hunter Miller, ed., *Treaties and Other International Acts of the United States of America*, II, 258–59.

[3] Bemis, *Jay's Treaty*, 358, 366. Alexander DeConde, *Entangling Alliance, Politics and Diplomacy Under George Washington*, 109.

repudiation of the "spirit" of that agreement.[4] Moreover, it made it impossible for America to stand as an unqualified neutral in the wars of the French Revolution. The alternatives open to Jay had provided little room for maneuver. He had been faced with the choice of a continuing crisis and possible war with England or an agreement with Britain that would in its application discriminate in favor of the British and against the French.

The passage of the treaty by the Senate in late June of 1795 placed the ultimate responsibility for the future of Anglo-American relations in the hands of President Washington, who was undecided as to whether or not he should ratify the treaty. Fully aware of the shortcomings of the agreement, he was also cognizant of the dangers of a war with Britain.[5] The President's position was made more difficult by the fact that, only a few days following the Senate's action, the exact stipulations of the treaty became known to the public, despite the hopes of both the Administration and the Federalists in the Senate to keep the precise nature of the treaty a secret until after a final decision on ratification had been reached. The leak set off protests throughout the country. From Charleston to Boston, Republican editorialists friendly to France denounced the treaty, while mass meetings and violent demonstrations were held to condemn it.[6] Partisanship now moved onto a defined battlefield.

To a significant degree partisan differences in the 1790's were closely related to economic interests. The Republicans, who garnered the majority of their support from among the back-country subsistence or semisubsistence farmers as well as from the small artisans and workingmen in the towns, found little support for their opposition to the treaty among the nation's powerful mercantile interests.[7] America's merchants were nearly unanimous in considering the ratification of the treaty as essential. It should not be as-

---

[4] DeConde, *Entangling Alliance*, 109.

[5] D. S. Freeman, J. A. Carroll, and M. W. Ashworth, *George Washington*, VII, 242–64.

[6] James B. McMaster, *A History of the People of the United States*, I, 216–31. Although many others have since described these events, McMaster's narrative remains the most vivid. Joseph Charles, *The Origins of the American Party System*, 91–140.

[7] Manning J. Dauer, *The Adams Federalists*, 3–34.

sumed, however, that merchants in the United States were delighted with the stipulations of the treaty. Most undoubtedly shared in the "deep and general aversion to the terms of the Jay Treaty." Even as a commercial agreement, it promised no improvement over the unsatisfactory commercial relationship that had existed between the United States and Britain since 1783.[8] The treaty's one advantage was that it promised the continuation of peace with Britain and thus the continuation of America's commercial prosperity.

The wars of the French Revolution had stimulated a phenomenal trade in both exports and re-exports, as both belligerents looked to the merchants of neutral America to carry their goods safely upon the high seas. Consequently, as the wars progressed, American merchants watched their profits soar. While trade and commerce with both belligerents increased during the war, that which developed between the United States and Great Britain was far the more extensive.[9] As a result, in 1794 the threat of war between the United States and England had stimulated fear in mercantile houses throughout the country. Jay's treaty brought the promise of peace. The treaty, most merchants agreed, could not be rejected. The alternative was war with England and economic disaster.

Inevitably, Secretary of War Pickering was among those who supported immediate and unqualified ratification of the Jay Treaty. There can be no doubt that his firm commitment was in large measure a product of his own New England commercial mentality. However, Pickering's support for the treaty, if partially based upon reasoned economic considerations, was heightened by an emotional reaction to the shrill, democratically-oriented opposition to it. He had seen mob action before. In the seventeen-sixties he had at first taken the Tory side at least partially as a reaction to the disorderly resistance offered by radicals to the Stamp Act and the Townshend duties. In the Wyoming Valley he stood for order and proved unbending even in the face of threats of physical violence and actual kidnapping. He now reacted negatively to the often violent and

---

[8] Charles, *American Party System*, 104.
[9] Curtis P. Nettels, *The Emergence of a National Economy, 1776–1815*, Table 17, 396; 230–32.

always insistent pro-French and antitreaty position taken by the Republicans, for violence was the antithesis of reason. The emotional public outcries of the Republicans served only to deepen Pickering's hostility toward democrats at home and revolutionaries in France.

The nature of the opposition seemed, to Pickering, to present a grave danger to that political unity and central governmental authority he had come so zealously to admire. He made no distinction between opposition to governmental policy and opposition to government per se. An extreme Federalist, he equated democracy with anarchy. When governmental authority allowed itself to be subverted from its logical course by the clamors of a mob, stability and order, the watchwords of eighteenth-century conservatism, vanished.

Within the Cabinet, Pickering, Wolcott, and Attorney General William Bradford, all New Englanders, formed a triumvirate in favor of immediate ratification of Jay's treaty.[10] Only Virginia's Edmund Randolph, the Secretary of State, opposed it. A nonpartisan figure, Randolph's opposition to the treaty stemmed from the nature of the agreement itself. He considered it a serious diplomatic defeat, not only for American foreign policy, but for himself personally, since he, as Secretary of State, was primarily responsible for the conduct of foreign relations.

The issue, of course, remained to be decided by the President, and Washington continued ambivalent. He agreed with Randolph that the treaty was diplomatically disastrous, but he was simultaneously impressed by the importance of maintaining peace with Great Britain; the security and prosperity of the nation seemed to depend upon it. Through the first week in July the President deliberated, considering all the elements in a set of alternatives that offered no really satisfactory choice. Then, in the midst of his contemplation, distressing news reached Philadelphia. The British had launched a new and vigorous assault upon American merchant vessels carrying provisions to French ports. The Royal Navy was acting in conse-

---

[10] Octavius Pickering and Charles W. Upham, *The Life of Timothy Pickering*, III, 218; Irving Brant, "Edmund Randolph, Not Guilty!" *William and Mary Quarterly*, 3d Series, VII, 185.

quence of a new order-in-council of April, 1795, similar to the re-
pealed order of June, 1793.[11]

The renewal of British attacks upon American commerce gave
Randolph strong leverage in his efforts to convince the President
that the treaty should not be ratified. He urged Washington to establish as a precondition to ratification the immediate repeal by Britain
of her latest order-in-council. Simultaneously, he pressed the President to try for entirely new talks with England designed to achieve
a more satisfactory treaty than the one Jay had managed to arrange.[12]
Randolph's advice seemed sensible to Washington, for, in any case,
the treaty could not honorably be ratified before these new depredations had been halted. Moreover, the situation might be used to
real advantage if the British could be forced to reopen negotiations.
Randolph had temporarily triumphed.

For the moment there was nothing to detain the President in
Philadelphia. Summer in the city had few attractions for him. The
heat, the discomfort of urban life, and the threat — constant during
the summers — of the dread yellow fever combined with Washington's love of his own lands and the Virginia countryside to persuade him to undertake the uncomfortable journey to Mount Vernon. There he would await news of Britain's next move.

In that summer of 1795, while the fate of the treaty remained in
doubt, the political atmosphere became violently charged as Republicans continued to agitate against ratification of the treaty. Boston
was a focal point for their activity, and, as the result of their debate
of the question, the Republican-controlled Town Meeting sent a
resolution, one of dozens from all parts of the country, urging the
President to reject the treaty. News of the Boston resolution soon
reached Secretary Pickering, who never lacked for correspondents
in that part of the country. Stephen Higginson, a former colleague
of Pickering's on Salem's first committee of correspondence and,
in 1795, an influential Boston merchant, was quick to assure the

---

[11] Samuel Flagg Bemis, *John Quincy Adams and the Foundations of Ameri-
can Foreign Policy*, 74; Freeman, Carroll, and Ashworth, *George Washington*,
VII, 260–61.
[12] Brant, "Edmund Randolph," 182; Freeman, Carroll, and Ashworth,
George Washington, VII, 260–63; Pickering and Upham, *Timothy Pickering*,
III, 216.

Secretary of War that the protests of Boston's democratic assembly were not representative of the thinking of the elite. "Men of reputation," he explained, "would not attend the meeting, being opposed to the town's taking up the subject. They were left wholly to themselves; no attempt was made to counteract them, though nine merchants out of ten reprobated the procedure, and a large majority of the whole body of citizens were averse to it." He went on to promise that within a week tempers would cool and supporters of the treaty would "be called patriots." [13]

Pickering's nephew Timothy Williams also wrote, ascribing the Boston Town Meeting's resolution to the efforts of a minority that, he believed, was anxious "either to throw this country into war and anarchy, or reduce us to a *Province* of *France*." Williams, like Higginson, believed that things would soon quiet down and that in the long run it was safe to "confide in the good sense and firmness of the people at large. An enlightened yeomanry," he believed, would "not be soon duped and misled by a few factious demagogues of Boston." [14]

Despite the optimism of Higginson, Williams, and others among the mercantile elite, Pickering grew tense as reports of mass demonstrations against the treaty accumulated in Philadelphia. At first he had assumed that Washington would abide by the decision of the Senate and ratify the treaty without delay. Uninformed of the President's intention to require that the British rescind their recent orders-in-council before ratifying the treaty, he grew restive as Washington apparently hesitated. Quickly enough he came to fear that Washington would weaken under the pressure being exerted by the Republican-sponsored mass protests. Committed to the view that in a representative republic the feelings of the people at large should have no influence upon policy decisions, he believed the many public resolutions opposing ratification of the treaty to be "flagrant violations of the fundamental principles of our republican govern-

---

[13] Higginson to Pickering, July 14, 1795, Pickering Papers (Massachusetts Historical Society), XX, 18.
[14] Williams to Pickering, July 17, 1795, Pickering Papers, XX, 20; for an account of the meeting, see the *Philadelphia Aurora and General Advertiser*, July 18, 1795.

ments, which are not simple democracies but governments by *representation*." [15]

Pickering's fear that Republican agitators might succeed in intimidating the President moved him to set to work at depreciating the significance of their protests. Higginson's letter, which testified to the unimportance of the recent resolutions of the Boston Town Meeting, seemed useful ammunition. He sent it on to the President, in the hope that the merchant's message could encourage Washington to ratify the treaty. [16] When Republicans in Philadelphia held a mass meeting similar to the one that had been held in Boston, Pickering attended. From the fringes of the crowd he watched in silent fury as resolutions condemning the treaty were passed. When they were sent on to the President as the sentiments of the people of Philadelphia and the surrounding area, Pickering again wrote to Washington, warning him not to take the resolutions seriously. Only a few men, he reported — most of them totally unqualified to sit on a jury, let alone to consider the merits of a major international agreement — had participated in the meeting. [17]

While Pickering fumed and fussed his way through the early days of Philadelphia's warm July, Randolph, in the offices of the Department of State, was kept busy preparing an official memorandum to be presented to the British Foreign Office as a statement of the American position on the treaty. After he had completed his task, he asked the other Cabinet members for their opinions on the matter. Pickering, who was willing to surrender almost anything in order to preserve peace with England, was both angered and dismayed when Randolph showed him the memorandum. He told Randolph that Britain would rebuff his proposals for a new negotiation and that a refusal to ratify Jay's treaty could lead only to disaster. [18]

Pickering's reply to Randolph stands as unquestionable evidence

---

[15] Pickering to Williams, undated letter cited in Pickering and Upham, *Timothy Pickering*, III, 181–82.

[16] Pickering to Washington, July 21, 1795, Pickering Papers, XXXV, 209.

[17] Pickering to Washington, July 27, 1795, Pickering Papers, Vol. VI, 91; far different accounts appear in the *Philadelphia Aurora*, July 24, 1795, and *Philadelphia Minerva*, July 25, 1795.

[18] Pickering and Upham, *Timothy Pickering*, III, 216–19.

of both his unswerving determination to see the treaty ratified and of his refusal to consider the political implications of policy decisions. Although he had devoted his mature life to politics and public administration, Pickering, it is obvious, failed as a political man. He consistently refused to accept the inadequacy of his elitist republicanism in an age deeply affected by the upsurge of democratic impulses. He was convinced that the Administration should pay no attention to the impact upon public opinion made by the renewed British maritime depredations. He argued that the new British orders-in-council should be ignored. If the public raised a cry against such a surrender, it too should be ignored, for it was the duty of the Government to respond, not to the whims of the populace (or a noisy portion thereof), but to act in the best interests of the nation. Only by ratification of the treaty without hesitation or reservation could the United States hope to avoid hostilities with the English.[19]

Despite his bold speech to Randolph, Pickering mourned for the treaty. The Secretary of State's opposition, renewed British naval depredations, and the violent public protests, all presaged disaster. Then, just a few days after the Secretary of State had shown him the proposed memorandum, events took a turn in the treaty's favor. Randolph had discussed with George Hammond, British Minister in Philadelphia, the whole question of the renewed British attacks and had indicated that the President would not agree to ratify the treaty until the British had changed this new aggressive policy.[20] Hammond struck back with the most potent weapon at hand; he turned over to Secretary of the Treasury Wolcott a dispatch from the former French Minister in Philadelphia, Joseph Fauchet, to the French Foreign Ministry — a dispatch that the British had intercepted and that seemed to indicate that Secretary Randolph had, a year previously, during the Whisky Rebellion of 1794, asked Fauchet for funds with which to foment rebellion against the Federalist Government.[21]

Wolcott was of course delighted when Hammond gave him the

---

[19] Pickering and Upham, *Timothy Pickering*, III, 216–19.
[20] Brant, "Edmund Randolph," 182; DeConde, *Entangling Alliance*, 121–22.
[21] Brant, "Edmund Randolph," 182–85. Brant's careful research has shown clearly that Randolph was falsely accused.

original and a certified copy of the dispatch. Because he read no French himself and was too careful with his secret to employ a translator who might or might not be trustworthy, he turned the dispatch over to Pickering. The Secretary of War had, upon learning of the contents of the dispatch, quickly volunteered to translate it. Already convinced that Randolph was risking disaster in attempting to prevent the immediate ratification of the treaty, Pickering now discovered, at least to his own satisfaction, the Secretary's reason: Randolph was a French sympathizer. Indeed, in his own anxiety to see the treaty ratified, Pickering came to believe that Randolph was actually a traitor.

The Secretary of War knew little French, yet, filled with fanatical ardor, he worked far into the night and, with the aid of a French-English dictionary, managed to complete a stilted translation of the original Fauchet dispatch. Now in command of a political weapon formidable enough to discredit Randolph in the eyes of Washington, he wrote to the President, who was still at Mount Vernon, urging his quick return to Philadelphia.[22]

Upon his arrival in the capital, the President, mystified by Pickering's urgency, sent a message asking him to wait upon him as soon as convenient. At the presidential mansion that same evening, Pickering was startled by the sight of Washington and Edmund Randolph dining together in quiet conviviality. The President offered the new arrival a glass of wine and, shortly thereafter, found an excuse to see him alone in an adjoining room. Asked the meaning of his strange letter, Pickering replied, pointing dramatically to the room from which they had just emerged, "That man in the other room is a traitor." Briefly, he explained to the stunned President the contents of Fauchet's incriminating dispatch. The President, determined for the moment to say nothing of the matter to Randolph, rejoined him at dinner.[23]

Washington was shaken by Pickering's disclosures and, as the New Englander had hoped, concluded that Randolph's opposition to the treaty stemmed from his sympathies for France. The Presi-

---

[22] Pickering to Washington, July 31, 1795, Pickering Papers, VI, 94; Pickering and Upham, *Timothy Pickering*, III, 217.
[23] Pickering and Upham, *Timothy Pickering*, III, 217.

dent apparently assumed that if this were true, a refusal to ratify the treaty would play directly into the hands of the French; perhaps it would mean war with England. He acted quickly, calling a Cabinet meeting to discuss the treaty again. Randolph, as the only opponent of ratification in the group, attended the meeting in certainty that the President was in agreement with him. To his amazement Washington overruled him and decided to sign the treaty with no further hesitation.[24]

The climax to this, the first of Pickering's many personal conflicts while in the Cabinet, came on the day following the signing of the treaty. Washington and the New Englanders in the Cabinet confronted Randolph with Fauchet's incriminating dispatch and demanded an explanation. Pickering watched silently and implacably as Randolph, who was fluent in French, read through the dispatch. The President, obviously agitated, look on. Upon concluding his reading, Randolph asked if he might retain the dispatch and promised to provide an explanation of his role in the matter. The President agreed, and the Secretary of State immediately left the meeting.[25]

Washington had been almost a father to Edmund Randolph. From the time of the Revolution, the two had been very close. When Washington had been called to the Presidency he had brought Randolph with him as his Attorney General. Then, in 1793, when Jefferson resigned, Randolph was appointed to replace him. Washington's accusations of near treason came as a crushing personal blow to Randolph.

Hurt beyond words by Washington's distrust of him after so long and close a personal and official relationship, Randolph made no effort to explain. Instead, he resigned from the Cabinet. For months thereafter he secluded himself, collecting evidence, which included a statement from Fauchet, and preparing his *Vindication*, which appeared in 1796. Randolph, however, used bad judgment and wasted his efforts in a denunciation of Washington.[26] Even Republicans seemed not to be impressed, and Washington felt merely insulted.

---

[24] Pickering and Upham, *Timothy Pickering*, III, 218.
[25] Pickering and Upham, *Timothy Pickering*, III, 218.
[26] Brant, "Edmund Randolph," 187–89; Pickering and Upham, *Timothy Pickering*, III, 225–26.

As for Timothy Pickering, throughout his life he continued to assert that Randolph had been a traitor. In Salem, Pickering's progenitors had perfected the technique of witch-hunting; a century later he applied it with both conviction and expertise.

Appointed Acting Secretary of State in the wake of Randolph's resignation, Pickering used his office to urge a confrontation with the democrats. Washington had requested that all members of the Cabinet draft replies to the antitreaty resolutions that had been submitted to him by popular mass meetings. Pickering, on his part, was eager to challenge the right of the people even to consider such important questions as treaties. He wrote a reply to the resolutions of the Boston Town Meeting which clearly demonstrated that as an elitist he had no sympathy with democratic interference in affairs of state.[27] Wholly unsympathetic to the democratic tendencies of American politics, his denunciation of the Boston resolutions showed no consideration for the political atmosphere in which he was operating. The Republican press, clamoring for the Administration's blood, was having a good deal of success in arousing popular sentiment against the Government, and the publication of Pickering's sentiments at such a time would have proven politically catastrophic. Washington's polite refusal to use the Secretary's draft replies in answering the resolutions avoided another major tempest.

Edmund Randolph's resignation created another serious problem for the harassed Chief Executive. Confronted with a continuing diplomatic crisis and a vacancy in the Department of State, he sought desperately but unsuccessfully to find a replacement. Weeks dragged by and the position remained unfilled. Almost in despair, he wrote to Alexander Hamilton: "What am I to do for a Secretary of State? I ask frankly, and with solicitude." New Jersey's William Paterson, Thomas Johnson of Maryland, General Charles C. Pinckney of South Carolina, and Virginia's Patrick Henry had each refused the office. He wondered, in his letter to Hamilton, if Rufus King would accept the post.[28] Hamilton replied in tones of equal

---

[27] Pickering to Washington, September 1 and 8, 1795, Pickering Papers, XXXV, 228.

[28] Washington to Hamilton, October 29, 1795, *Writings of George Washington*, J. C. Fitzpatrick, ed., XXXIV, 347–53.

despair that King had refused. The New Yorker candidly admitted that "for a Secretary of State I know not what to say." After canvassing thoroughly all of the likely candidates, he concluded rather sadly: "In fact, a first-rate character is not attainable. A second-rate must be taken with good dispositions and barely decent qualifications. I wish I could throw more light. 'Tis a sad omen for the government." [29]

Desperate, Washington offered the position to Pickering, who at first refused. To his credit the New Englander considered himself not only too inexperienced, but also temperamentally unfit for a diplomatic career. The President, however, implored him to accept. [30] Overcoming his own judgment, Pickering reconsidered and shortly thereafter became the third Secretary of State in the short history of the nation.

The new Secretary of State recognized that he was emotionally unsuited for a diplomatic career; he was quite correct. The same blunt frankness, righteousness, and zeal, which had served him well in domestic political scuffles, was of little advantage in conducting America's foreign relations. Even a friend such as Stephen Higginson had his doubts. He wrote:

> The new station may require more of the *suaviter* to qualify the *fortiter*; and this to me, would be the most difficult part of the business. In the intercourse between governments of different nations, especially those of state, custom has established a certain manner or style of communication, which we call courtly; and this is, in a certain degree, I suppose, indispensable to propriety. . . .

Not that Higginson disapproved of frankness, but might it not be carried too far?

> In a government like ours, an open and manly frankness, in all cases where no danger can result to our object from exposing it, is very proper. It is an engaging feature in the republican character. But cases will often arise, in our intercourse with the Europeans especially (who will not be equally

---

[29] Hamilton to Washington, November 5, 1795, *The Works of Alexander Hamilton*, H. C. Lodge, ed., X, 129–32.

[30] Pickering to Hamilton, November 17, 1795, Pickering Papers, VI, 150.

candid and open), in which we may hazard our interest by too much frankness and sincerity; with them it may be dangerous to avow our object. It is sufficient if we avoid duplicity, and become frank and open as the business ripens.[31]

The irony of Pickering's appointment is that, while he recognized one weakness in himself, he was blind to his principal failings. He never really understood the construction of the European state system nor America's place in it. The idea that a diplomat might need to set aside his own political philosophy in order to serve his nation's best interests never occurred to him. The view that nations that were at odds over questions of political ideology might tolerate one another if it were in the interests of each nation to do so seemed out of the question, an immoral proposition. Unlike his predecessors in the department, Pickering was a provincial with a narrow view of America's role in international politics. Both Jefferson and to a lesser degree Randolph had adapted to the demands of the office. Pickering would never make these adjustments. He was the first Secretary of State in American history to use a moral yardstick in assessing the international situation and then to base his foreign policy upon that moral judgment.

---

[31] Higginson to Pickering, December 30, 1795, Pickering Papers, XX, 120.

3

CHAMPION OF THE JAY TREATY

THE DEPARTMENT TIMOTHY PICKERING INHERITED from Edmund Randolph was an administrator's nightmare. As Secretary of State, he held a position analogous in the British context to those of both the foreign and the home secretaries. With a staff of five, headed by Chief Clerk George Taylor, Jr., Pickering was responsible for the implementation of policy and for the conduct of all correspondence with America's consular and diplomatic representatives abroad, as well as for an extensive correspondence with the representatives of foreign powers in the United States. His domestic chores added to what was an already burdensome task. As holder of the nation's seal, he was responsible for carrying out virtually all domestic administrative functions not directly managed by either the War or Treasury departments. It was the Secretary of State, for example, who drafted and sent all commissions to civilian officials appointed by the President. He also handled the affairs of the United States Mint, granted patents for inventions, was in charge of the printing of the census reports, and carried on an extensive correspondence with federal judges. Federally appointed marshals and attorneys received their instructions, not from the Attorney General, but from the Secretary of State. For discharging all of these duties, this official

33

received the munificent salary of thirty-five hundred dollars per annum.[1]

Inadequate salaries and the nearly overwhelming demands of administration were nothing new to Pickering. Indeed, he seemed to thrive under adverse administrative circumstances. Each new day, with its myriad of issues — some major, some insignificant — he viewed as a personal challenge. More diligent than most, Pickering was apparently thoroughly content when immersed in the details of administration.

Although the Secretary was a capable administrator, there were flaws in his performance. In contrast to Washington he never fully appreciated the importance of delegating authority or responsibility. Always uneasy when allowing subordinates to handle even routine affairs, he kept far too many details in his hands. The result was that he often paid too much attention to routine matters that could have been handled by one or another of his aides. Still, because Pickering was remarkably diligent, the business of the State Department seldom suffered.[2]

There were times, however, when his methods hampered the department. During one period of several months, from the summer of 1795 when he assumed office, to the spring of the following year, affairs were badly deranged. At this time, while familiarizing himself with his new duties as a secretary of state, Pickering was burdened with the extra responsibility of administering the War Department. Despite his habits of hard work, he was simply overwhelmed. In a letter to John Q. Adams, written early in 1796 after a few months of unremitting labor, he admitted that he was attending to far too many matters and that, as a result, both offices were suffering.[3]

The Harpers Ferry incident is a case in point. Early in 1795 Colonel Stephen Rochfontaine, an old acquaintance of Pickering's from his days in the Quartermaster's Department, completed a sur-

---

[1] Galliard Hunt, *The Department of State of the United States*, 90–93.

[2] Leonard D. White, *The Federalists: A Study in Administrative History*, 194–98. White considers Pickering one of the forgotten men of the period, a bureaucrat of great ability.

[3] Pickering to Adams, January 15, 1796, Diplomatic Instructions of the Department of State, III, 97.

vey of several sites for a projected arsenal on the Potomac. This survey, however, made no mention whatever of the site that President Washington thought most likely. In September, 1795, in complete disregard of Rochfontaine's report, Washington wrote Pickering that he had begun investigations into the possible purchase of land at Harpers Ferry at the confluence of the Potomac and the Shenandoah rivers. It would be up to the Secretary of War to handle the details.[4] Months passed and nothing happened. By November Washington was more than a little disturbed with the Secretary's inaction in the matter. Finally, in late January, 1796, Pickering submitted a report to Washington recommending the same site Washington had earlier considered for purchase.[5] It was as though Pickering had never seen or heard of Washington's earlier note. A puzzled President replied to Pickering's long report by urging the Secretary to get on with the purchase.[6] Then chance entered the negotiations. A letter from Pickering to Tobias Lear, Washington's business agent, that authorized Lear to purchase the land, was lost in the mails.[7] After waiting for more than two weeks for action by Pickering, Washington himself wrote to Lear, urging him to proceed with the transaction. Furious at the delay, he did not believe that Pickering had ever written to Lear. "The business relative to the arsenal," Washington wrote, "has been shamefully neglected." So much time had been wasted that Washington believed Pickering had some ulterior motive for delaying the purchase, for although he had been "continually reminding" the Secretary of the matter, nothing had been done.[8]

It is doubtful that there was any duplicity on Pickering's part. A man plagued by as many and as serious difficulties concerning foreign policy as he was encountering in his first months in office was probably too preoccupied with them to attend to the purchase of

---

[4] Washington to Pickering, September 28, 1795, *Writings of George Washington*, J. C. Fitzpatrick, ed., XXXIV, 318.

[5] Pickering to Washington, January 26, 1796, Papers of George Washington (Library of Congress), XXXVII, 57. Hereafter referred to as Washington Papers.

[6] Dandridge to Pickering, January 28, 1796, Pickering Papers (Massachusetts Historical Society), XXXVI, 15.

[7] Pickering to Lear, Pickering Papers, VI, 160.

[8] Washington to Lear, February 15, 1796, Washington, *Writings*, XXXIV, 465.

real estate on the Potomac. Indeed, he had little time for more important affairs in the War Department. For example, in November, 1795, he was asked to prepare a report on the state of the American military establishment, to be presented to the next session of Congress. The December session opened without the report. Congressional leaders complained to Washington, who reprimanded Pickering. The harried Secretary scribbled a reply, indicating that the reports would be completed soon. Pathetically, he wrote that the preparation of the report had "required more time than I had imagined." [9]

During this period the affairs of the State Department also suffered. Consider, for example, what may have been the single most embarrassing event of 1795, as far as Pickering was concerned. Thomas Pinckney, the American Minister to Spain, had just negotiated a very favorable treaty with that power. He was located in what was a very hot corner of Europe at a moment when Spanish diplomacy was undergoing a change that was to have a dramatic effect on Spanish-American relations. Early in October one of Pinckney's coded dispatches was received in Philadelphia. Search for the code key was fruitless and an embarrassed Secretary sent Pinckney's undecoded message to a puzzled Chief Executive with a note explaining that the State Department had lost the key to Pinckney's cipher. [10]

These instances of inefficiency are isolated and were confined to a time when Pickering was trying practically singlehandedly to administer two government departments. Once he was able to turn the War Department over to James McHenry, operation of both departments returned to normal. Although Pickering was never able or willing to delegate responsibility, he could, through diligence and persistence, successfully administer the affairs of the Department of State.

But the Secretary's obligations were not confined to the problems of management. He had also to prove his abilities as a diplomatist. It was here that Pickering, who lacked both the experience and insight to play his role wisely, failed. American diplomacy was faced

---

[9] Pickering to Washington, December 11, 1795, Pickering Papers, XXXV, 319.
[10] Pickering to Washington, October 5, 1795, Pickering Papers, XXXV, 285.

with the problem of arriving at a new *modus vivendi* with France without violating the Jay Treaty. This difficult task had to be accomplished in the face of the fact that France's Directory viewed that treaty as a deliberately hostile alteration in the neutral position of the United States.[11] Even the most dexterous diplomatist would have found the situation demanding.

Of course, and fortunately — considering his lack of experience — Pickering was not allowed a great deal of independent authority. There can be no doubt that Washington wished to be his own Secretary of State and that he viewed Pickering as his adviser and administrative assistant.[12] On the other hand, the Secretary was not completely without power. Although Washington carefully scrutinized the conduct of affairs in Pickering's department, neither he nor anyone else could have maintained total control. A certain amount of power comes with the office and cannot be denied. If Pickering did not have the authority to make policy, he could set its tone and influence its development through his role as adviser to the President, by his control over all diplomatic correspondence, and through his day-to-day conduct of routine affairs in the department.

The impact Pickering exercised on Franco-American relations was negative, for he conceived of himself as the guardian of the Jay Treaty and keeper of the insecure peace with England. Deeply suspicious of the French, he believed their ultimate objective to be a catastrophic war between England and the United States. The natural consequence of these views in a man of Pickering's temperament was an unfriendliness toward France that quickly came to characterize his diplomacy.

Pickering's hostility is alone not enough to explain the rapid deterioration of Franco-American relations. The growth of frictions in this area must also be understood as a result of America's ratification of the Jay Treaty and the French Directory's refusal to accept that treaty as a legitimate agent for alteration in the relationships

---

[11] Alexander DeConde, *Entangling Alliance, Politics and Diplomacy Under George Washington*, 199, 478–79; Albert Hall Bowman, "The Struggle for Neutrality: A History of the Diplomatic Relations Between the United States and France, 1790–1801," 252–53.

[12] White, *The Federalists*, 27.

between the United States, France, and England. From the time that the provisions of the treaty became known, French policy worked toward a break between England and America.[13]

It is apparent to anyone who compares the Treaty of 1778 between France and America with the Jay Treaty that the British acquired, as a result of their diplomacy, new and significant advantages in the competition for control of American commerce.[14] Aside from the impact of a general repudiation by the Americans of the principle of "freedom of the seas," possibly the worst disadvantage the French suffered as a result of the treaty was wrapped up in Article XVIII, which authorized the British to seize American ships carrying provisions to enemy ports. Provisions were not considered contraband under the stipulations of the treaty, for the British government agreed to purchase such cargoes at a fair price.[15] Nonetheless, the French considered American acquiescence in the seizure of provisions as seriously damaging to their interests. There was, first of all, an extensive trade between the United States and France in provisions, which would, by the terms of the treaty, be impeded. But worse than this, the French West Indies were entirely dependent upon American provisions. If the British succeeded in halting this trade, this part of the French Empire could be starved into submission.

Another noteworthy aspect of the Jay Treaty was Article XXIV, which dealt with foreign privateers. Such vessels would no longer be allowed to arm or to sell or to exchange their prizes in the ports of either party to the treaty.[16] Earlier, American policy had denied to the French the right to outfit privateers on this side of the Atlantic, but the French had retained the privilege of selling their prizes in American ports. Britain was the recognized Mistress of the Ocean. These new stipulations against the sale of prizes would create more difficulties for what remained of France's war at sea. French pri-

---

[13] Bowman, "Struggle for Neutrality," 249–52. Bowman's dissertation is exceptionally useful because of the extensive use of French Foreign Office materials not generally available in the United States.

[14] Hunter Miller, *Treaties and Other International Acts, etc.*, II, 3–33; 245–74.

[15] Miller, *Treaties*, II, 258–59.

[16] Miller, *Treaties*, II, 262.

vateersmen would now have to develop markets in the Caribbean or risk sending their prizes on the long and perilous journey to France or to a sympathetic Continental power for sale. When the President ratified the Jay Treaty, he institutionalized an inequality in the United States' relations toward the two belligerents. He further authorized an actual change in the American position regarding the rights of neutrals.

Most Federalists sought to resolve the unfortunate aspects of the situation by arguing that the agreement with England in no way violated any of the stipulations of the French treaty. This argument is, strictly speaking, correct. "Freedom of the seas," which was fundamental to the Franco-American agreement, constituted a special relationship agreed upon bilaterally between the two powers. Federalists generally held that the liberal maritime principles involved had not become part of international law and that the British view of neutral rights still prevailed. Thus, in adhering to British principles in the Jay Treaty, the United States had done nothing more than to accept as binding in her maritime relationship with Britain general principles of international law.[17]

Moreover — and this was a most important part of the Federalist argument — the Jay Treaty in no way violated the Franco-American pact because the two agreements were exclusively bilateral and had no relation to one another. The United States and France had agreed upon a special set of maritime relationships divergent from those predominantly accepted among nations. In the current international situation the French found themselves at a disadvantage as a result of the agreement, but the arrangement was nonetheless binding. At some time in the future the international situation might be reversed. Then, should the United States be a belligerent and France a neutral, American interests would suffer. In this sense, the Administration argued, there was reciprocity in the agreement.[18]

Despite the rigidly legalistic position adopted by the Federalist Administration and the sorry fact that the Jay Treaty did have an

---

[17] Pickering to Monroe, September 12, 1795, Diplomatic Instructions, III, 56.

[18] Pickering to Adet, November 1, 1796, *American State Papers, Foreign Relations*, Class I, Vol. 1, 578.

immediate and unfortunate impact upon the French, it would be an error to assume that Washington was following a deliberately provocative policy toward France. The treaty was the price the Administration had been forced to pay in order to eliminate — at least temporarily — potentially dangerous frictions with England.[19] Although difficulties with France might develop, the Government's objective continued, as before, to remain uninvolved in the European war. Alexander Hamilton, whose influence over Washington was constant and strong, was most responsible for this policy.[20] Within the limits fixed by the Jay Treaty, both Hamilton and Washington strove to avoid conflict with France.

At least two factors must have influenced Hamilton in his thinking. First, there could be no advantage to the United States in a war with France. So long as peace could be maintained, it was to America's economic and diplomatic advantage to avoid conflict. Second, it was politically expedient to adopt a friendly attitude toward France. This became a more compelling point as the elections of 1796 approached. By the spring of that year the Republicans were already making much of the issue of British impressment of American seamen and Federalists' un-neutrality. Federalists had to counter the effects of such Republican arguments, especially since popular sympathy for France was very strong. Certainly, then, there was nothing to be gained and much to be lost by adopting a hostile demeanor toward France. It would have been construed as solid evidence of the Federalist government's leaning toward the British and would have played directly into the hands of both the Republicans and the French.

Quite obviously the Administration was to experience difficulty in convincing either the government of France or French sympathizers in the United States that its pose of friendly neutrality was an accurate reflection of its policy. For one thing, the implementation of the Jay Treaty was sure to convince observers that the Government had in fact altered its course. At another level, the primary spokesman for the United States' policy, Timothy Pickering, was completely

---

[19] Samuel Flagg Bemis, *Jay's Treaty: A Study in Commerce and Diplomacy*, xiii–xiv.

[20] Stephen G. Kurtz, *The Presidency of John Adams*, 122–23.

out of sympathy with the Administration's intentions and emotionally incapable of playing the calm and even amicable role required of the diplomatist. He was never able to set aside his natural suspicion of, and hostility for, the government of France. Even within the limits imposed upon him by Washington he seriously damaged any hopes the President may have had of avoiding a crisis in Franco-American relations.

An early example of the failure of the Administration's policy at both the substantive and procedural levels was the unnecessarily violent dispute that erupted during the summer of 1795 between Pickering and the French Minister to the United States, Pierre Adet. The issue was an unusual one, the treatment of French vessels of war in American ports. But then, *Le Cassius* was an unusual ship.

Under the name of *Le Jumeaux*, this vessel had first been illegally outfitted as a privateer in Philadelphia. She had slipped out to sea over the objections of the American Government and in disregard of the futile efforts of the Delaware Militia to halt her. Later, she had been commissioned a public vessel of war in the French Navy and renamed *Le Cassius*. While cruising in the Caribbean *Le Cassius* took as prize a ship owned by the Philadelphia firm of Yard and Ketland and brought her to St. Domingue. There a French prize court of admiralty condemned both cargo and vessel. Later *Le Cassius* brazenly reappeared in Philadelphia, claiming the rights and prerogatives guaranteed to French warships in American harbors under the terms of the Franco-American Treaty of 1778. Despite her new public character, she was recognized as *Le Jumeaux* the illegally outfitted privateer. The merchant Mr. Yard, who had lost his ship and cargo to her, brought suit against both the ship and the captain, an American.[21]

Was *Le Cassius* a vessel of the French Navy and consequently beyond the reach of American courts of law, or was she *Le Jumeaux*, a privateer, illegally outfitted and armed in the United States and therefore subject to American law? Adet immediately protested the seizure, contending that the ship was a French public vessel and therefore beyond the jurisdiction of American courts.[22] Pickering's

---

[21] Pickering to Monroe, July 22, 1796, Pickering Papers, XXXVI, 166.
[22] Adet to Randolph, August 11, 1795, *A.S.P., F.R.*, I:1, 630.

reply evaded the fundamental issue by maintaining that, since the matter was presently before the courts, the executive branch of the government was powerless to interfere. The court would first have to decide its own competency and the vessel's fate. In his blunt and unnecessarily antagonistic note Pickering aggravated the situation by stating his own certainty that *Le Cassius* was the same vessel that as *Le Jumeaux* had violated American neutrality. Therefore, he felt, it should be no "surprise that *Le Cassius* should be subjected to the course of legal proofs, before the courts of the United States."[23]

The question was not a simple juridical matter. Both American neutrality and the preservation of peace with England were at issue. George Hammond, the British Minister in Philadelphia, had inquired as early as August 8, 1795, as to the United States' intentions relating to *Le Cassius*. He held a dubious view of privateers masquerading as men-of-war and using American ports as bases of operation perhaps against British commerce.[24] Moreover, there was always the likelihood that ships like *Le Cassius* might increase. Numerous privateers might thus legalize their depredations by putting to sea and accepting commissions as French vessels of war. American law against the outfitting of privateers would then not apply, and, protected by the Treaty of Amity and Commerce of 1778, these marauders could ravage British commerce. By the end of September reports circulated that ships suspiciously similar to *Le Cassius* were being clandestinely outfitted at both Baltimore and New York. The British government wanted the outfitting stopped.[25]

Pickering knew that time was short. Although his legal training was far in his past, he must have realized that it was doubtful that a federal court would actually try the suit brought by Yard and Ketland against *Le Cassius*, since this suit charged that their ship had been taken illegally as prize. A French court had already judged the question, and the American court certainly could not legitimately

---

[23] Pickering to Adet, August 25, 1795, Department of State, Domestic Letters, VIII, 382–83.

[24] Pickering to Rawle, September 2, 1795, Department of State, Domestic Letters, XXXV, 229.

[25] Pickering to Bond, September 30, 1795, Pickering Papers, XXXV, 276–77; Pickering to Harrison, October 1, 1795, XXXV, 279; Pickering to Wolcott, October 5, 1795, XXXV, 284.

evaluate the decision of a foreign court of admiralty. Still, it was imperative to end the career of *Le Cassius* and also prevent the sailing of any other illegally outfitted privateers before they too became part of the French Navy.

The Secretary wrote to William Rawle, United States District Attorney for Pennsylvania. With the private suit against the vessel still in the courts, he urged Rawle to bring federal charges against the ship as well. Complicating the situation further, he stated his disapproval of the idea of releasing the ship on bond while the courts were deliberating. The French, he asserted, could not be trusted; he did not wish the United States to be responsible for any British prizes taken by *Le Cassius* while she was free on bond.[26] On the day following, probably to urge him on, Pickering wrote once more to Rawle, reminding him that both he and the British chargé were anxious to know how the case was to be handled.[27]

Rawle proceeded carefully. For the Federal Government to bring suit voluntarily might be embarrassing. He therefore consulted with Mr. Yard, who agreed to bring suit against *Le Cassius* and her American captain for violation of federal law. Eventually, two suits were brought against her and one against the captain. On October 5 Pickering triumphantly reported to Phineas Bond, the British chargé, that the ship had been "dismantled" and was being held for trial on charges of violating the federal statute prohibiting the arming and outfitting of privateers for service to a foreign power.[28]

While Pickering proceeded to tie *Le Cassius* up in the courts, Adet renewed his demands for the release of the ship. But these demands elicited the same hostile and legalistic replies as had earlier protests. Despite the fact that it was he who had instructed Rawle to proceed in the suits against the vessel, the Secretary continued to maintain that the executive branch was helpless to take the matter out of the hands of the courts. Characteristically, however, he was again unable to keep his personal sentiments out of his reply to Adet and in a clearly antagonistic vein accused the French Minister of attempting

---

[26] Pickering to Rawle, September 1, 1795, Department of State, Domestic Letters, VIII, 384.

[27] Pickering to Rawle, September 2, 1795, Pickering Papers, XXXV, 229.

[28] Pickering to Bond, October 5, 1795, Pickering Papers, XXXV, 286.

to circumvent the federal law. In response to Adet's charges of un-neutrality, Pickering adopted the tone of an injured innocent, remarking that, after "the many assurances which have been given to the ministers of the French Republic, that the Government of the United States holds itself bound, as well by inclination as by duty, faithfully to observe its treaties, it is unpleasant to receive as frequent intimations of its violation or suffering them to be violated." With the cutting edge of his pen he suggested that "subterfuge" could not be used to avoid responsibility.[29]

For over a year, the case of *Le Cassius* remained in the courts while the vessel itself literally rotted at its wharf. Finally, in October, 1796, months after Adet had angrily surrendered French rights to the by-then practically valueless hulk, the court upheld the French contention and freed the remains of the vessel.[30]

Despite the court's decision, Pickering was gratified at the outcome of the case. *Le Cassius* had been stopped and Anglo-American amity preserved. Had France succeeded in this sham, he believed that the United States could have expected serious controversy with Britain. Illegally armed privateers like *Le Cassius*, disguised as French vessels of war, might well have proliferated. Using American ports as bases of operation from which to prey upon British merchantmen, they would have put serious strains upon Anglo-American friendship. The Secretary of State, by using the courts to detain *Le Cassius*, had demonstrated to the French that there were legal means of handling such chicanery as they had employed. The custodian of the Jay Treaty had, at least to his own satisfaction, thwarted a French move to undermine America's uneasy peace with England.

A far more serious issue that also revealed the inadequacy of the Administration's policy toward France was the article of the Jay Treaty that recognized the right of British cruisers to take provisions from American ships without protestation. On September 28, 1795, Adet condemned the treaty, on the grounds that its stipulations were in violation of some of the basic principles of the Treaty of Amity and Commerce of 1778. In his letter to Pickering he paid special

---

[29] Pickering to Adet, October 1, 1795, Department of State, Domestic Letters, VIII, 419–22.
[30] Pickering to Adet, October 19, 1796, *A.S.P., F.R.*, I:1, 643.

attention to the fact that British cruisers were taking large numbers of American vessels carrying provisions to French ports and that the cargoes of these vessels were being condemned as contraband of war. He reminded the Secretary that the Treaty of 1778 between France and the United States had carefully excluded food from the contraband list and that the United States had committed itself to the liberal principle of "freedom of the seas." Despite the terms of the treaty, Adet charged, the American Government had done nothing to protect either the cargoes of food or its own violated rights.

The French envoy went on to denounce the Jay Treaty as an outright violation of American neutrality. Under the circumstances, he wrote, France had a right to protest if the American Government

> by a perfidious condescension, . . . permitted the English to violate a right which it ought to defend for its honor and its interest: if under the cloak of neutrality, it presented to England a poniard to cut the throat of its faithful ally: if, in fine, participating in the tyrannic and homicidal rage of Great Britain, it concurred to plunge the French people into the horrors of famine.[31]

Earlier in the month Pickering had provided Adet with a full explanation and defense of the Administration's policy. Having received no reply, he had assumed that Adet was satisfied. When, almost a month later, he received this insulting message, he decided to ignore it. Moreover, he took an unusual liberty in not informing the President.[32]

---

[31] Adet to Pickering, September 28, 1795, *A.S.P., F.R.*, I:1, 644.

[32] Pickering himself later admitted that he had deliberately ignored this and other notes from Adet. (Pickering to Adet, November 1, 1796, *A.S.P., F.R.*, I:1, 578.) A letter from Washington to Hamilton also written in November indicates that he heard nothing of this, or of two other letters of protest written by Adet, until November, 1796. (Washington to Hamilton, November 2, 1796, Washington, *Writings*, XXXV, 252.) A further indication that Adet's protest was withheld from the President is the fact that nowhere in the correspondence between Pickering and Washington is there to be found any indication that this note was sent on to the President. Since there are numerous other notes covering letters from Adet and other envoys to Washington in both the Pickering collection and the Presidential Papers of George Washington (microfilm collection at Sacramento State College), it seems safe to assert that Pickering acted on his own on this and on at least two subsequent occasions to hold back French protests from the President.

Correspondence between Pickering and Adet for the remainder of 1795 and well into 1796 was sporadic and frigid. Adet wrote only occasionally, and Pickering confined his correspondence to routine matters. Thus, a crucial and divisive issue, the Jay Treaty, was allowed to remain unattended into the spring of 1796, when its potentialities for bitter debate were reinforced by the festering question of impressment.

In February, 1796, the Republicans in the House of Representatives began a vigorous assault upon the Administration's foreign policy and particularly upon the Federalists' inactivity with regard to the growing problem of impressment. They introduced a bill to authorize the issuance of certificates of citizenship to American seamen. These "protections" as they were called, would, it was hoped, protect American seamen against Britain's brutal practice of impressment. Over the following month a sporadic but vigorous debate took place on the question, despite the fact that members of the House were unanimous in their view that impressment was a serious problem. Eventually, and in a rather undramatic finish, the bill, which became known as "an Act for Relief and Protection of American Seamen," was passed by the House of Representatives and sent on to the Senate.[33]

On March 29, the morning following passage of the bill in the House, the Republican press began a vigorous campaign to focus the nation's attention upon the problems of impressment.[34] It was no accident that Adet's next diplomatic initiative was timed to coincide with this latest political assault upon the Administration. On the same day that Philadelphia's influential newspaper, the *Aurora*, devoted much space to British atrocities, Adet, in all likelihood attempting to exacerbate Anglo-American frictions, pressed the Secretary of State for vigorous action in dealing with the problem of

---

[33] *Debates and Proceedings in the Congress of the United States*, 4th Cong., 1st Sess., March 28, 1796, 820.

[34] The *Philadelphia Aurora* was especially active. On that day, under the headline "British Atrocity!" appeared the story of Captain Blackmore of the schooner *Hope* who had been shot through the face by a musket ball fired from a British frigate. Below this story was another entitled "British Amity" in which was reported the story of an especially brutal impressment in the Caribbean. Such stories continued unabated in the *Aurora* through the spring of 1796.

British impressment. In a long letter he explained that large numbers of Americans were being impressed into Britain's West Indian
squadron. France was deeply interested in finding out what measures the United States was taking to protest the impressment of her
seamen by England. French interest, Adet explained, stemmed directly from the fact that American manpower alone allowed the
British to maintain an effective naval force in the Indies. He went so
far as to suggest that the

> English division in the colonies is entirely recruited by mari-
> ners taken from on board your vessels. It is by their means
> that they block up republican ports; it is to their succor we
> ought to attribute the loss of these immense possessions, if
> the American government should not take the step which the
> duty of neutrality dictates to it.

Adet demanded that the Administration take vigorous action to
end impressment. He insisted, moreover, that American protests be
"prompt and efficacious." [35]

Again Pickering ignored an opportunity to take a reasonable
stance. It would have been a costless gesture for him to have informed Adet that the American Government was making serious
efforts at solving the problem of impressment. Such a response would
have committed the United States to nothing, but it would have
placed the Administration in a more defensible political position
at home. Instead, he again refused to reply to what he considered to
be nothing more than a combination of scurrilous accusations and
unjustified interference in affairs that should not concern Adet. Moreover, he once again failed to inform Washington of the insulting
note.[36] Within a month, the French envoy wrote once again to protest American inaction in the face of the continued impressment of
American seamen into the British Navy.[37] Again, the Secretary of
State refused to reply.[38]

Pickering's failure to answer Adet's charges and his unwilling-

---

[35] Adet to Pickering, March 29, 1796, *A.S.P., F.R.*, I:1, 644.
[36] Pickering to Adet, November 1, 1796, *A.S.P., F.R.*, I:1, 578; Washington to Hamilton, November 2, 1796, Washington, *Writings*, XXXV, 252.
[37] Adet to Pickering, April 21, 1796, *A.S.P., F.R.*, I:1, 644–45.
[38] Pickering to Adet, November 1, 1796, *A.S.P., F.R.*, I:1, 578.

ness to provide President Washington with information regarding them raise questions of motive. Pickering justified his refusal to reply, on the ground that Adet's notes were too insulting to be dignified by replies. Similar protests had either been answered earlier or, in some cases, merited no reply, since the envoy, Pickering charged, was improperly interfering in American affairs. Impressment was such an issue.

This explanation is unsatisfactory; while it explains why Pickering did not reply, it does not explain why the Secretary kept Adet's protests from Washington. Although it is only surmise, it is not unlikely that Pickering's decision to withhold the notes from Washington was a calculated one, since he was at odds with the conciliatory approach Hamilton and Washington were taking toward the French. He may well have feared that Washington would accept Adet's rebuke or, worse still, would weaken before the combined assault of the Republicans and the French and thus endanger the insecure peace with England either by violating the Jay Treaty or pursuing too vigorously the American case against impressment.

Few men ever fully appreciate the total significance of their actions, and certainly Pickering was not one of the few. He either did not understand or ignored the implications of his inaction for the internal political situation. Both the Jay Treaty and impressment were emotion-packed political issues. Later, when Adet looked for means of throwing his weight in support of Jefferson in the election of 1796, he would remember that the Administration had ignored his inquiries and would use these rebuffs as the bases for his public denunciations of the Federalists as not merely un-neutral but as actually unwilling to settle outstanding differences with his country. But this was all in the future. At the moment Pickering remained satisfied that the American Government would not be browbeaten by the representative of a foreign power.

On some occasions the Secretary of State did reply to Adet's notes, with unfortunate consequences. The results were not altogether his fault, however. He was, after all, caught in the gap between the Administration's contention that the Jay Treaty had changed nothing and the embarrassing fact that it had indeed changed much of significance in the nation's relations to other countries. On at least one occasion Pickering was forced to admit the truth of the situation. The issue in question was the privilege French privateers had enjoyed of selling British prizes in American ports. Under Article XXIV of the Jay Treaty, such sales were prohibited.

It was in the spring of 1796, with the political winds already blowing warm in preparation for the elections, that Adet raised the issue, protesting legislation that had just been passed by the House of Representatives, designed to prohibit the sale of prize vessels by belligerent ships in American ports. In a note to Pickering denouncing the passage of the bill by the House, Adet argued that the proposed law was in direct violation of Articles XVII and XXII of the Franco-American commercial agreement of 1778. While admitting that the articles in question did not specifically guarantee to French privateers the right to sell their prizes in American ports, he argued that the treaty did recognize the right of French privateers to bring prizes into American harbors. He believed it clear that the treaty "implicitly assured" French privateers "the right of . . . selling" their prizes in the United States. Adet concluded by remarking that, as interpreted by the American Government, the rights of French privateers in American ports had been so seriously limited as to be virtually worthless.[39]

Like Adet's preceding protests over impressment, this note makes more sense politically than it does from a diplomatic point of view. It was hardly two weeks since the Jay Treaty had passed its last great legislative hurdle in the House of Representatives. The debate had been long and bitter and had brought party differences to white heat. Although the debate was finished, its political effects remained. Adet was simply throwing new fuel on the coals. He knew full well that the law he was protesting was merely an act passed to implement one aspect of the treaty, and he had known for some months that, as a result of Article XXIV of the treaty, French privateers would be denied the privilege of selling prizes in American ports. Still, the best way to keep the party struggle going and to win support for the opponents of the Administration was to demonstrate how un-neutral the Government was.

---

[39] Adet to Pickering, May 18, 1796, *A.S.P., F.R.,* I:1, 650–51.

What prompted Pickering to reply to this challenge to the Jay Treaty is difficult to explain. Adet's note was sharply accusatory and not easily answered. Perhaps the President had received news of the note through other channels. Or perhaps Pickering viewed this letter as less importunate than others from Adet. In any case, the Secretary sent a sharp reply which pointed out that, even before the ratification of the Jay Treaty, Secretary of State Jefferson had made it clear that the Treaty of 1778 did "not contemplate a freedom for French privateers *to sell their prizes* here; but on the contrary, a *departure* to some other place, always to be expressed in their commission, where their validity is to be finally adjudged." So far so good; but then the Secretary entrapped himself. Argue as he might, there was one inescapable flaw in his position. He had to admit that, despite Jefferson's statement on the question, French privateers had, until recently, been allowed the "privilege" of selling their prizes in the United States. He admitted, too, that it was because of the stipulations of Article XXIV of the Jay Treaty that he himself had issued orders to all customs officials to refuse to allow any further sales of British prizes brought by French privateers into American ports.[40] Adet had made his point. The Jay Treaty had unfavorably altered, in this respect at least, the relationship of France to America.

Scarcely a week after this exchange of views Pickering demonstrated his determination to protect the British treaty on this score. At the end of June the Philadelphia press published a story about a French privateer and the two British prizes she had brought to Boston. The recently arrived British envoy, Robert Liston, requested that Pickering prohibit the sale of these prizes. The Secretary reacted instantly. Since at the time there was no federal district attorney in Massachusetts, he wrote to Harrison Gray Otis, a Federalist and one of the leaders of the Massachusetts bar, requesting him to serve as an acting district attorney in order to stop the sale of the prizes.[41] He next asked Benjamin Lincoln, Collector of Customs at Boston, and John Lowell, Federal District Judge for Massachu-

---

[40] Pickering to Adet, May 24, 1796, *A.S.P., F.R.*, I:1, 651–52.
[41] Pickering to Otis, June 30, 1796, Pickering Papers, XXXVI, 142.

setts, to cooperate with Otis in this affair.[42] Pickering was hoping
to obtain a court injunction to prohibit the sale of the ships. When,
by July 12, no injunction was forthcoming, he instructed Otis to
warn the owners of the prizes that, injunction or no injunction, the
sale of the prizes would constitute a violation of the Jay Treaty,
which was the law of the land.[43] In the end the Secretary triumphed
and the prizes remained unsold, but another item was added to
the growing list of irritations that were eroding Franco-American
relations.

In the late spring of 1796, while Pickering worked to defend the
British treaty, Franco-American relations were unexpectedly threatened from another direction. French privateers in the Caribbean
began to swarm over American shipping. Since American merchant
vessels had, prior to this time, sailed virtually unmolested by French
cruisers, American observers assumed that this was the beginning
of a new phase in Franco-American relations and that war was in
the offing. They were mistaken, for these attacks were completely
out of keeping with the objectives of French policy as they had developed to that time.[44]

Although France's Foreign Minister Charles Delacroix believed
the ratification of the Jay Treaty tantamount to a declaration of war
against France by the Federalists, he realized that actual combat
was out of the question. Such a conflict would merely unite the
American people in support of their government, drive the United
States more deeply into the arms of England, destroy all French
commerce with the United States, and create a whole new set of
threats to France's holdings in the West Indies. Delacroix set out
instead to find a peaceful way to reverse the direction of American
foreign policy. A technique he believed would prove fruitful was a
cautious interference in the internal political affairs of the United
States. His object was to unseat the Federalists in the coming elec-

---

[42] Pickering to Lowell, June 30, 1796, Pickering Papers, XXXVI, 143; Pickering to Lincoln, June 30, 1796, XXXVI, 141.

[43] Pickering to Otis, July 12, 1796, Pickering Papers, XXXVI, 149.

[44] DeConde, *Entangling Alliance*, 495. French colonial agents in the West
Indies and the Windward Islands were, without the knowledge or consent of
the government in Paris, privateering for profit.

tions. Delacroix believed that, with the more amicably disposed Republicans in control in Philadelphia, a change of American policy would come about quickly and war between the United States and England would become a distinct possibility.[45]

Delacroix's intrigues, of course, were unknown to the American leadership. News of the privateering raids set Philadelphia in turmoil, for it came after rumors had persisted for some time that French cruisers would take American provision ships bound for British ports.[46] Many Federalist leaders feared their tenuous grasp upon peace was slipping. Hamilton, for example, was in immediate contact with the Cabinet in an attempt to chart the Administration's course during the crisis. The object was to avoid the war the French might precipitate. The Directory must be convinced that a declaration of war would be foolish and that the people of the United States would make a vigorous and united response to foreign aggression. Moreover, it must be made evident that American foreign policy was founded upon a real desire to remain clear of Europe's conflict. To achieve these goals, Hamilton believed it advisable for the Administration to recall the American Minister to France, the Republican James Monroe, and to replace him with a man more representative of Federalist foreign policy.[47] Hamilton's reasoning, although based upon the false notion that France intended to declare war, was sound. The Republican Monroe was possibly the man least likely to make any serious effort at defending American foreign policy.

Monroe had never supported Federalist policy while in France. Originally, in 1794, he had been appointed Minister to France because of his deep sympathies for the French Revolution. The pressures of deepening Anglo-American hostility at that time made it imperative that the French be assured by a representative whom they trusted that the United States considered its treaty obligations to France as sacred and that John Jay, then poised to sail as a special

---

[45] Bowman, "Struggle for Neutrality," 285; Kurtz, *Presidency of John Adams*, 126–27.

[46] Pickering to Adet, October 12, 1795, Pickering Papers, XXXV, 296.

[47] Hamilton to Wolcott, June 15, 1796, *The Works of Alexander Hamilton*, H. C. Lodge, ed., X, 174.

envoy to London, would commit the United States to nothing that might in any way violate previous agreements with France.[48]

Subsequently, when the American Government ratified the Jay Treaty, Minister Monroe fell out with the Administration. He considered the treaty a virtual alliance with Britain and a repudiation of the long friendship between the United States and France.[49] Thus, at a moment when the United States sought, as inconspicuously as possible, to alter the course of its foreign policy in response to a new set of circumstances, and at a time when France was growing increasingly antagonistic, the American Minister in Paris was in complete disagreement with the policy he was to represent.

Despite his lack of sympathy for Federalist policy, Monroe had performed a useful function, especially after the ratification of the Jay Treaty. Fervently Republican, he feared war between France and America, which would destroy republicanism in the United States. He used his influence and all of his persuasive powers to convince the Directory that precipitate aggressive action against the American Government could only drive the United States further into the embrace of England and that there was nothing to be gained for France in a war with the United States. His arguments, which comported with the thinking of Foreign Minister Delacroix, his successor Talleyrand, and other French diplomatists, helped avoid a direct confrontation. Although indiscreet in his use of information and hostile to the Administration, Monroe nonetheless served Philadelphia's purposes well.[50]

Once it appeared that hostilities might actually begin, however, as was the case by the spring of 1796, Monroe's usefulness seemed at an end. Philadelphia began to debate the wisdom of his recall, and Pickering was among those who most avidly sought to remove him from his post. The Virginian's sympathies for the French Revolution were alone enough to condemn him in the Secretary's eyes,

---

[48] Randolph to Monroe, June 10, 1794, in *Writings of James Monroe*, S. M. Hamilton, ed., II, 8.

[49] Monroe to Secretary of State, September 10, 1795, *A.S.P., F.R.*, I:1, 721–22.

[50] DeConde, *Entangling Alliance*, 380; Beverley W. Bond, *The Monroe Mission to France, 1794–1796*, 44–56.

but the suspicious Yankee had developed some seemingly more substantial reasons for wanting a change of ministers. He believed that, at least since December, 1795, Monroe had deliberately neglected to carry out instructions sent him in early September. At that time Pickering had dispatched a long and careful defense of the Jay Treaty, which Monroe was instructed to use in explaining the agreement to the French government. Ten months later Pickering was still awaiting word that Monroe had carried out these instructions.[51] While Monroe's dispatches remained mute as to any efforts to defend the treaty, they were consistently filled with dark warnings of French anger over it.[52]

Pickering was convinced that Monroe wished to encourage a diplomatic crisis between France and the United States so long as it did not result in war. Such a crisis would mean great political advantage to the Republicans in the coming elections. Hadn't they for some time been charging the Administration with gross hostility to France? In July, 1796, Pickering admitted to Washington his "suspicions some months since entertained, that the ominous letters of Mr. Monroe composed . . . part of a solemn farce to answer certain party purposes in the U. States."[53] Despite the advice of Hamilton and pressure from Pickering, Washington was reluctant to act and allowed matters to continue unsettled into July, 1796. The President certainly understood Hamilton's arguments and probably was in general agreement with them. On the other hand, Monroe was very popular with the French. His recall might be regarded by the French as another Federalist insult. It would be very difficult to find a man who would both accurately represent the Adminis-

---

[51] Pickering to Monroe, September 12, 1795, Department of State, Diplomatic Instructions, III, 56–60; Pickering to Monroe, June 13, 1796, 173–76. By June, Pickering was furious with Monroe. In this sharply accusatory dispatch inquiring why, despite the fact that he continually warned of French discontent over the Jay Treaty, he had failed to use "such means in your hands — means amply sufficient to vindicate the conduct of the United States . . . ," Pickering noted that he and the President were both regretful and surprised "that no attempt was made to apply them to the highly important use for which they were sent."

[52] Monroe to Secretary of State, August 17, 1795, Department of State, Diplomatic Dispatches, France, VI, 297–98; September 10, 1795, 300–307; November 5, 1795, 335–37; December 5, 1795, 338–42. The examples are even more numerous.

[53] Pickering to Washington, July 21, 1796, Pickering Papers, VI, 206.

tration's policy and simultaneously be well received as a successor to Monroe. In June, while at Mount Vernon, he hit upon an alternative to outright recall of the Minister. He sought the Cabinet's opinion on whether it would be sensible to keep Monroe as the regular minister in Paris while dispatching a special envoy plenipotentiary to settle any differences arising out of the Jay Treaty. This was, after all, the procedure he had followed in 1794 when he sent John Jay on his special mission to London.

Pickering, who wanted no more of Monroe, drafted the Cabinet's reply, which was signed by Wolcott and the new Secretary of War, James McHenry. It was unconstitutional, Pickering argued, for the President to send an envoy extraordinary without the consent of the Senate, and the Congress was not in session. The only legal method of sending another man was to recall Monroe.

Washington probably would not have been impressed by such an argument alone, but Pickering reinforced it with a condemnation of Monroe's past failures. Despite the fact that he had "been amply furnished with documents to explain the views and conduct of the United States" and to alleviate tensions between France and the United States, Monroe had not done so. Instead, he had kept up a steady stream of warnings of French anger. If the Directory was perturbed, why did Monroe refrain from using the material he had at his disposal to explain American policy? Without subtlety, Pickering pointed out that there might well be political reasons for Monroe's refusal to carry out his earlier instructions. A letter from Monroe to Dr. George Logan, the prominent Pennsylvania Republican leader, had recently come to hand. Pickering included this note in his own message to Washington. From its contents it was clear that Monroe was in regular contact not only with Logan but also with John Beckley, another important Pennsylvania Republican, and Benjamin F. Bache, editor of the anti-Administration *Philadelphia Aurora*. This letter promised a series of letters from "a Gentleman in Paris" to his friend in Philadelphia for publication in the *Aurora*. These letters would inform the people of the United States as to the state of the revolution in France and also evaluate American policy toward that country. It was clear that such evaluations would not be sympathetic to the Administration.[54] In concluding his letter to Washington Pickering remarked:

> These anonymous communications from officers of the United States in a foreign country, on matters of a public nature; & which deeply concern the interests of the United States in relation to that foreign country are proofs of sinister designs, and show that the public interests are no longer safe in the hands of such men.[55]

Washington at last agreed, and on July 8 wrote Pickering of his intention to recall Monroe.

Although Pickering's arguments were deeply prejudiced and hardly fair to Monroe, his objections to Monroe as Minister to France had merit. The envoy had long since allowed his own anti-Administration prejudices to affect his diplomatic intercourse, and, although he was working to avoid a Franco-American war, he was also contributing to the belief in France that the American Government did not represent the true feelings of the people. He had even suggested to the French that in the coming November elections the Federalists would be repudiated and a Republican administration would execute a shift in American foreign policy that would unilaterally abrogate the Jay Treaty. Monroe spoke so frankly and with such vehemence regarding the Washington Administration and the internal divisions within his own country that France's Foreign Minister Delacroix, who was the frequent auditor of such outbursts, discounted much of what Monroe said. No minister, the French diplomatist believed, would, in the presence of the foreign minister of another nation, be so frank in the condemnation of his own government.[56]

Pickering viewed the imminent change of ministers with unmixed pleasure and was gratified when Charles C. Pinckney, a Southern Federalist, accepted the appointment. He felt far more secure in his department's negotiations, with the South Carolinian on his way

---

[54] Monroe to Logan, June 24, 1795, Pickering Papers, XLI, 227.

[55] Pickering to Washington, July 2, 1796, Washington Papers, XXX, 243–46.

[56] Bowman, "Struggle for Neutrality," 253–54.

to Paris. As a strong nationalist and defender of the Administration's policy, Pinckney would help to clarify those policies in France.

Pinckney's chances for success in pacifying the French were minimal from the outset. The American diplomatic position was perilously weak and totally lacking in flexibility. At the substantive level the Jay Treaty was an issue, and there was no room for compromise. The United States could not negotiate without endangering the crucial "British connection," and the French were determined to win their point, not through negotiation, but by encouraging popular dissatisfaction with Federalist policy within the United States.

The instructions Pickering drafted for Pinckney reflected the impossibility of the new Minister's task. Diplomacy was reduced to a rigid defense of previous American actions; Pinckney was given no powers to negotiate. He could offer the French no concession that would in the slightest way endanger the tenuous peace recently arrived at with Britain. He was armed with no new alternatives, no proposals for conciliation.[57] Any real possibility for his success hinged upon his ability to convince the French of the essential unity of the American people and of their support of Federalist policy.

Monroe's recall precipitated the crisis between France and the United States that had been presaged when the Jay Treaty first became public. From December, 1795, until the summer of 1796 the French Government had refrained from hostile action. News of the ratification of the treaty had been a blow to Franco-American relations, but it became apparent immediately that Republicans in the House of Representatives would test the treaty by attempting to withhold the appropriations needed to implement it. When news arrived in Paris that this maneuver had failed in the Congress and that the treaty had been implemented, it shocked the French deeply. Still, the Directory restrained itself, realizing that firm measures against the United States would weaken republicanism within the United States. But when, in the autumn of 1796, news arrived that the friendly Monroe would be recalled to be replaced by the Federalist Pinckney, the French Government decided, if only to drama-

---

[57] Pickering to Pinckney, September 14, 1797, Pickering Papers, XXXVII, 228.

tize the perils of the situation, to take a measured step in the direction of a break in diplomatic relations. It had no intention of actually inviting war with the United States, but some expression of dissatisfaction seemed in order. If handled correctly, such expression would help and not harm the Republican chances in the coming American elections.

Thus, when the new American Minister reached Paris after more than two months of hazardous travel, he found that he was not to be received officially. Furthermore, he was informed that the Executive Directory would refuse accreditation to any minister from the United States until that government had acted to redress French grievances. Principal among French demands was the requirement that the United States renounce the Jay Treaty.[58] For over a month, the unaccredited Minister lingered in Paris, awaiting either orders from his own Government or an ultimatum from the Directory. Finally, late in January, 1797, just after Adams' victory in the presidential elections became known in Paris, the Directory ordered Pinckney out of France.[59]

Even before Pinckney arrived in France Delacroix had implemented his earlier decision to take a hand in the American elections. In Philadelphia Pierre Adet was charged with carrying out this aspect of French policy.[60] During his stay in America, this perceptive envoy developed doubts about the strength of the attachment that bound the Republicans to France. In fact, he came to believe that it was only the internal political conflict with the Federalists that motivated the Jeffersonians to seek support from abroad. For instance, he was quick to note that, while the Republicans delighted in French attacks against Washington and the Federalists, they took offense at similar affronts directed against American institutions. Adet believed that, like all other Americans, the Republicans "could not forgive the Directory for destroying their illusion that they were

[58] C. C. Pinckney to Pickering, Dispatch #1, November 17, 1796, Department of State, Diplomatic Dispatches, France, V, 1–5.

[59] Pinckney to Pickering, Dispatch #5, January 24, 1797, Department of State, Diplomatic Dispatches, France, V, 33–37.

[60] F. J. Turner, ed., "Correspondence of French Ministers to the United States 1791–1797," *American Historical Association Annual Report for 1903*, II, 948–49.

'the first people of the earth' if it had not at the same time given them the means of avenging themselves on Washington and of fighting with stronger weapons the Britannic faction."[61] Nonetheless, when in the late summer of 1796 instructions arrived from Paris, authorizing Adet to do what he could to influence the outcome of the American elections, he set aside his misgivings and gave thought to what he might attempt.

Political activity accelerated as the first true contest for the Presidency in the nation's history approached. It was agreed that the choice between Jefferson and Adams would be very close and would probably turn on a few electoral votes. Adams' chances were dimmed by divisions within the Federalist coalition and by the almost public conspiracy organized by Alexander Hamilton to arrange the election of Thomas Pinckney, the South Carolina Federalist. Pennsylvania, with its fifteen closely contested electoral votes, seemed to hold the key to success or failure for both major candidates.[62]

The Federalist faction in Pennsylvania was badly divided, for here the movement to bring Pinckney in ahead of Adams had caused great consternation and division. Pickering, Wolcott, and numerous others including the powerful Senator from Pennsylvania William Bingham, were convinced that Adams' chances were slim. "It is therefore deemed expedient," Bingham wrote, "to recommend to Federal Electors an uniform vote to give for Mr. Pinckney, which with those he will obtain to the Southward, detached from Mr. Adams, will give him a decided majority over the other candidates."[63] Since others vehemently disagreed with Bingham, the result in Pennsylvania was schism and disorganization.

Republicans in Pennsylvania were far better organized than the Federalists and, under the able leadership of John Beckley, had prepared well for the contest. Organizing secretly, Beckley had not only fashioned a well-oiled political machine but had also put together a slate of prospective presidential electors known throughout Pennsylvania. McKean, Gallatin, Maclay, Smilie, Irvine, Muhlen-

---

[61] Cited in Bowman, "Struggle for Neutrality," 285.

[62] Manning J. Dauer, *The Adams Federalists*, 92–111. This is an excellent survey of the election of 1796; Kurtz, *Presidency of John Adams*, 177–91.

[63] Cited in Dauer, *The Adams Federalists*, 98.

berg — these and others on the Republican slate were names that
would attract the voters. When, in October, 1796, the Republican
slate of electors became known, the Federalists were thrown into
further confusion, for theirs, a list of relatively undistinguished and
unknown people, had already been made public. Nothing could be
done to correct this miscalculation.[64]

Beckley had another trick up his sleeve. The entire campaign focused at the national level upon two issues, the ostensible monarchi-
cal convictions of Adams and the alleged pro-British, anti-Gallican
position adopted by the retiring Administration. Although most Republican leaders disagreed with him, Beckley believed that if he
moved carefully, he might be able to use, as a neat fillip to the campaign, a public statement denouncing Federalist foreign policy, to be
made by the French envoy to the United States.[65]

It was probably at this point, in October, 1796, that Beckley enlisted the services of Pierre Adet. The Frenchman, who had since
the spring been working closely in support of the Republicans,
quickly turned his attention to Beckley's project. He realized that
he could make no direct appeal to the voters; Genêt had attempted
this in 1793, with disastrous consequences. But if he addressed a
diplomatic note to the Secretary of State, which would somehow
find its way into print, this would be a different matter.

Adet knew that his greatest political advantage lay in the tradition of friendship between the peoples of France and the United
States. He set out to demonstrate to the American people that the
friendship remained and that Franco-American differences were
the results of the Federalist faction's hostility for France. Nor did
Adet lack evidence for this assault on the Federalists. The last
eighteen months had provided him with a vast reservoir of useful
material, which he could use to support his charges that the Administration had not only violated the meaning of the Treaty of 1778
by adhering to Jay's treaty but that the Secretary of State had also

---

[64] Kurtz, *Presidency of John Adams*, 182–83.
[65] Kurtz, *Presidency of John Adams*, 178. It should be noted that Kurtz has
only circumstantial evidence of an arrangement between Beckley and Adet.
Whether or not there was such an arrangement, the efforts of both men certainly worked to produce the same result.

arrogantly refused to discuss matters of great consequence to the future of relations between France and the United States. Pickering was about to pay for his silence.

The voters of Pennsylvania were scheduled to go to the polls on Friday, November 6. On the preceding Friday, Adet sent a long diplomatic message to Timothy Pickering, which appeared in the *Philadelphia Aurora* on the following Monday.[66] The ostensible purpose of the note was to announce a new maritime decree of the Directory that established a more restrictive policy with regard to American vessels carrying provisions and naval stores to English ports. The French Government, Adet wrote, would treat neutrals as they "allow themselves to be treated by the British." He went on to explain, in terms highly critical of the Administration's policy, that when the British first began to violate America's neutral rights the Government of France had assumed that the United States would be quick to "take steps in favor of her violated neutrality." Yet, since the beginning of the war between England and France, Britain had trampled on American rights on the high seas with no discernible indication that the Government of the United States intended any response other than submission.

Adet took full political advantage of Pickering's long silence. In a damning attack on Federalist policy he noted that on three separate occasions he had protested the Administration's inaction in the face of British violations of American neutral rights and of the impressment of American seamen into the British Navy. His protests, he noted, had not been dignified by replies; the Department of State had refused to indicate in any way "the steps taken to obtain satisfaction for this violation of neutrality."

Adet tried to make clear that the new French maritime decree was being issued only in self-defense. It was only because of British violations of American neutrality and the American Government's refusal to protest that France was forced to act. This need not be a permanent situation. No neutral, he wrote, need fear France so long as it kept an honest and unprejudiced neutrality. "But," he remarked, in a slashing indictment of the Federalists,

---

[66] Adet to Pickering, October 27, 1796, *A.S.P., F.R.*, I:1, 577.

if through weakness, partiality, or other motives they should suffer the English to sport with that neutrality and turn it to their advantage, could they then complain when France, to restore the balance of neutrality to its equilibrium, shall act in the same manner as the English? [67]

All in all, Adet's note was a shrewd piece of political propaganda, and it served as an effective campaign statement for the Republicans. He avoided making a direct plea for the election of Republicans over Federalists, yet the only conclusion voters could draw from his little leaflet was that the Republicans would be more trustworthy guardians of American neutrality than the Federalists had been.

When Washington read Adet's letter in the *Aurora*, he was confused as to how to respond. A public reply would be undignified, yet if no reply were made, he feared that the American people would believe that Adet's charges were just. Most deeply disturbing to him was the probable truth of the allegation that Pickering had not replied to earlier protests. Annoyed at being kept in the dark by Pickering, Washington nevertheless accepted the Secretary's rather lame explanations as to why he had not replied to the earlier notes: They were "accompanied by as indecent charges, and as offensive expressions as the letters of Genêt were ever marked with," and "the same things on former occasions, had been replied to . . . over and over again." [68] Certainly, the Chief Executive must have felt that the entire affair would have been much less serious had Pickering acted differently.

The President's immediate reaction under the circumstances was to seek the advice of Alexander Hamilton, then in New York. On the same day Adet's note appeared in the *Aurora* he wrote to Hamilton, imploring his help.[69] But time was short, and both Pickering and Wolcott believed that, with the election only four days off and Pennsylvania hanging in the balance, an immediate public reply was absolutely necessary. Reluctantly and without waiting for Hamil-

---

[67] Adet to Pickering, October 17, 1796, *A.S.P., F.R.*, I:1, 577.

[68] Washington to Hamilton, November 2, 1796, Washington, *Writings*, XXXV, 252.

[69] Washington to Hamilton, November 2, 1796, Washington, *Writings*, XXXV, 252.

ton's answer, Washington agreed, and Pickering set to work on a response to Adet's charges.[70]

Pickering's letter, which the Administration published in reply to Adet's, appeared in the *Gazette of the United States* on November 3. Drafted only the day before, it was an altogether wrathful, indignant, and defensive response. Washington's approval of it is perplexing, for the letter was completely out of keeping with the Administration's policies.

In his letter Pickering took up Adet's charges one by one, beginning with the accusation that the United States had repudiated its commitment under the stipulations of the Treaty of 1778 to defend its neutral rights. The question of the defense of "freedom of the seas," Pickering argued, was a closed matter. Adopting a narrow and inflexible interpretation of American obligations, the Secretary admitted only that the United States had maintained a traditionally sympathetic attitude toward the idea of "freedom of the seas." However, he continued, when the first major test of American policy came with the outbreak of the wars of the French Revolution, the United States made clear that it would not defend its view of neutral rights against the armed might of Britain. Pickering even went so far as to suggest that the British interpretation of belligerent and neutral rights was that which was generally accepted in international law. Freedom of the seas, he asserted, was little more than a dream for the future.

Pickering argued that the Treaty of 1778 had established a special commercial relationship between France and the United States. As a result of the treaty, French goods found on American vessels by British cruisers were legally subject to capture; the French, however,

---

[70] Liston to Grenville, November 15, 1796, Foreign Office, F.O. 115 (microfilm available at Library of Congress). Robert Liston, the British Minister and a confidant of Pickering's, explained in a dispatch to Lord Grenville that "the American ministry found the effect of the step [Adet's letter] to be so strong and so very unfavorable to themselves, particularly on account of their pretended neglect in leaving Mr. Adet's former note unanswered that they thought themselves constrained to make an immediate reply and to give their defence the same publicity that the minister had given to his attack. This last circumstance was reluctantly consented to by General Washington, who felt it to be inconsistent with that degree of dignity which he is desirous of preserving in every action particularly of his publick life."

did not have the reciprocal right to seize British goods carried on American vessels. France had sacrificed this right by the Treaty of 1778. Reciprocal advantage for the French would occur when they were neutral in a war in which the United States was a belligerent. Thus, as far as Timothy Pickering was concerned, the Jay Treaty had in no way altered the international situation; it had merely institutionalized it.

Pickering continued his reply to Adet by noting that the French Government had demanded that the United States renounce rights guaranteed it by special agreement with France simply because these placed France at a disadvantage. Angrily he contended: "The American Government Sir, conscious of the laws of neutrality, and of its inviolable regard to treaties, cannot for a moment admit that it has forfeited the right to claim a reciprocal observance of stipulations on the part of the French Republic; . . ." In answer to the charge that the Department of State had not replied to notes protesting the Administration's refusal to defend American seamen from British impressment, Pickering flatly stated that the matter was none of France's business. "As an independent nation, we were not bound to render an account to any other, of the measures we deemed proper for the protection of our own citizens." Furthermore, Pickering continued, Adet's notes had been phrased in such an insulting manner and were so full of unjustified insinuations, that "for the sake of preserving harmony, silence was preferred to a comment upon these insinuations." It is apparent from this letter that the Secretary was himself no longer interested in "preserving harmony."[71]

Certainly, Pickering did a creditable job of representing the American position on neutral rights. It was a stand that had been upheld by Jefferson earlier and would be maintained by John Adams later. Accuracy in representing the Administration's position was not, however, the real issue, for Pickering's public reply to Adet had much greater political than diplomatic significance. Adet had accused the Federalists of surrendering the principle of "freedom of the seas" in the face of British pressure; the Secretary substantively admitted that the United States recognized the British position as legitimate

---

[71] Pickering to Adet, November 1, 1796, *A.S.P., F.R.*, I:1, 578.

and that the Administration had no intention of defending the nation's neutral rights. Adet had accused the Administration of inaction in the face of British impressment of American seamen; Pickering replied by rebuking the French envoy for interfering in a question that was not his concern. Yet, as an ally, France had every right to inquire into this matter. Finally, Adet had strongly implied that the Federalists had long been openly hostile to France; anyone reading Pickering's outburst would instantly have become convinced that Adet's charges were well founded. In short, Pickering's note proved to be a monumental political blunder that stood as public testimony to the accuracy of Adet's charges.

It is impossible to assess correctly the impact of Adet's and Pickering's letters on the voting public in Pennsylvania. There are factors, however, that should be considered in an attempt to measure their effect. First of all, in the election in Pennsylvania there was a high degree of party regularity, which is to say that the mass of voters cast their ballots, not for individual electors, but for a slate of electors. Jefferson won 14 of the state's 15 electoral votes, but the majority that determined the victory for the Republican electors was razor thin. Out of a total of 24,487 votes cast, on the average only 125 more were given to Republican electors than to Federalists. In short, Adet's letter and the negative impact of Pickering's response did not have to impress a large number of voters in order to be significant.[72]

Perhaps it is only the weeping of the losers, but many Federalists believed that this exchange of letters between Adet and Pickering had had a drastic impact on the outcome of the election in Pennsylvania. Benjamin Goodhue, Federalist Senator from Massachusetts, believed that Adet's efforts had "an effect to establish the Anti-Ticket of Electors in this state."[73] William Bingham agreed: "We are unfortunate in the election in this state: . . . The most unwearied

---

[72] Kurtz, *Presidency of John Adams*, 184–90. Kurtz notes that, at the time, John Adams wrote: "Adet's note had some effect in Pennsylvania and proved a terror to some Quakers; and that is all the ill effect it had." As Professor Kurtz so aptly points out, if Adams was correct, then Adet achieved what he set out to do. It might also be argued that Pickering proved a useful assistant.

[73] Goodhue to King, December 12, 1796, cited in Rufus King, *Life and Correspondence of Rufus King*, C. R. King, ed., II, 124.

exertions accompanied by some bribery, and not a little chicane, have been practiced on this occasion by the anti-federal Party. They were essentially aided in their views by some of Mr. Adet's strokes of diplomatic finesse." [74]

Aside from the politics of the matter, there was diplomacy to be considered. Alexander Hamilton, who saw his carefully constructed pacific policy toward France disintegrating, was deeply distressed by Pickering's published harangue. Realizing that the New Englander did not take criticism well, he did not write directly to him, but instead warned both Washington and Oliver Wolcott, Jr., the Secretary of the Treasury, of the effects of such emotionalism in politics and diplomacy. The situation, he wrote, was very delicate, and hostilities with France were to be avoided if at all possible. If such diatribes as Pickering had just published were to continue, the United States could easily find itself in an unsolicited and undesirable war with France. "Nations," he noted, "like individuals sometimes get into squabbles from the manner more than the matter of what passes between them." Pickering, Hamilton warned, needed to be watched more carefully. [75]

Hamilton's warnings were important, for at this juncture the last scene between Pierre Adet and Timothy Pickering had yet to be played. On November 15, 1796, Adet published an open letter to the people of the United States, which was unquestionably designed to influence the meetings of presidential electors to be held in December. Carefully cataloging the sins of the Federalists, including the ill treatment of French privateers in American ports and the implementation of the Jay Treaty — which he referred to as "equivalent to a treaty of alliance with Great Britain" — Adet announced that his mission to the United States had been suspended. Affirming the friendship that Frenchmen everywhere felt for the American people, he made it clear that the restoration of amicable relations between the two nations would be simple, once the Government of

---

[74] Bingham to King, November 29, 1796, King, *Life and Correspondence*, II, 113.
[75] Hamilton to Washington, November 5, 1796, Papers of Alexander Hamilton (Library of Congress), XXIX; Hamilton to Wolcott, November 9, 1796, *ibid.*

the United States returned to the principles of neutrality from which it had strayed. In a wonderfully romanticized ending, Adet reached for the heartstrings of the American people: Reminding them of their Revolution and the sympathetic role played by France in that struggle, he called for reconciliation through the repudiation of Federalist policy:

> O! Americans covered with noble scars! O! You who have so often flown to death and to victory with French soldiers! You who know those generous sentiments which distinguish the true warrior! Whose hearts have always vibrated with those of your companions in arms! Consult them today, to know what they experience; recollect, at the same time, that, if magnanimous souls with liveliness resent an affront they also know how to forget one. Let your government return to itself, and you will still find in Frenchmen faithful friends and generous allies.[76]

Pickering's anger at this new evidence of French temerity was unbounded. Left unhindered, he would undoubtedly have produced a tirade that would have paled his earlier utterances. This time, however, the President saw no need for an immediate reply and, instead, wrote Hamilton for advice on how to treat Adet's second letter. The former Secretary of the Treasury, while emphasizing the importance of caution and reason, advised Washington to order a measured statement of the American position on neutral rights and other issues troubling Franco-American relations to be drafted by the Department of State and sent to Minister Pinckney for delivery to the Directory. A copy of this document, together with "a short auxiliary statement of the facts," should be sent to the House of Representatives. According to general practice the House would publish the statement, and it would be distributed throughout the country.[77]

The circumspection with which Washington proceeded in this case is in direct contrast to his earlier unfortunate and precipitate decision. He set Pickering to work on the painful job of developing a reasoned statement of American foreign policy — hardly a task congenial to one given, as Pickering was, to passionate outbursts. For

---

[76] Adet to Pickering, November 15, 1796, *A.S.P., F.R.*, I:1, 583.
[77] Hamilton to Washington, November 19, 1796, Hamilton, *Works*, 429–30.

more than a month the Secretary labored while Washington scrutinized. In early January the President explained to Pickering his reasons for taking such precautions:

> from a desire that the statement may be full, fair, calm, and argumentative; without asperity or anything more irritating in the comments than the narration of facts which expose unfounded charges and assertions, do themselves produce, I have wished that this letter to Mr. Pinckney may be revised over and over again. Much depends upon it as it relates to ourselves and in the eyes of the world; whatever may be the effect as it respects the governing powers of France.[78]

When the work was completed Washington took one last precaution: A copy of the letter to Pinckney was sent to Hamilton for his comment before publication.[79]

Eventually, after almost two months of unhurried preparation, Pickering's reply to Adet's later letter appeared in the form of a long and temperate address to Charles C. Pinckney, the American Minister to France.[80] In this paper the Secretary of State reviewed Franco-American relations from the outbreak of the European conflict. In it he made a clear, cogent, and dispassionate defense of American foreign policy, which gained for him the unanimous applause of his Federalist colleagues.[81] This paper, however, was a command performance and certainly did not reflect the attitudes of the Secretary himself.

As the Washington Administration wound toward its conclusion, Franco-American relations were in serious disarray. Undoubtedly, at bottom real issues divided the two nations. It would not be out of keeping, however, to suggest that the bitterness that had developed was at least exacerbated through the hostile ministrations of Timothy Pickering. Into a situation that required finesse, flexibility, and above

---

[78] Washington to Pickering, January 4, 1797, Washington, *Writings*, XXXV, 351–52.
[79] Washington to Hamilton, January 22, 1797, Washington, *Writings*, XXXV, 372–73.
[80] Pickering to Pinckney, January 21, 1797, Pickering Papers, XXXVII, 10.
[81] Cabot to Pickering, February 2, 1797, Pickering Papers, XXI, 26; Hamilton to Pickering, February 7, 1797, *ibid.*, 28; Jay to Pickering, January 31, 1797, *ibid.*, 23.

all a keen political sensitivity, he brought moral self-righteousness, rigidity, and an open and inveterate enmity for France. Intent upon preserving peace with England and convinced that the French were determined to precipitate a break in Anglo-American relations, he allowed his emotions to characterize his diplomacy. Pickering could have done little more to endanger both the peace and the Federalist hopes in the election of 1796.

4

ANGLOPHILIA, 1795-1796

$\mathcal{W}$HILE PRESIDING WITH DEVASTATING EFFECT over the conduct
of Franco-American relations, Pickering simultaneously struggled
to maintain a tenuous peace with the Mistress of the Seas. Despite
the recently negotiated Jay Treaty, the remaining months of the
Washington Administration were scarcely a time of real amity with
Britain. They were, rather, a time of trial and strain during which
the *modus vivendi* arrived at in 1794 was put to a severe test. Pickering was, of course, acutely aware of the economic importance for
New England of continued peace with the British. Beyond any
economic considerations was his deep admiration of England as a
powerful defender of political conservatism. He believed British
naval power to be the one force capable of thwarting the advance of
French arms and revolutionary ideology.[1]

Fitting complement to Pickering's attitude were the pacific sentiments of Britain's Foreign Secretary, William Wyndham, Lord
Grenville. Within the limits established by the Jay Treaty and the
requirements of British national security, Grenville also sought

---

[1] Pickering to J. Q. Adams, March 17, 1798, Pickering Papers (Massachusetts
Historical Society), VIII, 206.

friendly relations with the United States. He demonstrated this desire as early as the spring of 1795, when he responded affirmatively to John Jay's suggestion that a change of ministers at Philadelphia would aid in the maintenance of peace between the two nations.[2] Within six months, George Hammond, the cold and often arrogant British envoy who had become repugnant to American Federalists and Republicans alike, was recalled. His replacement was the congenial Robert Liston. A Scot and a career man in the British diplomatic service, Liston held very friendly predispositions toward the United States.[3]

The portents seemed good for continued peace and friendship between Britain and the United States. Yet, despite good intentions on both sides, maritime problems continued to threaten their amity, as far too often the insolence of British naval commanders promised to upset the unstable *status quo.* Even in August, 1795, at the height of the crisis over the President's ratification of the Jay Treaty, the actions of the captain of a British ship seriously endangered Anglo-American relations. For some time, Rodham Home, commanding H. M. S. *Africa,* had been prowling the waters off the coast of Rhode Island. Antagonized by the privileged sanctuary the French frigate *Medusa* had found at Newport, the British Commander was further angered by the unfriendly treatment his men had encountered ashore. Frustrated by his inability to strike at the *Medusa* and enraged by American hostility, Home apparently lost all sense of proportion when in late July he received news that a British naval officer, a prisoner on board the *Medusa,* had been given his parole in Newport. Although the British sloop upon which this unnamed officer had served had been taken at sea and brought to Newport by the French frigate, Home believed — or pretended to believe — that she had been illegally seized while riding at anchor in the American harbor. He addressed a blustering letter to Governor Fenner of Rhode Island, demanding the return to his ship not only of

---

[2] Jay to Grenville, March 21, 1795, in William Wyndham, Lord Grenville, *Report of the Manuscripts of J. B. Fortescue, Esq., Preserved at Dropmore,* W. Fitzpatrick, ed., III, 38–39.

[3] T. Pinckney to Pickering, March 7, 1796, Department of State, Diplomatic Dispatches, Great Britain, IV, unnumbered dispatch (National Archives).

the parolled officer but of "all British *or others* who have been captured in any vessels, and set at liberty in these states." The letter continued by demanding "not a *feigned* and *pretended* aid; but such as the British nation has a right to expect from the United States." Finally, Home wrote, he expected to be allowed to reprovision at Newport. While they were ashore for this purpose, he expected his officers and men to be treated with respect. If they were not, he would bring the town under his guns "to protect them." [4]

Home followed his ill-timed show of arrogance on the next day with a clumsy effort to capture the former French Minister, Joseph Fauchet, reportedly traveling on board an American coasting sloop. [5] His search of the little ship while it was well within American territorial waters was a clear violation of American sovereignty, the serious nature of which was compounded by his intention of abducting the former French Minister.

At the time these events were taking place, the President was at Mount Vernon, Edmund Randolph was still Secretary of State, and the Jay Treaty had not yet received Presidential ratification. In fact, July 31, the date upon which Home addressed his insulting letter to Rhode Island's Governor Fenner, was the same day that Pickering wrote to urge Washington's return to Philadelphia for the confrontation with Randolph. Quite naturally, considering the events of the days that followed, affairs at the capital were rather badly deranged, and the Administration was slow to respond to this new British challenge.

It was not until August 19 that Randolph resigned and Pickering stepped in as Acting Secretary. Naturally, he was furious with Captain Home, in view of the danger to Anglo-American relations created by that arrogant officer at so crucial a moment. He was also anxious to extract an apology from the British chargé, Phineas Bond. But Bond would put nothing in writing and at the oral level strove to

---

[4] Home to Gov. Arthur Fenner, July 31, 1795, *American State Papers, Foreign Relations,* I:1, 667; Pickering to Bond, September 2, 1795, Pickering Papers, XXXV, 105-8. My italics.

[5] Notarized affidavit signed by Captain Thomas Bliss of the sloop *Peggy* and by Louis Amédée Pichon, former French Secretary of Legation at Philadelphia, *A.S.P., F.R.,* I:1, 663; Republican newspapers made much of Home's actions. *Aurora,* August 16, 1795; *Philadelphia Minerva,* August 29, 1795.

defend Home. Still, Pickering remained cautious, and throughout the remainder of August, apparently with the approval of Washington, he patiently awaited British explanations.

In the end it was Home and not Pickering or Washington who forced the issue. At the close of August he added to his already impressive list of offences by stopping the American sloop *Anne* at the entrance to Newport harbor, well within American territorial waters. An armed party boarded the *Anne* and impressed three seamen. This latest violation of American sovereignty finally moved the Administration to action. On Washington's instructions Pickering lodged a vigorous protest with Bond, in which he excoriated the British Commander and denied to the *Africa* any further hospitality in American waters. Moreover, the British vice-consul at Newport, for having delivered Home's earlier letter to Governor Fenner, was stripped of his exequatur.

Even in anger, however, Pickering revealed his essential Anglophilia. He made it clear to Bond that he did not believe Home to be representative of the true attitudes of the British Ministry, and he once again affirmed his belief that His Majesty's Government sought only peace and friendly relations with the United States. Feeling it necessary to emphasize the dangers to peace should American opinion become overwrought at the irresponsible actions of men like Captain Home, Pickering concluded his note in a pessimistic vein and expressed "regret that, at the moment when an amicable adjustment of past difficulties, after years of alienation, gave hopes of returning friendship and goodwill — at the moment when the respective interests of our two nations required a careful avoidance of every act that could excite animosities afresh, — the disagreeable transactions, which are the subject of this letter, should have taken place."[6]

Home's actions were a subject of serious concern to Pickering. The Jay Treaty, while it had preserved peace, had not ended the hostility Americans felt for Britain. Pickering feared that the aggressions of blustering naval commanders, such as Home, and the continued

---

[6] Pickering to Bond, September 2, 1795, Octavius Pickering and Charles W. Upham, *The Life of Timothy Pickering*, III, 233-37.

depredations by British cruisers on American commerce would re-
vive popular anger and frustrate his efforts for peace. Adding to his
anxieties were the activities of the Republican press, determined to
exploit every evidence of British hostility in its efforts to undercut
the position of the Federalist Administration. The Secretary believed
that the effect such British aggressions might have upon an already
aroused American public could be catastrophic both for the Federalist coalition in the coming elections and for the cause of peace with
England.

The danger of stumbling into war with Great Britain was ever
present in the thoughts of the Secretary. Only a few days after having taken action against Captain Home, he again expressed his fears
in a dispatch to John Quincy Adams, who was then journeying to
London. He reiterated both his belief that Home's actions were not
representative of British policy and his fear that their effect might
be disastrous in any case: "If Britain studied to keep up the irritation in the minds of Americans, and wished to prevent the return
of our good will, some of her naval commanders appear perfectly
qualified for the object." [7]

Vexations caused by British aggressions on the high seas were
not confined to the belligerent acts of intransigent naval officers.
Throughout 1795 and into 1796, English privateers based in the
West Indies, particularly those sailing out of Bermuda, continued
almost daily to capture American merchant vessels. William Fitz-
simmons, chairman of the Committee of Merchants of Philadelphia,
was urgent in his demands that officials put an end to the attacks.
Theodore Lyman from Massachusetts, Marcus and Clausland, merchants of Baltimore, and numerous others pressed the State Department for action.[8] Pickering responded vigorously to this new British

---

[7] Pickering to J. Q. Adams, September 12, 1795, Department of State, Diplomatic Instructions, III, 40–41 (National Archives). It is an interesting com-
mentary on Pickering's perceptions to note that the British Ministry refused to
punish Home. King to Pickering, April 29, 1797, Department of State, Diplomatic Dispatches, Great Britain, IV.

[8] Pickering to Pinckney, October 22, 1795, Pickering Papers, XXXV, 304–5;
Pickering to Marcus and Clausland, November 27, 1795, 320; Lyman to Pickering, November 15, 1795, XX, 100–101.

challenge, for here not merely national honor, but commerce as well, was threatened.

In October, 1795, he wrote to Bond, protesting the actions of the marauders in the Caribbean and of their local courts of admiralty. How long, he wondered, could peace be maintained between the two nations when adventurers who flew the British flag continued to capture American merchant vessels?[9] Unless the British authorities took preventive action, the United States would be driven to hostilities, despite the Secretary's efforts to maintain peace. Later in the month he wrote the American Minister in London, Thomas Pinckney, urging him to bring the matter to the attention of the Ministry: "The American commerce if not soon suspended will be annihilated, if it is to become the sport of so many plunderers, on such light pretenses." If the British Government wished to cultivate our friendship, he informed Pinckney, the excesses of the renegades in Bermuda must be curbed.[10] Eventually, Pickering took his case to the Governor of Bermuda, appealing to him for aid in halting the depredations.[11]

Pickering's fears may be traced not only to a natural concern for the security of American commerce but to political considerations as well. The growing strength of republicanism within the United States and the impetus given it by constant reports in the press of new acts of British hostility were sources of grave concern to the Secretary. In the face of continued British aggressions, it was almost impossible for Federalists to justify the Jay Treaty or the entire tendency of their foreign policy. With the presidential elections only a year in the future, it was imperative that Britain alter her policy of harassment. Unless she did, America might have a Republican

---

[9] Pickering to Bond, October 12, 1795, Department of State, Domestic Letters, VIII, 434–35; for a few of the numerous newspaper stories dealing with the Bermudans, see the *Philadelphia Aurora*, January 6, February 6, March 27, October 8, 1795. Especially interesting is the *Philadelphia Minerva*'s account of how an angry Boston mob burned to the water line a suspected British privateer that had been docked at Boston's long wharf, June 27, 1795.

[10] Pickering to T. Pinckney, October 22, 1795, Department of State, Diplomatic Instructions, III, 76–80.

[11] Pickering to Crawford, April 21, 1796, Pickering Papers, XXXVI, 49.

President in 1797. Such a circumstance, Pickering believed, although it might not bring about a social revolution, would surely move the United States into the orbit of France.

The British Government was slow to react to Pickering's urgings. While the Foreign Secretary certainly desired friendship with the United States, his concern in this direction should not be overestimated. Fully occupied by the war in Europe, Grenville had little time to deal with Anglo-American relations. Once aroused to the dangers of the situation, however, he moved to halt the worst excesses of the "Bermuda privateers." Throughout 1796 and 1797, British captures of American vessels steadily declined, and by June, 1797, while French captures were mounting into the hundreds, British seizures had dwindled to insignificance.[12] Timothy Pickering could claim a certain tactical diplomatic success. He had made the British Ministry aware of a dangerous situation, and it had been alleviated.

Lord Grenville's lack of any vital concern over the problems clouding Anglo-American relations was due, of course, to the fact that Britain was at war with France. War placed serious limitations upon the pacific quality of the Ministry's American policy. Britain would do nothing, consent to nothing, that in any way might endanger the security or strength of the English nation. As a result, one major source of irritation — impressment — continued. England's survival rested upon her ability to maintain naval superiority, and Britain, always with more ships than seamen to man them, was unwilling to negotiate the question with the United States.[13]

The issue of impressment had been serious enough to cause con-

---

[12] Pickering to John Adams, June 21, 1797, Pickering Papers, VI, 369.

[13] British and American diplomats were unable to agree upon a satisfactory definition of American citizenship that might be used to judge whether an impressed seaman was British or American. The American government recognized the right of foreigners to become American citizens; but Britain, for her part, denied this right to her citizens. By British definition, citizens of the United States included only persons born in the United States (either before or after American independence was recognized) or persons who had migrated to the United States before 1783. In his decisions of February 9, 1797, Sir William Scott, justice of Britain's most important court of admiralty, set the long-standing precedent in writing. A copy of this decision may be found in the Rufus King Papers (New York Historical Society), under the date of the decision.

cern even before John Jay's mission to London. It became far more serious early in 1796, when the British, who had previously confined acts of impressment to their own ports, began to impress seamen from the decks of American ships at sea. The very sovereignty of the United States was threatened. Was an American ship American territory? If so, the Royal Navy had no more right to impress men aboard American vessels than it had to send press gangs into the streets of Boston.

Prior to February, 1796, the Administration had been unwilling to make an issue of impressment. Jay had held conversations with Grenville about it in 1794, but he had never really urged action on the matter and the British treaty was silent on the subject. Had it not been for the fact that in 1796 the question became partisan in nature, the Government might have continued to ignore it officially. It was Edward Livingston, Republican Representative from New York, who focused national attention on impressment when he introduced legislation to provide seamen serving on board American vessels with certification of identification as protection against impressment into the Royal Navy.[14] The bill authorized the President to send agents to the West Indies and England to investigate reported acts of impressment and to work to free Americans unjustly seized. One of the controversial aspects of the bill was the fact that it made no distinction between native and naturalized Americans, authorizing the issuance of protections to both groups on equal terms. It further authorized the issuance of certificates of identification to citizens of neutral nations serving on American ships.[15]

In part, the Republicans were honestly distressed that the Administration had been so inactive with regard to impressment. Their distress had been apparent for some time. One of the less known objections raised by opponents of the Jay Treaty, for example, had been its failure to settle this question. Legislation would force the Government to action. Even if the bill failed, a legislative debate,

---

[14] *Debates and Proceedings in the Congress of the United States*, 4th Cong., 1st Sess., 802; James F. Zimmerman, *Impressment of American Seamen*, 55–59.
[15] Zimmerman, *Impressment*, 58.

complemented by press coverage of impressments at sea, would arouse public interest and force the Administration to act.

Looking at the situation from another standpoint, it is difficult to avoid the conclusion that there were political as well as humanitarian reasons behind Livingston's proposal. Certainly the bill at least made sense politically. Soon the House would be the last battleground for opponents of the Jay Treaty. The fight over appropriations for its implementation would be a bitter one. The more publicity of a negative nature for both the Administration and England at this point, the better were the Republicans' chances of blocking the treaty in the House.

It was difficult for Federalists in the House to oppose the bill. A question of national honor was involved, and even though Federalist diplomacy was in many ways based upon the sacrifice of honor to preserve peace, it was unwise to admit this publicly. Some Federalists did speak out. Representative Joshua Coit of Connecticut, one of the more vocal and extreme Federalists in the House, agreed that impressment was a serious problem but argued that the Livingston bill did not offer an effective solution. Indeed, he believed it would cause more problems with Britain, for in the first place the proofs of citizenship required by the measure were inadequate. Any sailor who could bring one witness to swear to his citizenship before a justice of the peace was entitled to official protection. This procedure allowed too much room for fraud and, this being the case, the British would refuse to respect the certificates. Coit also questioned the right of Congress to legislate on impressment. This, it seemed to him, was a matter for diplomacy; legislation not only could not help, but would be an infringement upon the executive authority.

Coit's argument is of considerable interest to the student of Federalist diplomacy. His position was founded upon the assumptions that the British actually had a right to search American merchant ships for deserters and that the United States would have to find a way to reconcile its interest with the rights of England. Livingston's bill offended Coit and like-minded colleagues because it was an assertion that an American flag flying from the masthead of a merchant ship made of that ship American territory. Coit would not accept this idea. To his way of thinking the proposed bill solved no problems and created only greater difficulties for Anglo-American relations.[16]

Uriah Tracy, a Connecticut colleague of Coit's and possibly the most extreme Federalist in the House, went even further in his objections to Livingston's bill. Not only did Britain have the right to seize deserters from on board American vessels, but she could also consider every former Briton who had taken American citizenship as a deserter. Naturalization, Tracy argued, did not give a man the right to renounce his obligations to his native land. It was "one of the first laws of society" that the natives of a nation had an obligation to defend it in time of trial. No one ought to be surprised or angered, then, when Great Britain, in the midst of a great war, used every means at her disposal to call her sons to her service.[17]

In defense of his bill, Livingston pointed out first that Congress was not exceeding its authority in legislating on the matter. Clearly, the President had no constitutional power to send agents to the West Indies or England to investigate impressments. He needed legislative authorization.[18] Albert Gallatin, in a more devastating reply to the charge of interference in affairs of the executive, argued that diplomacy had had its chance, that the Jay Treaty was silent on the question of impressment, and that the British Government seemed unwilling to make any concessions. Certainly all pacific means short of war should be used in an attempt to solve the problem. The issuance of protections might be of help.[19]

Getting at the essence of the Federalist argument, Livingston, Gallatin, William Branch Giles of Virginia, and others struck hard at its embarrassing weakness. Livingston, for example, noted that the Federalists' opposition was founded on the view that the British had the right to search American vessels and impress British deserters from their decks. Livingston denied this right. Each time an act of impressment took place on board an American vessel, he argued, it was "the grossest violation of the rights of nations. . . . [T]he vessels of the United States . . . were as much the territory

---

[16] *Debates and Proceedings*, 4th Congress, 802–3.
[17] *Debates and Proceedings, ibid.*, 807.
[18] *Debates and Proceedings, ibid.*, 804.
[19] *Debates and Proceedings, ibid.*, 806.

of the United States as the ground of the territory itself." Livingston was not surprised that the British so misused ships and seamen of the United States and so trampled on American rights; it was the Federalist Administration that was at fault for not defending those rights. "We are weary . . . of their oppressions; and when they see us determined to defend and protect our seamen, they will beware how they offend a great nation; . . ."[20]

Opposition to Livingston's bill was futile, for national honor was at stake and there were few Federalists who were willing to take a stand against that. A vain effort to recommit the measure failed, and it passed the House of Representatives on March 28, by an overwhelming majority.[21] The bill, however, had yet to pass the Senate.

The Administration was forced to action by the political pressures brought to bear upon it by the Republicans. Only a little more than a week before Livingston's bill passed the House, Pickering suddenly became vitally interested in impressment and addressed a strong note to the British chargé, protesting the outrageous acts of impressment committed "almost daily by His Majesty's naval forces in the West Indies." He warned that American opinion would not long tolerate such indignities.[22] Bond replied, noting that Pickering had used as the basis for his protest a series of unsubstantiated reports of impressments carried in the American press. Considering the well-known Anglophobia of some American journalists, Bond refused to accept such reports as legitimate grounds for action. Pickering, recognizing the need for official data on impressment, dispatched a circular letter to the collectors of customs in all ports on the Atlantic seaboard to urge that they obtain affidavits from witnesses to British acts of impressment and that these be immediately forwarded to the Department of State.[23]

Throughout the spring of 1796 reports of impressments streamed

---

[20] *Debates and Proceedings, ibid.*, 804.

[21] *Debates and Proceedings, ibid.*, 810.

[22] Pickering to Bond, March 19, 1796, Department of State, Domestic Letters, IX, 78 (National Archives).

[23] Pickering to Benjamin Lincoln, March 22, 1796, Department of State, Domestic Letters, IX, 80. See also Pickering to all Collectors of Customs, March 25, 1796, *ibid.*, 83–84.

in, and Pickering made numerous requests for the release of American seamen, accompanying each request with affidavits of witnesses to the act of impressment. Thus, the Secretary adopted a piecemeal approach to the problem. Time and a great deal of energy were being wasted in these efforts, while American seamen remained subject to the indignity and danger of impressment. Furthermore, newspaper reports of impressments continued to appear in the Republican press, dimming the Federalists' chances in the approaching presidential elections. It was obvious that the Livingston bill offered an immediate solution by providing a method of identifying seamen as Americans, prior to impressment.

Under the circumstances even the Federalist-controlled Senate had little choice but to pass the bill. The Senate's changes forced a meeting of a Senate-House conference committee, which agreed to the Livingston bill as it had passed the House, with only one amendment: Applicants for certificates of protection were required to produce proof of birth or baptism in addition to one creditable witness in order to qualify. On May 28, 1796, "An Act for Relief and Protection of American Seamen" was signed into law. Ironically, the Senate amendment was inexplicably omitted from the law in its final form. The President attempted to correct this fault by issuing an executive order to collectors of customs to require certificates of birth or baptism before issuing the certificates of protection. The British Government, however, never accepted this executive order as having the force of law.[24] By the time the law came into effect the diplomatic situation had become quite serious. Pickering now was furious with the British, for he honestly believed they were in the wrong. Beyond the diplomatic level, however, as reports of impressment continued, public opinion in the United States — never friendly to Great Britain — grew more bitterly antagonistic. By May, 1796, a thoroughly agitated Secretary of State wrote to Thomas Pinckney in London, declaring that British policy was not only unjust, but that it was also endangering the peace between the two nations. Pickering deplored Britain's inability to "restrain so many oppressive acts" on the part of her naval commanders, acts that were often

---

24 Zimmerman, *Impressment*, 60.

committed in full knowledge of the American nationality of the seamen impressed. The acts of Britain's naval officers, he believed, kept anti-British sentiment at a high pitch in the United States and worked a serious hardship upon those who sought to preserve peace.[25]

Moved by the urgency of the situation, the Secretary acted immediately to implement the new law. David Lenox was appointed as the American agent in Great Britain for the relief of impressed seamen, while Silas Talbot, a war hero of the Revolution soon to become the first commander of the famed U.S.S. *Constitution*, was sent to the West Indies. Talbot's mission was crucial, for the Caribbean was the area where the problem of impressment was most serious.[26]

It was clear that without the cooperation of the British Ministry Talbot had no chance of success. Therefore, Pickering urged the newly arrived British Minister, Robert Liston, to write letters of introduction for Talbot, suggesting to British officials in the West Indies that they help him in his mission. In making this unusual request, Pickering reminded the new Minister that in his first meeting with the President he had stated his desire to foster conciliation between the United States and Great Britain. The Secretary warned that, unless something was done about impressment, "conciliation" would "be a visionary idea." [27]

Pickering's unusual request put Liston in a quandary. Though truly eager to see relations between the United States and Great Britain improve, he realized that for him to write such letters would be to exceed his instructions in a way that might create serious problems for him in London. Nevertheless, his first impulse was to comply with Pickering's request, and early in July he actually wrote a letter to the Governor of Barbados urging cooperation with Talbot.[28]

---

[25] Pickering to Pinckney, May 3, 1796, Department of State, Diplomatic Instructions, IV, 127–28.

[26] Pickering to Talbot, June 3, 1796, Department of State, Domestic Letters, IX, 149.

[27] Pickering to Liston, June 25, 1796, Department of State, Domestic Letters, IX, 181–83.

[28] Liston to the Governor of Barbados, July 7, 1796, Department of State, Notes from Foreign Legations, Great Britain, II (National Archives).

Liston immediately had second thoughts, however, and he temporarily withheld his letter.

Liston's hesitancy was justified, for on May 19, 1796, Grenville had dispatched specific instructions to govern the British Minister's actions in this matter. Specifically referring to the legislation regarding impressment, which was, he understood, then under consideration in the American Congress, the Foreign Secretary categorically rejected the proposal to dispatch an agent to the West Indies and made it clear that protections issued to American seamen would not be accepted by the British as proof of American citizenship. In Grenville's words "it cannot be expected that His Majesty's Government will so far depart from the policy which it has invariably observed with regard to its foreign dependencies, as to tolerate the residence in them of Official agents appointed by the American Government, or that the certificate of Citizenship granted by the United States will be considered here as evidence of the fact so conclusive as to supersede the necessity of any farther enquiry." It was Grenville's view that the impressment of native Americans was at most of minor consequence and that the vast majority of impressed seamen were in actuality Britons. The Foreign Secretary was quick to assert that in cases where error could be proved Great Britain would act promptly to rectify injustice.[29]

Had Robert Liston received this dispatch in time, he undoubtedly would have withheld his letter to the Governor of Barbados, but Grenville's dispatch was delayed and Liston acted before it arrived. Ironically, it was the brutal action of a British naval officer that convinced Liston of the utility of Talbot's mission and precipitated his decision to issue letters in support of the American agent. Captain Hugh Pigot of the frigate *Success* had halted the American merchant vessel *Mercury*, flogged her captain, and impressed six American seamen. Liston was aghast at the violent American reaction to the British Commander's brutality.[30] Convinced that Pigot was the ex-

[29] Grenville to Bond, Dispatch #12, May 19, 1796, in Bernard Mayo, ed., "Instructions to the British Ministers to the United States, 1791–1812," *American Historical Association Annual Report, 1936*, III, 118–19.

[30] Liston to Grenville, August 13, 1796, Great Britain, Foreign Office, F.O. 115, Archives, America, United States of America, Correspondence of British Diplomatic Representatives, Selections, 1791–1902, P.R.O.

ception and not the rule among British naval commanders, he believed an investigation, even if conducted by an American agent, would reveal that impressment of American seamen was of little significance. Therefore, Liston, who considered the current of hostility in the United States as dangerous, decided to transmit his letter introducing Talbot to the Governor of Barbados. He also sent a circular letter to civil and naval officials in the Caribbean, urging full cooperation with Talbot. In these and other private communications to the West Indies the Minister urged British naval officers to be circumspect in the impressment of seamen claiming to be Americans. He even went so far as to advise the wisdom of allowing suspected Englishmen to remain in the American merchant service rather than to run the risk of unjustly impressing native Americans.[31]

Two weeks later Liston received Grenville's overdue dispatch and immediately acted to extricate himself from his difficulties. In midmorning of August 12 he paid a personal call upon the Secretary of State and informed him that the Ministry would refuse to allow the United States to maintain a resident agent in the West Indies. Liston remarked that, in dispatching his letter to the Governor of Barbados and his circular letter to other governors and naval officers in the Caribbean, he had gone far beyond his instructions. He had issued them, he said, in the hope that the Ministry would see the value of cooperation in this matter. As the Ministry did not regard the matter in the same light, Liston now urged Talbot's immediate recall.

Startled by this serious reversal, Pickering complimented Liston on his own farsighted attitude and deplored the fact that Lord Grenville apparently did not share it. At some time, either during this conversation or one that may have followed and is unrecorded, Pickering learned the exact stipulations of the Foreign Secretary's instructions. His intent was perfectly clear: to stop the United States from making any investigation of impressment in the West Indies. But the instructions Liston received left a loophole: A *permanent*

---

[31] Later, Liston was to take a far less liberal approach to the question. See, for example, Liston to Sir John Temple, March 31, 1798, in the Bowdoin and Temple Papers, Part II, in Massachusetts Historical Society, *Collections*, Series 7, VI, 216–20.

resident agent was prohibited; Grenville had said nothing about a roving envoy in the islands.

Pickering decided to proceed with Talbot's mission, though it was clear the British Ministry disapproved. Prospects for Talbot's success were "unpromising" from the start, but American public opinion would be outraged if he were not permitted to investigate impressment. Furthermore, what would the opposition make of this new example of "British amity"? Pickering wrote Talbot to inform him that the British Foreign Office had prohibited his permanent residence in the Indies. However, as his withdrawal was not officially demanded by Grenville, there was nothing to stop him from acting there as a roving agent. In fact, the nature of his assignment required that he move about from port to port.[32]

A scene similar to the one that occurred between Pickering and Liston in Philadelphia had taken place a few days earlier between Grenville and Rufus King, the new American Minister to the Court of Saint James's. Perhaps a bit naïve, and undoubtedly anxious, King had barely arrived in London before he sought his first audience with the Foreign Secretary. The American Minister has left a vivid description of that meeting which indicates that Grenville firmly disapproved of Talbot's agency in the Caribbean and warned that the governors of the various British West Indian islands could not permit the agent's residence within their jurisdiction. Furthermore, without special instructions, they might even refuse Talbot permission to land in the islands. Grenville wanted Talbot recalled and King knew it, but King refused to yield.[33] What followed between the two men is unrecorded. Perhaps the American convinced the Foreign Secretary of the importance to the Federalist party of allowing Talbot to continue his mission, or perhaps Grenville merely decided that Talbot's agency might help Anglo-American relations. At any rate, Grenville withdrew his opposition and agreed to allow Talbot to operate as a roving American agent in the West Indies.

---

[32] See Pickering's notes on a conversation with Robert Liston on August 24, 1796, Department of State, Notes to Foreign Legations, I, 97–99 (National Archives).

[33] Rufus King to Pickering, August 10, 1796, Department of State, Diplomatic Dispatches, Great Britain, V, Dispatch #1.

Silas Talbot's mission proved a mixed blessing. Throughout the last months of 1796 and well into 1797, he encountered a cooperative and, in some instances, a friendly spirit among British officialdom in the West Indies. Furthermore, he did not uncover the hundreds of unjustly impressed Americans most of the American people had expected. He learned instead that the instances of British impressment, although serious, had been exaggerated in the American press. Most encouragingly, during almost six months of investigation, Talbot was informed of only one new case of impressment, indicating that with Talbot on the scene British commanders were demonstrating a wholly new circumspection with regard to the practice of impressment.[34] It appeared that Pickering had achieved another partial diplomatic success.

Unfortunately, however, in the late spring of 1797, the spirit of cooperation on the part of the British command in the West Indies changed to one of fixed opposition. Admiral Sir Hyde Parker, who was in command in the area, began to have the men in his command who sought Talbot's aid summarily and brutally punished. When Talbot obtained writs of habeas corpus from British courts, ordering British commanders to produce alleged impressed Americans, Parker ordered that the writs be ignored.[35] By July, 1797, what had begun as a promising experiment threatened to become a dangerous disadvantage to Federalism.

Pickering sought desperately to save the situation by a direct appeal to Liston.[36] The Minister could do little. He tried to soothe the Secretary's temper, but without success. "The ill treatment of American seamen," he reported to the Foreign Secretary, "is the only subject upon which I have never been able to get him to speak with moderation."[37] In fact, Admiral Parker had the complete sympathy of the Ministry and Liston knew it. The Ministry's attitude was linked closely to the growing problem of desertion by British seamen into the American merchant service, a problem that reached near

---

[34] Pickering to John Adams, June 21, 1797, Pickering Papers, VI, 369; Zimmerman, *Impressment*, 62–69.

[35] Talbot to Pickering, July 4, 1797, Pickering Papers, VI, 393.

[36] Pickering to Liston, August 11, 1797, Pickering Papers, VII, 68.

[37] Liston to Grenville, August 30, 1797, Great Britain, Foreign Office, F.O., 115.

epidemic proportions by early 1797. In May, Liston himself had warned the Ministry of this increasing danger and had urged that it required "the serious attention of His Majesty's Ministers. If the progress of this evil is alarming," he warned, "the consequence that may possibly arise from it to the disturbance of the harmony between the two nations appear to be no less dangerous."[38]

The British proposed as a solution to the impasse an additional article to the Jay Treaty to provide for mutual exchange of deserters. Such a solution was unsatisfactory to the Americans because it totally ignored the entire question of impressment. "This proposal," King warned, "embraces only part of a subject of great extent and importance and it does not appear to me that it would be consistent with good policy to enter into any partial stipulations respecting it: more especially when our repeated overtures to adjust the entire subject on principles of liberality and mutual advantage if not neglected, have not been received in the manner we had a right to expect."[39] Pickering refused to discuss the issue of desertion as a question separate from impressment, and deadlock ensued. One result of deadlock was that the Ministry gave its complete support to Sir Hyde Parker. So long as America would not agree to the mutual return of deserters, American agents would not be allowed to roam about among British squadrons in search of impressed seamen. By October, 1797, it was clear to Pickering that "Colonel Talbot's agency in the West Indies" was "no longer very important," and he was recalled.[40]

Silas Talbot's mission had served to highlight the issue of impressment. Great Britain retained the initiative, but the Secretary of State continued to seek a satisfactory agreement. He believed that Congress had provided the basis for one in its plan for issuing protections to American seamen, and he hoped that the British would agree to accept such papers as positive proof of American citizenship — this, despite the fact that such hopes should earlier have been shattered by disheartening reports from Minister King. In the first place

---

[38] Liston to Grenville, May 12, 1797, Great Britain, Foreign Office, F.O., 115.
[39] King to Pickering, July 27, 1797, Department of State, Diplomatic Dispatches, Great Britain, V, Dispatch #40.
[40] Pickering to King, October 3, 1797, Pickering Papers, XXXVII, 239.

Grenville had refused to accept as positive proof of citizenship the protections carried by American sailors. Moreover, he angrily protested and later prohibited the distribution of protections by American consular agents in the British Isles.[41] The Foreign Secretary took this position even though European consular officials resident in England were allowed precisely this privilege.[42] Grenville's discriminatory actions were, like so much else, linked directly to the growing problem of desertion by British seamen to the American merchant marine. Once a deserter had made his move, it was ridiculously simple for him to pretend to be an American and thus obtain false papers from American consular agents in England. The proof of citizenship required by America's representatives before conferring such papers was at best vague.

Rufus King refused to believe that desertions were the reason behind British obduracy. For some time he had felt that Britain was discriminating against the United States in a purely cynical effort to retain in her naval service not only British subjects but Americans as well. Thoroughly discouraged, the American Minister had written, "I cannot allow myself to believe that ultimately they will decline entering into a reasonable convention on this subject. But as they believe that their national safety depends essentially upon their marine they feel unusual caution relative to a stipulation that by mere possibility can deprive their navy of a single seaman who is a real British subject or that may even diminish the chance of obtaining the services of those who are not British subjects, but who by various pretences are detained in service as such."[43] In King's view, the United States might go on achieving the release of a seaman here and there upon presentation to the British Government of positive proof that the man in question was an American citizen, but it seemed that Great Britain would never relinquish its initiative by entering into an agreement on the subject.

The efforts of Timothy Pickering and the Washington Adminis-

---

[41] King to Pickering, April 13, 1797, Pickering Papers, VIII, 173.
[42] King to Grenville, January 28, 1797, in *Life and Correspondence of Rufus King*, Charles R. King, ed., II, 139.
[43] In King to Pickering, October 16, 1796, Department of State, Diplomatic Dispatches, Great Britain, V, Dispatch #9; Robert Ernst, *Rufus King*, 239.

tration to reach a satisfactory agreement with Britain on impressment had failed. Nevertheless, Pickering's diplomacy had yielded certain political and diplomatic gains. Seamen were being released when actual proof of American citizenship was presented to British authorities. More important, during the crucial election autumn of 1796 British impressments had become much less aggravating as British commanders heeded the urgings of Robert Liston to be more circumspect in the practice.

These first eighteen months of Pickering's stewardship in the Department of State had not seen any considerable lessening of tensions between London and Philadelphia. The unstable but peaceful *status quo* had merely been preserved. The cost of even this small accomplishment, in terms of national honor, had been high. Yet it had been a price Pickering proved personally willing to pay. Often angered by the outrages of British cruisers or by the impressment of American seamen, he never allowed his emotions to go out of control. Convinced of Britain's peaceful intentions and of the desirability of friendly relations with her, he doggedly pressed for agreements that would satisfy his government, pacify American opinion, and justify Federalist policy.

When John Adams succeeded Washington as President on March 4, 1797, he did not inherit a stable and friendly relationship with Great Britain. Rather, he faced the prospect of dealing with the deteriorating French situation while confronted by the distinct possibility that at any time the unstable *modus vivendi* that had been maintained between Philadelphia and London might collapse. A new rash of impressments in the Caribbean, or a grievous insult to the flag perpetrated by an arrogant British naval officer might precipitate disaster.

5

A NEW NEGOTIATION

*D*ESPITE THE CHANGE OF ADMINISTRATIONS in March, 1797, Pickering remained firmly seated in the Cabinet as Secretary of State. Adams was content to retain Washington's Cabinet, and there can be no doubt that the Secretary of State was pleased to remain. But frictions between the two men were inevitable. Throughout the period in which he served as Secretary of State for Washington, Pickering had exercised rather wide administrative autonomy. In a fashion, he had been able to set the tone of American policy on a day-to-day basis. Moreover, during this entire period, he had never been called upon to represent a policy of which he did not approve — an important factor, for the ruggedly independent Secretary took his own administrative autonomy seriously. He had never served as subordinate to anyone, even Washington, without chafing. As Secretary of State, he fancied himself not as an administrative appendage of the President but as an independent officer of the government. The suggestion that Cabinet officers who could not in good conscience carry out the orders of the President should resign their offices drew from him the startling observation that obstruction, not subordination, to the President's wishes was the real duty of Cabinet members. "I should think it their duty," he once remarked, "to prevent as far as practicable the mischievous measures of a wrong headed President."[1]

Pickering's pride and strong sense of individualism were bound to bring him into conflict with Adams. The new President, after all, was at least as proud and as independent as his Secretary of State. Moreover, his was the constitutional power, and he was determined to assert it. Policy, Adams believed, was made by the President. Cabinet members were to carry out the President's orders quickly and unquestioningly.

The potential for conflict between the new President and his inherited Secretary of State, then, lay deep within the personalities of the two men. Still, the battle that eventually took place between them might never have occurred had it not been for their differences over the conduct of foreign policy. Pickering's essentially unbalanced approach to diplomacy, his trust of the English in particular, ran directly counter to Adams' more realistic view of the nature of international relations. The President's long diplomatic career had taught him to set aside his political and moral predispositions when making judgments in the area of diplomacy. He accepted the general view that all European nations served only their own "true interests" and that friendship could never be relied upon as an agent in international affairs. He adhered consistently to the old views he had been so insistent upon during the American Revolution, that America must choose a rigidly neutral course, bending benevolently toward no European power. In 1796, a few weeks following the November election, he wrote a testament to this view to his wife, then at home in Quincy, Massachusetts. He feared, he said, English "kindness as much as French severity"; he intended to be "the dupe of neither."[2]

Another nascent source of conflict between the two men lay in the Secretary of State's friendly relationship with Alexander Hamilton. Fiercely independent, Pickering seldom played the willing pawn for Hamilton, but he admired the New Yorker both for his political

---

[1] Pickering to McHenry, February 13, 1811, in James McHenry, *Life and Correspondence of James McHenry*, Bernard C. Steiner, ed., 568.

[2] Page Smith, *John Adams*, II, 903.

convictions and for his personal decisiveness. Hamilton could always count upon a friendly listener in Timothy Pickering.

On the other hand, Hamilton and Adams were, to say the least, cool toward one another. Indeed, during the campaign of 1796, Hamilton had gone so far as to work for Adams' defeat. Adams, on his part, considered Hamilton "a proud spirited, conceited aspiring mortal always pretending to morality, with as debauched morals as old Franklin." He was quite willing to admit that the New Yorker was a man of talent, but these were not talents Adams admired. As President-elect, he had already decided to "take no notice of his puppyhood but retain the same opinion of him I always had and maintain the same conduct towards him I always did, that is keep him at a distance." [3]

Even as President-elect, Adams had been warned by some of his closest friends that the Cabinet he was about to inherit was filled with his enemies. Elbridge Gerry, often erratic but always loyal, did his best, prior to the inauguration, to warn Adams of the danger he saw in retaining Washington's appointees. The new President's enemies, he wrote, "who would always endeavour to be nearest his person, [would] be the most officious with their information and council, and the most assiduous with their flattery." Gerry asserted that, though he had the deepest respect for Washington, he believed that the General had been unduly influenced by lesser men who had dictated his appointments. Terrible errors had been made by appointing men "totally lacking in virtue and national morality." [4]

Gerry later singled out the Secretary of State as especially un-

---

[3] Adams to Abigail Adams, January 9, 1797, Adams Papers (Massachusetts Historical Society), Letters Received and Other Loose Papers, January to March, 1797, microfilm reel #383. Hamilton's biographers all note the bitterness that existed between the two men. The most recent of these, John C. Miller, *Alexander Hamilton and the Growth of the New Nation*, and Broadus Mitchell, *Alexander Hamilton*, Vol. II, *The National Adventure*, both find the basis for a political split between the two men in Hamilton's machinations against Adams in 1796. Manning Dauer, however, points out that Hamilton had never been a keen supporter of Adams and that even in 1789 and 1792 his support for the New Englander had been only passive. Manning J. Dauer, *The Adams Federalists.*

[4] Gerry to Abigail Adams, January 7, 1797, Adams Papers, Letters Received and Other Loose Papers, January to March, 1797, reel #383.

qualified for his office. His recent and violent exchanges with the French Minister, Adams' friend charged, had been needlessly provocative.[5] Adams, not at all sympathetic to this "French" point of view, replied that the debate with France had gone beyond the point where the United States could worry about French sensibilities. "The people of this country must not lose their conscious integrity, their sense of honor, nor their sentiment of their own power and force, so far as to be upbraided in the most opprobrious and contumelious language, and be wholly silent and passive under it, and that in the face of all mankind."[6]

It would have been amazing if the President had not been aware of the unreliable nature, not only of his Secretary of State, but of both Wolcott in the Treasury Department and James McHenry in the Department of War as well. Certainly he was at least generally sure that his advisers had Hamiltonian predispositions. Nevertheless, Adams did not deem this cause for their dismissal. In the first place, satisfactory replacements would not be easy to find. More importantly, the dismissal of Pickering and his colleagues would have precipitated an open battle within Federalist ranks, which would have been politically disastrous and would also have indicated to the French that the United States was even more disunited than had previously been believed. Adams would have enough trouble with the Republicans without precipitating conflict with those who at least tended to support him. Furthermore, since Adams viewed the Cabinet as simply an administrative arm of the executive, his advisers' Hamiltonian tendencies were of little consequence. Not wishing to admit to Gerry, however, that he was right about the unreliable nature of the Cabinet, Adams resorted to *double-entendre*, stating: "Pickering and all his colleagues are as much attached to me as I desire. I have no jealousies from that quarter."[7]

---

[5] Gerry to John Adams, February 3, 1797, Adams Papers, Letters Received and Other Loose Papers, January to March, 1797, reel #383.

[6] Adams to Gerry, February 13, 1797, Adams Papers, Letterbook, January 18, 1797 — February 22, 1799, reel #117.

[7] Adams to Gerry, February 13, 1797, Adams Papers. Stephen G. Kurtz, *The Presidency of John Adams*, 268–70. Kurtz suggests that partisan differences made a large reservoir of talent unavailable to Adams. This, combined with the very poor pay for Cabinet officers and the difficulty of attracting talent, encour-

The key to Adams' real feelings about Pickering lies in the fact that he did not rely upon his Secretary of State for information about or analyses of the European situation. There were, of course, personal reasons for this. Adams, who could hardly be considered a man of great humility himself, found Pickering's often ostentatious vanity oppressive. The two men, both proud and self-righteous, just could not get along. Moreover, Pickering was a provincial, barely acquainted with European politics. Adams had, in his son John Quincy Adams, the American Minister at The Hague and later at Berlin, a far better source of accurate information and knowledgeable analysis. There was no one else he so thoroughly trusted. Unprepared to dismiss Pickering, Adams was prepared to ignore him.

Almost every communication John Quincy Adams sent from Europe confirmed the President-elect's feelings. The young diplomatist played upon a constant theme — the need for unity at home. He was convinced that the French had no intention of declaring war upon America. He believed, however, that they would keep up a constant pressure, hoping to foment an upheaval within the United States that would bring to power in America the leaders with French sympathies. The pressures the Directory would, in the future, exert upon the new Administration, would, he believed, be in direct proportion to "the support they [received] from their party" in America. "If our Government discover a single symptom of a disposition to yield, or if the House of Representatives for the ensuing Congress should from its complexion, encourage the hopes of obtaining a majority adverse to the system of the Executive, the Directory will not scruple at any measure of hostility which they may imagine or be persuaded will increase their influence by the augmentation of fear." On the other hand, if the United States, under the

---

aged Adams to keep the Washington Cabinet intact; Dauer, *The Adams Federalists*, 114. Dauer believes that Adams actually trusted the Cabinet and discounted Gerry's warnings. His secondary justification for Adams' seeming simplicity is, however, more convincing. He suggests that Adams was unwilling to precipitate a political split within the Federalist coalition at the outset of his Administration; Smith, *John Adams*, II, 922. Smith believes Adams was "aware in a general way, that most of the members of the cabinet . . . were strong Hamilton men." Smith, however, also believes that Adams was "trusting" at the outset.

leadership of the new President, could maintain a united front, the French would "inevitably retreat." [8]

The President-elect completely agreed with his son and was especially concerned over the nation's seeming inability to view realistically the nature of the French Revolution. In a mixture of foreboding and frustration, he wrote to his wife only a few weeks before the inauguration:

> The people of America, must awake out of their golden dreams, consider where they are, and what they are about. The foolish idolatry of France . . . has brought us into snares and dangers which we might have avoided. . . . The ignorance in which our people will keep themselves of the true character of the French nation in general and of their present government as well as all their former governments since the revolution is astonishing. [9]

Internal unity was the keystone around which John Adams believed a neutral foreign policy might be built. If the French believed that the United States was firmly committed to the Jay Treaty and that there existed no chance of fomenting internal revolution in the United States, they would probably adopt a more amicable and less aggressive foreign policy. Adams hoped to create a united front with the new Vice-President, Thomas Jefferson, in order to produce the image of national purpose that he believed necessary if America were to remain neutral. Jefferson's friendly predispositions served to raise Adams' hopes. [10] As for Jefferson's connection with the so-called "French party" in the United States, Adams was willing to believe that the Vice-President, while he had kept some bad company in the past, might be saved and that "the Senate, an excellent school" would "correct him." [11]

---

[8] John Q. Adams to John Adams, January 14, 1797, Adams Papers, Letters Received and Other Loose Papers, January to March, 1797, reel #383.

[9] John Adams to Abigail Adams, January 18, 1797, Adams Papers, Letters Received and Other Loose Papers, January to March, 1797, reel #383.

[10] Adams to Tristram Dalton, January 19, 1797, Adams Papers, Letterbook, January 18, 1797, to February 22, 1799, reel #117; Kurtz, *Presidency of John Adams*, 219–22. Alexander DeConde, *The Quasi-War*, 8.

[11] Adams to Tristram Dalton, January 19, 1797, Adams Papers, Letterbook, January 18, 1797, to February 22, 1799, reel #117.

Adams was overly optimistic, for the obstacles to cooperation between himself and Jefferson were insurmountable. While Adams viewed the danger to the national unity as issuing from the "French party" within the United States, Jefferson believed as fervently in the malevolence of the "English" faction that had dominated the Washington Administration. Further, the new President sought to found his foreign policy upon the Jay Treaty and to retain it intact,[12] while Jefferson based his hopes for better Franco-American relations upon a belief that Adams would repudiate the Jay Treaty and move to regain the lost neutrality of 1793. In the enthusiastic beginning of his Administration, however, Adams ignored all such considerations and hoped that cooperation with Jefferson might be the key to peace and neutrality.

The President-elect decided upon a bold move to settle the issues dividing France and the United States. He hoped to impress upon all concerned his ardent desire for a settlement by appointing a special commission of three ministers extraordinary to visit Paris and deal with the French. Although Pinckney had been rejected by the French Government, a bipartisan commission might be received. Adams was determined that Jefferson or perhaps James Madison should serve on the commission, along with two moderates, Charles C. Pinckney and Elbridge Gerry.[13]

With the appointment of the commission in mind, the President-elect visited Jefferson in his rooms in Philadelphia on the evening preceding the inauguration. Jefferson declined the mission to Paris, but he agreed to sound out Madison on the subject.[14] Adams was temporarily encouraged. A mission such as the one he had outlined would serve two purposes: It would help to heal the breach between

---

[12] Adams to Gerry, May 3, 1797, Letterbook, January 18, 1797, to February 22, 1799, reel #117.

[13] Thomas Jefferson, *The Complete Anas of Thomas Jefferson*, F. B. Sawvel, ed., 184–85. Jefferson's version of the story differs from Adams' in that, according to the Vice-President, Adams did not suggest that he go but thought that a commission including Madison, Gerry, and Pinckney would be advisable. For Adams' version of the meeting, see Adams' "Letters to the Boston Patriot," Letter XIII, reprinted in Oliver Wolcott, *Memoirs of the Administrations of Washington and Adams*, George Gibbs, ed., I, 462–66.

[14] Wolcott, *Memoirs of the Administrations of Washington and Adams*, I, 462–66.

the two political factions within the country, and it would also give promise that his Administration might begin with a diplomatic victory.

Less than a day following the inauguration, Adams, still apparently incompletely acquainted with the depths of party animosity that divided the extreme Federalists from the Republicans, broached the subject of a possible mission headed by Madison to Oliver Wolcott, Jr. As a result, the first open clash within the infant administration developed. Although the Cabinet members could have had no prior information of Adams' intentions, there must have been some sort of agreement among them to act as a unit in opposing any eccentricities they might encounter on the part of their new chief. Scarcely had Adams made his proposal when the Connecticut Federalist, speaking for Pickering, McHenry, and apparently for the new Attorney General Charles Lee as well, offered the resignations of the entire Cabinet if Madison were sent to Paris.[15]

Recognizing the political dangers of an open schism within his young Administration, the President retreated. When Jefferson reported that Madison had refused to serve on the proposed commission, Adams was very much relieved. Jefferson noted the change of attitude on the President's part and shrewdly ascribed it to the reaction his proposal must have received in the Cabinet.[16] Adams, on his part, was disillusioned and disgusted with his situation. Some days later he wrote to Abigail that if "the Federalists go to playing pranks I will resign the office and let Jefferson lead them to peace, wealth and power if he will. From the situation, where I now am, I see a scene of ambition, beyond all my former suspicions or imaginations."[17] The obstructionism that marked the technique of Wolcott, Pickering, and McHenry in thwarting the policies of a "wrongheaded" President was thus early begun.

The news that Charles C. Pinckney had not only been refused

---

[15] John Adams, "Letters to the Boston Patriot," Letter XIII, in Wolcott, *Administrations of Washington and Adams*, I, 465.

[16] Jefferson, *Anas*, 184–85.

[17] Adams to Abigail Adams, March 17, 1797, Adams Papers, Letters Received and Other Loose Papers, January to March, 1797, reel #383; Smith, *John Adams*, II, 914–36. Smith gives an excellent summary of these early days of the Adams Administration.

accreditation but had been driven ignominiously from French soil arrived in the United States hard upon Adams' inauguration and set off a major debate on foreign policy within Federalist ranks. All agreed that the fundamental problems facing the nation in this period of crisis were internal disunity and threatened ideological subversion. Moreover, it was apparent that the crisis that had developed between the United States and France was closely linked to domestic affairs and that the response of the Government to French insults would have the most important repercussions upon the internal American political situation. While there was general agreement upon the nature of the problem, Federalist leaders sharply differed over what response should be made.

Apparently convinced that the Cabinet could be crucially influential in deciding American policy, Alexander Hamilton, a moderate in the debate, urged a dual course of action upon Pickering and Wolcott. First, he emphasized the importance of girding the nation for defense against the French. He suggested that the President call a special session of Congress and, to dramatize the gravity of the situation, set aside a national day of fasting and prayer. Furthermore, the President, he believed, should ask Congress to pass legislation for the augmentation of America's meager naval force, for the arming of merchant vessels, for the fortification of the large port cities, and for the establishment of a provisional army to be called into service only in the likelihood of an invasion of the United States by France.[18] Second — still clinging to his pacific policy — Hamilton hoped to avoid a war, for he believed that such a clash would bring disaster to the United States; the nation would not only face the might of France but would probably be confronted also with civil conflict at home as the partisans of the French within the United States rose in rebellion.[19] Hamilton, doubting America's ability to remain united in such a crisis, urged that, simultaneously with the preparations for defense, the United States send a new set of envoys to Paris to negotiate a settlement. Like the President, Hamilton be-

---

[18] Hamilton to Pickering, March 22, 1797, Pickering Papers (Massachusetts Historical Society), XXI, 67.

[19] Hamilton to Pickering, March 29, 1797, Pickering Papers, XXI, 73.

lieved that it was of prime importance that this commission include among its members a representative of the Republican faction, preferably Jefferson or Madison; the second member of the commission should be a moderate, the logical choice being Charles C. Pinckney; the third commissioner should be solidly Federalist, say George Cabot.[20]

The purpose of the commission would be frankly dual. If possible, it was to explain the American position to the French and work out some settlement that would not infringe upon prior commitments made to Great Britain under the Jay Treaty. If, however, such an agreement could not be made, or if the commissioners were treated in the same manner as Pinckney had been, then the mission would still have served a very useful purpose, for the repudiation by France of a commission that included an important leader of the Republican faction would serve to disarm that party at home. It would be impossible for Republicans to contend that such a commission as Hamilton proposed had been rejected because of an unfriendly or openly antagonistic attitude on the part of the American agents. Consequently, even if the new effort at negotiation should fail, the United States would benefit. The tendency for the breach within the American political fabric to widen would be reversed, and the Government could count upon national unity in the face of a war with France.[21]

Hamilton realized that the broad cross section of the American people wanted to avoid an armed clash with France. He was also aware that the moderates in Congress, who controlled the balance of power in both houses, wanted peaceful settlement. Without moderate support, no important legislation for the augmentation of the American military machine could be passed. If the Government did not first seek peace, the moderates would not support a more aggressive policy. In Hamilton's mind, one more serious effort at a peaceful settlement with France was, therefore, imperative.

At first, the weight of Hamilton's arguments seemed lost upon Wolcott and Pickering. The Secretary of the Treasury believed that

---

[20] Hamilton to McHenry, March 22, 1797, Papers of Alexander Hamilton (Library of Congress); Dauer, *The Adams Federalists*, 126–27; Miller, *Alexander Hamilton*, 455–56.

[21] Hamilton to Pickering, March 29, 1797, Pickering Papers, XXI, 73.

the time for the United States to initiate efforts at negotiation had passed. The insulting repudiation of Pinckney had been the last straw and, in the Connecticut Federalist's mind, indicated the true nature of French policy. The United States was being forced to choose between war and complete submission to France's will. Wolcott believed that what was really at issue was not the Jay Treaty, but America's right to trade with France's enemies. So long as America's shipping and trade helped to sustain Britain, the United States would be under attack. Nevertheless, Wolcott believed that America might yet avoid a declared war. A limited clash with the French upon the seas, however, seemed unavoidable. Consequently, he agreed with Hamilton that the nation should gird itself for such a struggle. He even accepted the idea of keeping a minister in Europe who would be empowered to negotiate, in case the French should decide on such a course. The United States would not, however, submit to the indignity of its minister's once again seeking to initiate negotiations. Moreover, Hamilton's proposal to include on the commission Madison "or anyone like him" was completely unacceptable. The disadvantages, he feared, outweighed the advantages. Wolcott was convinced that such a person would block any efforts at a "moderate" settlement and would insist upon a complete surrender to French demands.[22]

Timothy Pickering proved even more resistant than Wolcott to Hamilton's arguments. After receiving news of Pinckney's disgraceful treatment, his emotions completely overcame what was left of his reason in the matter. War now seemed the only honorable alternative; in fact, by mid-March, 1797, he was busily preparing for conflict. A coded dispatch to John Quincy Adams, then negotiating the renewal of commercial treaties with Prussia and Sweden, clearly indicates as much. In earlier agreements with the two nations, the United States had adhered to the liberal principle of "freedom of the seas." Of particular concern to Pickering was the position, which until this time the United States had adhered to, that belligerent goods were immune from seizure when being carried by a neutral. With the United States on the verge of becoming a belligerent, Pickering

---

[22] Wolcott to Hamilton, April 1, 1797, in Wolcott, *Administrations of Washington and Adams*, I, 485–88.

instructed Adams to negotiate no agreement that held to the principle that "free ships make free goods."[23] If the United States were to engage in a naval war with France, it would not be to her advantage to cleave to these liberal maritime principles, for French goods on the high seas would thus be given the sanctuary of neutral bottoms. In a later dispatch, Pickering cynically noted that it would be wise to abandon "freedom of the seas" forever, since it had "not been regarded in respect to the United States when it would operate to her benefit; and may be insisted on only when it will prove injurious to their interests."[24]

Pickering's militant attitude dictated the nature of his reply to Hamilton's enlightened plea for a peaceful negotiation with France. In rather haughty fashion, he wrote that the suggestions of the New Yorker had "been contemplated" and would "receive attention" from himself and his colleagues. The rest of his letter made clear his rejection of Hamilton's views. He believed that no new effort at negotiation should be made. He justified his stand with the obviously inadequate explanation that such a commission as Hamilton proposed would be rejected by the French.[25] Like Wolcott, Pickering viewed Hamilton's proposal for a bipartisan commission as sheer foolishness. He missed the entire thrust of Hamilton's argument, which was that the nation could not face a war with France without the support of the moderates.

Many ultra-Federalists, of course, agreed with Pickering. Jeremiah Wadsworth, the New Hampshire Federalist, for example, thought war a better alternative than the "present state" of the nation.[26] The father of the Secretary of the Treasury and the recognized leader of Connecticut Federalism, Oliver Wolcott, Sr., while he did not believe that a declared war would necessarily be the outcome of the developing antagonisms between the United States and France,

---

[23] Pickering to John Q. Adams, March 17, 1797, Adams Papers, Letters Received and Other Loose Papers, January to March, 1797, reel #383.

[24] Pickering to John Q. Adams, July 15, 1797, Department of State, Diplomatic Instructions, IV, 95–96.

[25] Pickering to Hamilton, March 26, 1797, Hamilton Papers.

[26] Wadsworth to Wolcott, March 26, 1797, cited in Wolcott, *Administrations of Washington and Adams*, II, 478–79.

agreed in every respect with his son.[27] Stephen Higginson, too, believed that the time for negotiation had passed and hoped that the Government would move speedily to suspend the Treaty of 1778, raise new revenue for defense, and assume a more militant posture.[28]

Hamilton, however, refused to abandon his efforts at convincing the two obstinate Cabinet officers of the importance of further negotiations. In a letter to Pickering that in part reiterated his earlier remarks, Hamilton sought to convince him by introducing a new theme. He noted that "there is an opinion industriously inculcated . . . that the actual administration [the Cabinet] are endeavouring to provoke a war. It is all important by the last possible sacrifice to confound this charge. I cannot but add that I have not only a strong wish, but an *extreme anxiety* that the measure in question be adopted." [29] In an almost exact copy of his letter to Pickering, Hamilton pressed this same point of view upon Secretary Wolcott. Noting the general tendency to credit the Cabinet with sentiments favoring war, he emphasized the importance of "obviating" such thoughts "from the public mind." [30]

Wolcott, replying for both Pickering and himself, indicated that anger was replacing patience on his part. In almost peremptory tones, he denied that he or anyone else in the Administration sought war, but he made it apparent that he continued to believe that it would be a disgrace for the nation to bend any more to the will of the French.[31] Despite Wolcott's almost angry reply, Hamilton pressed further. Resorting to a different theme from those he had employed earlier, he warned that the European political situation was far too unstable for the United States to become involved in war with a Continental power. Relying on information he had received from Rufus King in

---

[27] Oliver Wolcott, Sr., to Oliver Wolcott, Jr., March 29, 1797, Wolcott, *Administrations of Washington and Adams*, II, 481–82.

[28] Higginson to Pickering, May 11, 1797, Pickering Papers, XXI, 115.

[29] Hamilton to Pickering, March 29, 1797, Pickering Papers, XXI, 73.

[30] Hamilton to Wolcott, March 30, 1797, in Alexander Hamilton, *The Works of Alexander Hamilton*, H. C. Lodge, ed., X, 248–49; Dauer, *The Adams Federalists*, 122. Dauer points out that Wolcott and Pickering were, when left to themselves, sadly deficient in their concern for what the public might think. Hamilton realized this and worked assiduously to bring these key members of Adams' Cabinet around to a position in keeping with moderate opinion.

[31] Wolcott to Hamilton, March 31, 1797, Hamilton Papers.

London, Hamilton warned that Austria was tottering on the brink
of defeat and might at any moment leave the war. Moreover, there
was every indication that even the British lion was faltering. The
credit structure of the Empire was in a seriously weakened condition,
and England would, if possible on honorable terms, shortly seek
peace with France.[32] Hamilton warned that

> to be in rupture with France, united with England alone, or
> singly, as is possible, would be a most unwelcome situation.
> Divided as we are, who can say what would be hazarded by
> it? In such a situation, it appears to me we should rather err
> on the side of condescension, than on the opposite side. We
> ought to do everything to avoid rupture without unworthy
> sacrifices and to keep in view as a primary object, union at
> home. No measure can tend more to this than an extraordi-
> nary mission. And it is certain, to fulfill these ends, proposed,
> it ought to embrace a character in whom France and the op-
> position have full credit.[33]

This time Hamilton touched a nerve. Neither Pickering nor Wolcott
wished for a war with France without the aid of England.

In the spring of 1797 it was clear that the weight of Federalist opinion supported Hamilton. For example, even such a warm Francophobe
as George Cabot fatalistically accepted some sort of new negotiation as
unavoidable. He realized that whatever danger there might be in
such talks, public opinion strongly favored one more effort at peaceable
settlement of Franco-American differences.[34]

The cynical squire of Dedham, Fisher Ames, also sought to influence the stubborn secretaries. War, he wrote, was "dreaded as it
ought to be, and after that . . . as it ought not to be." He believed
that within the United States the vast majority of the people preferred
"peace to honor and real independence."[35] Even though there was
more than enough justification for war in the plundering of Amer-

[32] Hamilton to Pickering, May 11, 1797, Hamilton, *Works*, X, 266; see also
Hamilton to Wolcott, April 5, 1797, Hamilton Papers.

[33] Hamilton to Wolcott, April 5, 1797, Hamilton Papers.

[34] Cabot to Wolcott, April 17, 1797, cited in George Cabot, *Life and Letters
of George Cabot*, Henry Cabot Lodge, ed., 128–30.

[35] Ames to Wolcott, April 17, 1797, cited in Wolcott, *Administrations of
Washington and Adams*, II, 477.

ican commerce and in the indignities heaped upon the American nation by the French Government, the American people wanted no war if it could be avoided. "Whether it proceeds from timidity, avarice, French fanaticism, . . . or the stupor which every public falls into, when for want of an impression from government, it is left to the anarchy of its own opinions, the fact appears to me that the dread of war is stronger still than the sense of honour or of injury. We the people, are in truth more kickable than I could have conceived."[36] In Ames's view the nation was too divided internally and the moderate majority too bent upon a policy of peace for the only really honorable course of action, war, to be commenced. Consequently, to create the necessary national unity and to assuage the moderates at large and in Congress, a new negotiation, designed to include Republican representation, would have to be attempted. The importance of moderate support could not be ignored. Ames argued that the moderates would have to be pacified and won over, for they controlled the balance of political power within the country.

Pickering and Wolcott gradually gave ground before the views of political advisers of the stature of Hamilton, Cabot, and Ames. Their withdrawal from an earlier militancy becomes even more understandable in light of the gloomy news being received from London in April of 1797. Rufus King, America's Anglophile Minister to the Court of St. James's, was despondent over the declining fortunes of the British and as emphatic as Hamilton had been in his urgings that the United States do everything in its power to avoid a war with France. He was especially concerned over the recent suspension of specie payments by the Bank of England. This, he believed, signaled England's inevitable national bankruptcy and collapse.[37] The British might soon be forced to seek peace with France, leaving that power dominant upon the Continent and perhaps, depending upon the extent of the English defeat, upon the seas as well.

By the beginning of May, 1797, Pickering was ready to agree that one more try at negotiation was perhaps wise. His advice to Adams

---

[36] Ames to Wolcott, April 24, 1797, Wolcott, *Administrations of Washington and Adams*, 497–98.

[37] King to Pickering, March 5, 1797, Rufus King, *Life and Correspondence of Rufus King*, Charles R. King, ed., II, 152.

on what should be included in the President's speech at the opening of the impending special session of Congress indicates, however, that he was much more concerned with preparing for war than with negotiating a peace. Adams ought to make it clear, the Secretary believed, that responsibility for the deterioration of Franco-American relations rested squarely upon the shoulders of the French and that French encroachments against the rights of neutral American merchant vessels "surpass those of all nations." The President ought also to ask Congress for appropriations to establish a provisional army of at least 30,000 men while simultaneously building up the Navy. Convoys should be provided for unarmed merchant ships, and merchants should be authorized to arm their vessels for defense. The nation needed to prepare against internal threat as well. Congress ought to authorize the President "to cause spies and persons justly suspected of designs hostile or injurious to the United States to be apprehended — offenders against the provisions of the law to be tried and punished — and foreigners compelled to quit the territories of the United States." To finance these increased expenditures, Pickering proposed a general land tax.[38] Agricultural America was to pay for the costs of defending New England's commerce.

---

[38] Pickering to Adams, May 1, 1797, Pickering Papers, VI, 267–68.

6

A PERIOD OF VACILLATION

*A*LTHOUGH HIS SECRETARY OF STATE lent only a skeptic's approval to further talks with the French, John Adams remained committed to seeking a peaceful settlement to the diplomatic impasse. He was confirmed in his intentions by the apparently pacific sentiments of the American people. Moderates from many areas wrote to him, urging peace. Elbridge Gerry, as yet uncommitted to either faction and a strong Adams man, wrote to suggest virtually the same solution to the French imbroglio that Adams himself had earlier struck upon, namely, the immediate dispatch of Thomas Jefferson to Paris to settle America's differences with France.[1] Gerry was joined in his enthusiasm for this idea by Henry Knox, former Secretary of War, who believed that the mere presence of Jefferson in Paris would work wonders on the collective mind of the Directory.[2] To both, Adams replied that he too had believed it would be a diplomatic stroke to send Jefferson to France and had suggested such a mission to the

---

[1] Gerry to Adams, March 27, 1797, Adams Papers (Massachusetts Historical Society), Letters Received and Other Loose Papers, January to March, 1797, reel #383.
[2] Knox to Adams, March 19, 1797, Adams Papers, Letters Received and Other Loose Papers, January to March, 1797, reel #383.

Virginian, but Jefferson had refused. Adams added that it was a good thing the Vice-President had done so, for it would have been a public "degradation" for a man as important in the nation's government as the Vice-President to deal with mere ministers of another government.[3] What Adams did not disclose in this rather lame reply to the two moderates was that the Cabinet had nearly rebelled at the proposal to send Madison to Paris and that his own political position, caught between his desire for peace and the Cabinet's opposition to measures that might best achieve that goal, was creating serious problems for him.

The policy Adams eventually proposed was in most respects similar to that which Alexander Hamilton had earlier outlined to Pickering, McHenry, and Wolcott. Adams was convinced that the people of the nation wished peace and that a belligerent policy would have the effect of alienating large numbers of citizens. He also believed the best possible course of action was to raise the olive branch while baring the sword. Consequently, to dramatize the situation, he moved to set aside a day of fasting and prayer for the nation and simultaneously called a special session of Congress to meet on May 16, 1797. Congress would consider the nominations of three envoys to negotiate a settlement with France and would also weigh the President's suggestions for the augmentation of American naval power and coastal defense in preparation for the war with France that might ensue.

Their differences notwithstanding, Pickering and Adams shared some basic viewpoints. They were agreed, for instance, that the envoys to be sent to Paris should make no concessions that might endanger the peace with Great Britain. The Jay Treaty, both believed, was a justifiable assertion of national sovereignty and was in no way a violation of the stipulations of the Treaty of 1778 with France. Certainly Adams was no more willing than Pickering to surrender tamely to French demands for the abrogation of the Jay agreement. He believed that the issue was far greater than the treaty itself.[4] The French Gov-

---

[3] Adams to Gerry, April 6, 1797, John Adams, *The Works of John Adams*, C. F. Adams, ed., VIII, 539–40.

[4] Adams to Elbridge Gerry, May 3, 1797, Adams Papers, Letterbook, January 18, 1797, to February 22, 1799, reel #117.

ernment, he felt, had acted deliberately from 1778 onward to alienate Great Britain from her former colonies and to keep the young United States weak. The creation of a republican government in France had done nothing to alter French policy. The Directory, he thought, was following the line laid down by the monarchy and was merely using the Anglo-American treaty as a lever in its efforts to keep the United States debilitated and to stifle any *rapprochement* between Britain and the United States. As a result, Adams, like Pickering, was determined that any settlement between France and the United States should be on terms dictated from Philadelphia.[5]

The President's address to the opening of the special session of Congress in May, 1797, was further proof that a surprisingly broad area of agreement existed between the President and his Secretary of State. In an analysis that drew Pickering's vociferous applause, Adams reviewed the delicate diplomatic situation and blamed the French for the decay of Franco-American relations. Affirming his determination to do everything possible to maintain the peace "on terms compatible with the rights, engagements and honor" of the nation, he informed Congress that he would appoint a special commission to negotiate with France. He also emphasized the importance of vigorous legislative action for the augmentation of America's military capabilities. He pled for unity within the nation and lashed out at dissenters who would destroy that unity. It would soon "be decided, whether the American people will support the government established by their voluntary consent or whether by surrendering themselves to the direction of foreign and domestic factions, they will forfeit that honorable distinction which they have hither to maintained." [6] The entire speech was a call for strength and unity in the face of French hostility and a ringing denunciation of internal opposition.

Jefferson, stung by Adams' denunciation of Republicanism, believed that the President intended the negotiation to fail and that

---

[5] Stephen G. Kurtz, *The Presidency of John Adams*, 286; Page Smith, *John Adams*, II, 913.

[6] Draft of the Speech of the President to the opening of the special session of Congress, May 16, 1797, Adams Papers, Letters Received and Other Loose Papers, April to June, 1797, reel #384.

he was really intent upon war.[7] Pickering, on the other hand, thought Adams had made a fine speech.[8] Any optimism, however, that might have been generated in Pickering's mind regarding prospects for a friendly cooperation between himself and the President were quickly dashed as a result of Adams' nomination of his old friend Elbridge Gerry as one of the envoys to be sent to France. Gerry had originally been suggested by Adams as a possible envoy to serve along with the Virginia Federalist John Marshall and Charles C. Pinckney. At that time there had been such vigorous opposition in the Cabinet to Gerry's nomination, however, that Adams had given in, offering third place on the commission to Francis Dana, Chief Justice of the Massachusetts Supreme Court. When Dana refused the mission, the President turned back to Gerry and presented his name for Senate approval over the objections of most of the Cabinet.[9]

Few people could have held such diametrically opposite views as did Gerry and Pickering. Like the Secretary of State, Gerry conceived of the European war in moral and ideological terms; in his eyes, France seemed the natural ally for the United States, while England appeared an inveterate enemy. "Republics," Gerry once observed, "should cultivate the friendship of each other, it being more than probable that had the coalesced powers of Europe succeeded against France, they would have eradicated republicanism as the bane of good government from the earth." [10]

The nomination of Gerry as one of the special envoys seemed a disastrous stroke to the Secretary of State. Gerry was a Republican in everything but name. His emotions surging, Pickering moved to block Gerry's appointment and in so doing precipitated the first public break between himself and the President. Working through his Massachusetts friends in the Senate, he sought to muster enough

---

[7] Jefferson to Strother, June 8, 1797, Thomas Jefferson, *The Writings of Thomas Jefferson*, Paul L. Ford, ed., VII, 138–39; Smith, *John Adams*, II, 930–31.

[8] Pickering to King, May 16, 1797, Pickering Papers (Massachusetts Historical Society), VI, 315.

[9] Smith, *John Adams*, II, 933.

[10] Gerry to Adams, March 7, 1797, Adams Papers, Letters Received and Other Loose Papers, January to March, 1797, reel #383; Smith, *John Adams*, II, 933–34.

opposition to reject the appointment and to force the President to nominate a safely Federalist envoy instead. The President, Pickering rationalized, had to be saved from his own "eccentricities." Pickering's efforts fell short. The Senate, with both of Massachusetts' senators voting in the minority, approved the appointment.[11]

Adams had appointed Gerry because he had a great deal of faith in the man's integrity and honesty. He realized, however, that his appointee was naïve, had little understanding of the nature of European diplomacy, and held overly romanticized views of the French Revolution. Adams, therefore, wrote to this friend to remind him of the importance of unanimity among the members of the commission and to warn him to avoid division "like a rock or quick sand."[12] Should the French successfully divide the envoys, then the entire diplomatic game would be reversed, with the French holding the winning hand. Should the negotiations fail under such circumstances, the French might persuasively contend that failure was the result of the hostility of a portion of the American commission. Even more seriously, Republicans at home might argue that the Administration had never intended the negotiations to succeed. From the American point of view a split commission would be a disaster, exacerbating instead of healing internal divisions within the United States. Gerry saw no probability of disagreement with his comrades and assured Adams that he understood completely the need for unity. He was, however, concerned over the efforts of Pickering and others to block his nomination. He believed that, while he was away, these same persons would attempt to undercut the President's confidence in him. He hoped the President would not be fooled by these "designing" men.[13]

In July, 1797, with the envoys on their way, a weary Adams wrote to his son in Berlin, "My mind is made up. I believe in a providence

---

[11] Abigail Adams to John Q. Adams, June 22, 1797, Adams Papers, Letters Received and Other Loose Papers, April to June, 1797, reel #384.

[12] Adams to Gerry, July 8, 1797, Adams Papers, Letterbook, January 18, 1797 — February 22, 1799, reel #117.

[13] Gerry to Adams, July 10, 1797, Papers of Elbridge Gerry (Massachusetts Historical Society).

over all and am determined to submit to it alone, in the faithful steady discharge of my duty. . . . I hope the French will not push us beyond our bearing." [14] Within four months of taking office, the President had clashed with the Secretary of State on two major issues. He had also offended the Republicans by defending Washington's foreign policy. He was an independent and, as a political realist, was ready to suffer for his independence.

Throughout the first quarter of 1797, Pickering had never wavered in his opposition to the initiation of further negotiations with the Directory. By May, he had come unwillingly to the conclusion that one more try at negotiation was unavoidable. Even as late as June, he continued to express the deep distrust of France that had dominated his earlier frame of reference. "As little as we ought to rely on the justice and good faith of any nation," he wrote to former President Washington, "France is most of all to be distrusted, because she has the power, and because more than any nation, since Europe became civilized, she has most unjustly and atrociously abused it." [15] He seemed not at all anxious to see the new negotiations succeed.

Yet, even as Pickering wrote to Washington, developments were taking place that would force a great shift in his position. By the end of June, this transformation was complete. No longer did the French seem dangerous and untrustworthy to Pickering; instead, they were sincere and eager for peace. Perhaps more interesting is the fact that Pickering himself now seemed anxious for the success of the negotiations. He wrote in the most optimistic vein to his friend Major Ulrich Rivardi, commanding at Fort Niagara, that nothing seemed "more evident than that the *desire for peace* is in France *a profound* national sentiment: and this with various other strong considerations, I hope in God will procure it." [16] Less than a month following, in corresponding with another close personal friend, Colonel Stephen Rochfontaine, he expressed the fervent conviction that French opinion

---

[14] John Adams to John Q. Adams, July 15, 1797, Adams Papers, Letters Received and Other Loose Papers, July–September, 1797, reel #385.

[15] Pickering to Washington, June 6, 1797, Pickering Papers, XXXVII, 176.

[16] Pickering to Rivardi, June 30, 1797, Pickering Papers, VI, 399.

was "sitting strongly in favor of the United States" and judged that the envoys extraordinary would "be cordially received"; "God knows," he exclaimed, "I am heartily desirous of the continuance of peace." [17] The Secretary had executed a major shift in his position.

Pickering's change of attitude may have been the result of a series of optimistic dispatches from Charles C. Pinckney, then in Amsterdam. Referring to the recent elections in France, Pinckney observed that the make-up of the legislature had been so altered that the Directory would not have a majority in support of its aggressive American policy.[18] Late in May, Pinckney reported that "friends of America draw a favorable augury from" the recent elections in France. In a dispatch sent two weeks later he recounted a conversation between the former American consul in Paris, Major James C. Mountflorence, and a member of the French Council of Five Hundred in which the unnamed legislator assured the American that he would make every effort to prevent a rupture with the United States. He further assured Mountflorence that a majority of the legislature felt as he did.[19] Shortly thereafter, Pinckney reported that this same unnamed legislator had spoken with François Barthélemy, one of the newly elected directors, and that he too opposed the "hostile measures adopted against us." [20] It appeared that the Directory was divided, 3 to 2, in favor of a continuation of the pressures being exerted against the United States. The minority, in this case, however, had the support of a majority in both houses of the French legislature and apparently had the popular support of the French people.

Since Pickering had earlier demonstrated a total distrust of France, it is doubtful that these pacific indications alone played a major role in deciding him upon a change of course. The continued decline in the military fortunes of the powers fighting against France was perhaps a more significant factor. Rufus King, in London, continued steeped in gloom and urgent in his pleas that the Government avoid,

---

[17] Pickering to Rochfontaine, June 26, 1797, Pickering Papers, XXII, 381.
[18] Pinckney to Pickering, Dispatch #17, May 28, 1797, Department of State, Diplomatic Dispatches, France, V, 114–15 (National Archives).
[19] Pinckney to Pickering, *ibid*.
[20] Pinckney to Pickering, Dispatch #20, June 22, 1797, Department of State, Diplomatic Dispatches, France, V, 145–49.

at all reasonable costs, a war with France.[21] The European situation was grave. Russia, King reported, could not be depended upon. Austria was weak, and the King of Prussia would serve only his own best interests. Britain, he believed, had reached nearly the limit of her endurance. Her strength could be measured by her wealth and her navy, but her wealth was a serious question mark; her navy had just suffered a widespread and successful mutiny and could not be relied upon; the entire nation was weary of the war, and few Englishmen saw any advantages to its continuation.[22]

King also warned that Britain would soon be forced to seek peace. It was this factor that was most significant in Pickering's turnabout. In the late spring of 1797 rumors that England was seeking peace talks with the Directory began to circulate. Pickering knew that for some time the British had been trying to arrange a settlement with France. An earlier effort had led to long discussions between the two powers at Rastatt, but in December, 1796, these talks had been broken off by the French. Throughout these early conversations both the British and American observers were convinced that the Directory had no intention of negotiating a settlement but was conducting the nonproductive talks in order to pacify domestic French sentiment.[23] When, however, in the spring of 1797 it became apparent that a pacific sentiment was growing within France, the British might once again seek a renewal of the discussions, this time with real hope for success.

By midsummer of 1797, then, as Pickering viewed the changed European situation from Philadelphia, the circumstances had radically altered. A weakened England sought peace. All of Europe

---

[21] King to Hamilton, April 1, 1797, Rufus King, *Life and Correspondence of Rufus King*, Charles R. King, ed., 162.

[22] King to Pickering, April 19, 1797, King, *Life and Correspondence*, 172–76; throughout the spring the newspapers were filled with reports of England's desperate situation. The impending collapse of the Bank of England, mutiny in the Channel fleet, rebellion in Ireland, the threat of a separate peace between Austria and France, and an impending French invasion were some of the stories that vied with each other for public attention; see, for example, the *New York Timepiece and Literary Companion*, March 27, 31, April 7, 10, 17, 21, May 1, 3, 5, 8, 18, 22, 24.

[23] Malmesbury to Grenville, November 28, 1796, William Wyndham, *Report on the Manuscripts of J. B. Fortescue, Esq.*, W. Fitzpatrick, ed., V, 278–79.

would surely follow to the peace table, once England and France had settled their differences. Pickering understood that under such circumstances a Franco-American war would be unthinkable.[24]

At first, many keen observers agreed with Pickering's new view that the French would settle with the United States. The American Minister in Berlin, John Quincy Adams, believed the success of renewed negotiations very likely. Only a few months earlier he had been convinced that the Directory would never settle with a Federalist administration.[25] In the spring of 1797 he even became concerned over the growing potentiality of the French Navy and believed that France would soon have the power to land and supply a large force of French troops in North America — a possibility he had not previously considered.[26] As a result of the elections in France, however, Adams' views changed. "The character which the legislative councils have assumed since the entrance of the new third part, and the choice of Barthelemi [*sic*] as a member of the Directory, fully convince me that much might be done at this time by way of conciliation."[27]

But John Quincy Adams was not optimistic for long. Soon he saw signs threatening to conciliation in Paris. He feared "a great struggle by the party who have hitherto governed with so much injustice and oppression, both at home and abroad. New conspiracies or new revolutions are apparently forming and whatever party prevails, will hold its power by no other tenure than that of violence."[28] These fears were shared by William Vans Murray at The Hague. Early in August, 1797, Murray discouraged the idea that peace in Europe would soon be restored. His source of information seemed unimpeachable: M. Noel, the French Minister at The Hague. To Murray it appeared

---

[24] Pickering to Andrew Ellicott, August 30, 1797, Department of State, Domestic Letters, X, 154–60. Pickering took this position three days after definite news had arrived that Britain was already negotiating for a settlement with France. See the *Gazette of the United States*, August 27, 1797.

[25] John Q. Adams to John Adams, March 18, 1797, Adams Papers, Letters Received and Other Loose Papers, January–March, 1797, reel #383.

[26] John Q. Adams to John Adams, April 3, 1797, Adams Papers, Letters Received and Other Loose Papers, April–June, 1797, reel #384.

[27] John Q. Adams to John Adams, June 7, 1797, Adams Papers, Letters Received and Other Loose Papers, April–June, 1797, reel #384.

[28] John Q. Adams to Abigail Adams, June 26, 1797, Letters Received and Other Loose Papers, April–June, 1797, reel #384.

that little — if anything — had changed as a result of the altered political situation within France.[29]

The information filtering into Philadelphia in the summer and autumn of 1797 indicated that the situation in France was the key to peace or war in Europe. If another revolution should take place in France the peace talks at Lisle might yet fail. Confused and frustrated, Pickering awaited further developments while clinging hesitantly to his new peaceful predispositions.

The President, however, on the basis of information he was receiving from his son and from Murray, was making some remarkably accurate predictions. Struck by the open schism within the Directory, he argued that the majority, being opposed by a majority of the legislature, would seek support from the Army and would probably precipitate civil war.[30] The result of internal conflict in France would determine the success or failure of the American mission then en route to France. If the moderates should emerge victorious, peace might be attained; if the Directorial majority should triumph, the continuation of French depredations might be expected and war would be likely.

Whatever Adams or Pickering thought of the diplomatic situation, they had no means to influence the course of events. The internal political situation in France was central in the crisis, and time was the principal factor in resolving it. Powerless in one sense, both the President and the Secretary were further frustrated in that summer of 1797 by the opposition of Republicans in the House of Representatives to proposed expenditures for defense. A crucial factor in their policy had been the augmentation of America's military capability, especially upon the seas. This required congressional authorization. Here the Republicans made their stand. The little House chamber became a desperate battleground. Giving in only when forced, the Republicans conceded little to the Administration. When Congress adjourned, most of the President's legislative program remained unenacted. Moreover — and more importantly in the eyes of some —

---

[29] Murray to John Adams, August 4, 1797, Papers of William Vans Murray (Pierpont Morgan Library).

[30] Adams to Pickering, October 31, 1797, Adams Papers, Letterbook, October 17, 1797–July 8, 1799, reel #119.

Republican obstructionism made it clear to all who were interested that America was sharply divided over questions of foreign policy.

Indignant at Republican hindrance, Pickering believed "the debates and proceedings of the sitting Congress will certainly excite in the French . . . and in all Europe an idea that we are that wretched, divided and spiritless people which the Directory have conceived us to be." [31] Righteous in his new desire for peace, Pickering believed that the American people were far more amenable to the measures proposed by the President than the Republicans in the House had been. He noted that, if peace should be preserved, the Republicans themselves would be "mortified and vexed" for, although they were opposed to a war with France, they would in an instant have plunged the country into a war with England. Disdainful of their accusations of Federalist un-neutrality, he excoriated the Republicans: "There is a malignancy in the slander of these parricides which heightened by disappointment surpasses all bounds . . . God knows that I am heartily desirous of the continuance of peace." [32]

Pickering's close friend Stephen Higginson was also enraged by Republican obstructionism in Congress, and he blamed America's weak constitutional system for the collapse of unity. "Indecision and imbecility," he believed, would forever mark congressional conduct "under such a Constitution." "Faction" too would be an ever-present aspect of the American governmental structure and would "be too powerful for the national strength of the government unless restrained by the people." On the surface, the Congress might look strong, but so long as that body could be factionalized so easily, it would never function satisfactorily. Congress would ever be "divided and reduced from a strong phalanx in appearance, to a set of blind timid wanderers in fact, without a guide or a leader; and the worst of it is, that all this arises out of our case, it results from the weakness of our machine." [33]

Events decisive for the future of Franco-American relations were taking place in Paris. September saw the violent outbreak of the

---

[31] Pickering to Winthrop Sargent, June 23, 1797, Pickering Papers, VI, 376.
[32] Pickering to Rochfontaine, July 22, 1797, Pickering Papers, VI, 451.
[33] Higginson to Pickering, July 1, 1797, Pickering Papers, XXI, 160.

smoldering quarrel between the majority of the Directory, backed by the Army, and the Directorial minority of Barthélemy and Lazare Carnot, supported by the majority of both houses of the French legislature and by the majority of the French people. Carnot and Barthélemy were driven from the Directory and some fifty moderates in the Council of Five Hundred, and the Council of the Ancients were arrested. Constitutional government was at an end in France, and a new and more arrogantly aggressive Directory, supported by the Army, was in control. One of the first acts of the new government was to call a halt to the talks with England and to order the British envoy, Lord Malmesbury, from Lisle immediately.

The outcome of the coup in Paris shattered American hopes that the envoys, who had not yet arrived in France, might succeed in their mission. John Quincy Adams, writing to his father from London, stated his belief that there was no longer any justification for the hope "that the new commission" would "succeed to make any satisfactory arrangement. . . . From the councils of such men as Sieyès, and Merlin de Douai [the two who replaced Barthélemy and Carnot on the Directory] we are to expect nothing but the most unqualified injustice, under the Machiavellian mockery with which they have so long duped the world." [34] He urged unity and warned,

> if the House . . . and Executive do not harmonize together for the protection and defence of our citizens and their property better than they have done for the last two or three years, we may boast of our government and Constitution as much as we will, the plain unequivocal and lamentable fact will be that neither of them will be adequate to the purposes for which all governments ought to exist, and we shall be plundered and insulted at the pleasure of every foreign robber or bully who may find a profit or a pleasure in attacking us. [35]

---

[34] John Q. Adams to John Adams, September 21, 1797, Adams Papers, Letters Received and Other Loose Papers, July–September, 1797, reel #385. In the United States the Republican press tried rather lamely to justify the coup and the overthrow of constitutionalism in France as necessary to thwart a royalist counterrevolution. See, for example, the *Philadelphia Aurora*, November 7, 1797; *New York Timepiece*, November 15, 1797.

[35] John Q. Adams to John Adams, September 21, 1797, Adams Papers, Letters Received and Other Loose Papers, July–September, 1797, reel #385.

John Marshall was at The Hague, awaiting the arrival of Gerry from the United States, when the news of the Paris revolution broke. Like the younger Adams, he was thoroughly dejected at the prospects for the success of his mission. "The wounds inflicted on the constitution by the three directors," he wrote to Washington, "seem to be mortal." The government of the nation was in the hands of the Directory and the Army, while law was blatantly overruled by force. "With their form of Government or Revolutions," Marshall admitted, "we have certainly no right to intermeddle, but my regrets at the present state of things are increased by an apprehension that the rights of our country will not be deemed so sacred under the existing system as they would have been had the legislature preserved its legitimate authority." [36] Even before Marshall and his colleagues reached Paris, the internal political situation in France had taken a turn toward absolutism, and at least Marshall was convinced that little could be expected from the Directory.

The coup of September, 1797, and its aftereffects also worked to alter once again the attitudes of America's Secretary of State. His earlier conversion to pacifism had been dictated by changed circumstances in Europe. Now the situation had again been transformed, and Pickering again altered his course. The cessation of the talks at Lisle made it apparent that the war would continue and that England would be unable to obtain peace within the near future. Moreover, news indicating that Britain was perhaps stronger than Minister King had previously believed began to flow into the Department of State in late 1797. The British had met the challenge of the Batavian fleet and in the resultant battle had captured "the greater part" of that navy.[37] Not long after this heartening news reached Philadelphia, a dispatch arrived suggesting King's own renewed confidence in British staying power. While "a general desire of peace" prevailed in England, King believed that the predominant attitude among Englishmen was "that this Government has sought peace with sin-

---

[36] Marshall to Washington, September 15, 1797, Papers of John Marshall (Library of Congress).

[37] King to Pickering, October 17, 1797, King, *Life and Correspondence*, II, 235. News of the Dutch defeat appeared in the American press in late December. *New York Timepiece,* December 20, 1797.

cerity, and that France has not been willing to make it on terms consistent with the safety and independence of England." He therefore thought that the people generally, while unenthusiastic, would "support the Government in carrying on the War, and that they will give this support in the belief, that without it the nation must sink beneath the blows of the Enemy."[38]

By late 1797, as Britain regained her strength and her determination to fight on, so too did the Secretary of State. His ever-present hostility toward France and his concern for the security of American commerce once more became compatible aspects of his foreign policy.

---

[38] King to Pickering, Dispatch #59, November 12, 1797, Department of State, Diplomatic Dispatches, Great Britain, V (National Archives).

7

PICKERING AND YRUJO

*T*HROUGHOUT 1797, while Pickering sought grimly to focus on the violently changing character of the European political situation, his attention was constantly diverted by a smoldering dispute with Spain that arose out of that nation's difficulties in Europe. In 1795 the Spanish had agreed to significant political concessions to the United States in the Treaty of San Lorenzo, negotiated by Thomas Pinckney, younger brother to the emissary to France. The treaty settled practically all questions at issue between the two nations on terms very favorable to the United States. Since that time, Spain had been engaged in a gradual alteration of her international commitments. She had found the alliance with England both unnatural and unprofitable and had, as a result, agreed secretly in 1795 to a separate peace with the French. On October 5, 1796, the Spanish Ministry completed a diplomatic revolution when it declared war upon the country's former ally, Great Britain, and joined in alliance with the French.

Spain's alliance with France was viewed with considerable concern by Secretary Pickering, because Louisiana, controlled by the Spaniards, was coveted also by the French. It was common knowledge that for two years, at the very least, the French had been unsuccessfully exerting pressure upon the Spanish for the retrocession of the territory. The formation of an alliance indicated that Spain might weaken in her determination to withhold Louisiana from France. Pickering viewed the possible retrocession of the territory to France as a serious threat to the United States. He had accepted Spanish control of the area only because of Spain's weakness and because the Spaniards considered Louisiana and Florida only as defensive buffers for the protection of their more valuable holdings farther to the south. France, however, sought Louisiana for its own sake, as the beginning of a new empire in North America, which would endanger the security of the United States. Moreover, he feared the ideological danger French control of Louisiana would produce. Recalling the recent bloody slave uprising in Santo Domingo, Pickering dreaded that the French might spread their revolutionary ideas among Southern slaves and precipitate a ruinous and bloody revolt.[1] It was, then, not only the strategic danger of exchanging a weak neighbor for a strong one that troubled Pickering, but also the thought that France in control of Louisiana would use the area as a base of operations from which to spread its revolutionary gospel among the enslaved Negroes of the American South.

The New Englander's fears were reflected in his diplomatic correspondence. He wrote to the new American Minister at Madrid, David Humphreys, reminding him that a prime object of his mission was to "ascertain what the disposition of Louisiana" would be, and, if the cession to France had "not already been made . . . to prevent it."[2] Humphreys was urged to use every possible means to convince the Spanish Ministry of the danger to its own holdings in South America should the aggressive French gain a foothold on the North American continent. Not content with importuning the Spaniards against the retrocession, Pickering sought through Minister Charles C. Pinckney (who at the time he did not know had been rejected by the Directory) to convince the French that it would be unwise for them to take Louisiana. "Competitions and quarrels," he

---

[1] Pickering to Pinckney, February 25, 1797, Pickering Papers (Massachusetts Historical Society), XXXVII, 54.

[2] Pickering to Humphreys, February 1, 1797, Pickering Papers, XXXVII, 16.

prophesied, would result from two active and energetic nations' bordering upon one another. On the other hand, if the French were to confine "themselves to the islands and to their territory on the southern continent, our reciprocal wants demanding reciprocal supplies, would render permanent the friendly relations subsisting between us."[3] Although the threat rings a bit hollow, given his already firm commitment to a close relationship between the United States and Britain, Pickering warned, just as Jefferson would five years later, that if France should take Louisiana and conflicts erupt between the United States and France, "the United States could not fail to associate themselves with Great Britain and make a common cause against France." Pickering sought to take advantage of France's traditional desire to keep the United States and Britain divided.[4]

The Secretary's concern over French designs in North America was further increased by rumored efforts of the French, in cooperation with certain Americans, to overthrow British rule in Canada. It was late in 1796 when Minister Robert Liston first became enough concerned about the possibility of such a coup to warn London on the subject.[5] Subsequent events, which included the British capture of an American vessel laden with arms for the projected uprising, the implication of the Governor of Vermont as well as of General Ira Allen — another Vermonter — in the business, and the capture and execution in Canada by the British of three spies for the French (all of whom were Americans) exacerbated still further Pickering's fears. "We are not without apprehensions," he wrote to Rufus King, "that France means to regain Louisiana, and to renew the ancient plan of her monarchs of *circumscribing* and encircling what now constitute the Atlantic states."[6]

Concerned as he was over the ultimate disposition of Louisiana,

---

[3] Pickering to Pinckney, February 25, 1797, Pickering Papers, XXXVII, 54.

[4] Pickering to Pinckney, February 25, 1797, Pickering Papers, XXXVII, 54; E. W. Lyon, *Louisiana in French Diplomacy, 1759–1804*, 268. Lyon proves conclusively that the French remained very interested in recovering Louisiana throughout the entire period.

[5] Liston to Grenville, November 18, 1796, Great Britain, Foreign Office, F.O. 115, United States of America, Correspondence of British Diplomatic Representatives, selections, 1791–1902, P.R.O.

[6] Pickering to King, June 20, 1797, Pickering Papers, XXXVII, 189.

the Secretary of State would have been even more troubled had he known that the diplomatic revolution Spain had just completed would create serious new problems for Spanish-American relations. The Spaniards had negotiated Pinckney's treaty at a moment of weakness, when they were in the process of privately making a separate peace with the French. Spain's First Minister, Manuel de Godoy, recognized that British hostility would become virulent over the separate peace. He therefore sought to pacify the Americans and thus make a friend in the Western Hemisphere out of a potential enemy by surrendering to the United States on all major questions dividing the two nations. The treaty that had emerged from the negotiations, therefore, was most favorable to the United States.[7] By late 1796, the European situation had been radically altered. Spain was now bolstered by the power of France, while England seemed anxious for peace. Godoy, repenting his earlier concessions to the United States, decided to abandon plans for the implementation of the treaty agreement with the United States and secretly ordered Francisco Luis Hector Baron de Carondolet, Governor of the Louisiana Territory to refuse to run the boundary line agreed upon in 1795. He further ordered Spanish military forces to hold the posts at Walnut Hills and Natchez, both of which were above the agreed boundary and in what would be, according to the treaty agreement, American territory.[8]

Pickering faced a very delicate problem. On the one hand, he was deeply concerned over the fate of Louisiana and anxious to prevent France from regaining this foothold. On the other hand, the treaty between Spain and the United States was not fully implemented. Just how hard could he push the Spanish? Did he run the risk of antagonizing them to the point where they would retrocede Louisiana, a territory that at best was costing them a fortune, to the French? Was it not possible that they might be convinced that the power of

---

[7] The treaty set the southern American boundary at latitude 31° N., called for the Spanish to evacuate their military posts above this line, and stipulated that a team of surveyors from both nations should work together in running the line. See Samuel F. Bemis, *Pinckney's Treaty: A Study of America's Advantage from Europe's Distresses, 1783–1800.*

[8] Arthur P. Whitaker, *The Mississippi Question, 1795–1803: A Study in Trade, Politics and Diplomacy,* 56–57.

France was perhaps the best possible buffer against the future aggressions of their energetic American neighbor to the north?

If Pickering faced a dilemma, the Spanish Minister in Philadelphia did not. The Chevalier Casa de Yrujo was charged with the duty of justifying Spanish refusals to consummate the treaty. One such justification was an imagined large-scale British attack upon the upper Louisiana Territory, which, Yrujo asserted, was being prepared upon the Great Lakes and which would be launched from within the American boundaries. This charge had twin advantages for the Spaniards. In the first place there was a germ of truth to it, since the British had already demonstrated a mild interest in Louisiana by establishing a post on the Missouri River. Moreover, if the British were believed to be readying an attack upon the area, Spain's refusal to evacuate her military posts above latitude 31°N. could be rationalized.[9]

Pickering, who had for some time been on the friendliest of terms with the British Minister and whose distrust of the Spanish was augmented by their alliance with France, gave Yrujo's allegations no credence. The Spaniard had provided no evidence for his charges, and intelligence from American military commanders on the Great Lakes indicated no preparations of the magnitude that would be necessary for such an expedition. Pickering simply dismissed the Spanish allegations from his mind, not even mentioning them to the new President. This was a serious error, for within a week, in a chance meeting with President Adams, Yrujo himself informed the President of the supposed danger in the Northwest. Adams immediately met with the Secretary, and together they worked out a reply to Yrujo. Although Adams was as skeptical as Pickering, he realized that the situation required an official reply. Under his direction, Pickering assured the Spanish Minister that the United States was prepared to take every measure necessary to protect American neutrality.[10] This affirmation of America's intention to remain neutral was a mere formality for the Secretary. He did not believe Yrujo's

---

[9] Yrujo to Pickering, March 2, 1797, Department of State, Notes from the Spanish Legation, II (National Archives).

[10] Pickering to Yrujo, March 11, 1797, *American State Papers, Foreign Relations*, I:2, 68.

charges and considered it inconceivable that the British would be so foolhardy as to precipitate a dangerous crisis with the United States for the sake of attacking a few insignificant Spanish posts in the Far West. At this point, however, Pickering had made no connection between these wild charges and the fact that the Spanish had consummated only a part of the treaty with the United States and that they as yet had neither evacuated all of their military posts above latitude 31°N. nor agreed to run the new boundary line between Spanish Florida and the United States.

Yrujo could not have been surprised when Pickering questioned him regarding the implementation of the agreements made at San Lorenzo in 1795. More than a year had passed, and still the Spanish had made no move to run the boundary line. Some time since, the United States had dispatched Andrew Ellicott, respected member of the American Philosophical Society and an expert surveyor, as America's representative on the commission that was to draw the new boundary line. Ellicott had been idled in Natchez for some weeks, awaiting Spanish action. When queried about the delay, Yrujo simply claimed ignorance, falsely asserting that he had heard nothing from Governor Carondolet in months.[11] Just four days later Yrujo took the offensive again, informing the Secretary of another British plot, this time against Florida. As in his charges of aggression in the Great Lakes region, this attack was to be mounted in American territory, with the aid, in this case, of General Elisha Clarke of Georgia.[12]

Concerned by the increasingly difficult Spanish situation, Pickering consulted with Adams regarding his next move. Under normal circumstances the forthright and combative Secretary might have been expected to reject as unsubstantiated the charges made against Britain and to press for immediate action on the part of Spain by withdrawing her troops from American territory and by running the new boundary line. Perhaps because he feared he might exasperate the Spanish or perhaps because Adams feared he would, Pickering adopted an approach more circumspect than usual for him. He first wrote to

---

[11] Yrujo to Pickering, April 17, 1797, Department of State, Notes from the Spanish Legation, II.
[12] Yrujo to Pickering, April 21, 1797, *A.S.P., F.R.*, I:2, 68.

Minister Liston, informing him of the charges leveled against Britain by the Spanish Minister and warning him that the United States, "desirous of living on terms of amity with their neighbours, on one side and the other, agreeably to subsisting treaties . . . cannot consent that either should march troops through the territory of the United States to attack the other." [13] Liston replied immediately, denying any personal knowledge of such projects and promising to write to the Governor General of Canada to request any information he might have. Pickering next wrote to Yrujo, affirming once more the American determination to defend its neutrality whether in the Northwest or in Georgia. He further informed the Spanish Minister that he had told Liston of the allegations made by the Spaniards concerning British intent, and had warned him against any violation of American neutral rights. [14]

In May, 1797, Pickering threw off diplomatic restraint, lost his temper, and set aside the caution that had marked his earlier exchanges with Yrujo. The cause of this alteration in his approach to the Minister was a rancorous attack Yrujo made upon the Jay Treaty that was sharply reminiscent of Pierre Adet's earlier broadsides. The United States, Yrujo contended, had received generous concessions from Spain in hopes that these would cement amicable relations between the two nations. Instead, an ungrateful Federalist Administration had negotiated Jay's treaty and placed Spain at a serious disadvantage vis à vis Britain. Accusing the American Government of bad faith and worse, Yrujo wondered: "What should be the surprise of His Majesty on knowing that this country had contracted engagements with England prejudicial to his rights, and to the interests of his subjects, nearly at the same time in which, with so much liberality, he was giving to the United States the most striking proofs of the most sincere friendship." Specifically, Yrujo charged that while the Treaty of San Lorenzo stipulated that free ships make free goods, this very same precept was denied by Article XVII of the Jay Treaty. His Majesty, the Minister contended, was thus "reduced

---

[13] Pickering to Liston, April 28, 1797, Department of State, Domestic Letters, X, 35–36 (National Archives).

[14] Pickering to Yrujo, April 28, 1797, Department of State, Domestic Letters, X, 36–37.

to the disadvantageous situation of seeing the property of his subjects seized with impunity under the safeguard of neutrality, whilst a state of war requires that his squadrons and ships should respect English property on board of American vessels." Contraband was also defined differently in the two agreements. Naval stores and supplies, which were considered as free goods under Pinckney's treaty, were contraband of war under the agreement between the United States and Britain. Finally, rising to a fever pitch of indignation, Yrujo accused the United States of granting to the British a privilege that was not theirs to give, namely, the right to navigate the Mississippi River. This, he charged, was a privilege that had been bestowed upon the United States by His Catholic Majesty and was not transferable to any third power.[15]

Convinced by this echo of Pierre Adet that Spain was little more than a pawn of her ally France, Pickering set to work upon a reply to prove that fiery Latin tempers were no match for the cold heat of New England disdain. For the Government of Spain, which had been dragging its heels for more than a year rather than put into effect the Treaty of 1795, to accuse the American Government of bad faith in negotiating the Jay Treaty, was offensive, especially since Pickering was sure that Godoy had been furnished with a copy of the Anglo-American agreement long before he and Pinckney had finished their negotiations.[16]

In his reply, Pickering went over the same ground he had covered earlier in his squabble with Adet. The Jay Treaty and Pinckney's treaty had only one thing in common. They had both been negotiated by the United States. Other than that, it was fatuous to compare them, for each was reciprocal in nature and had nothing to do with the other. Referring to the surprise expressed by Yrujo at the policy followed by the United States in acquiescing to British interpretations of international maritime law, Pickering, who had always viewed the British interpretation of neutral rights as that which was accepted in International Law, wondered seriously if His Catholic

---

[15] Yrujo to Pickering, May 6, 1797, *A.S.P., F.R.,* I:2, 14.
[16] Pickering's report to the President on Spanish-American relations, January 23, 1798, *A.S.P., FR.,* I:2, 83.

Majesty had expected "that Great Britain would relinquish her legal rights to a nation which abounded in materials for building and equipping ships, and whose vessels adapted to the carrying trade traversed every sea and visited every quarter of the globe?"

The charge that the American Government, in allowing the British the right to navigate the Mississippi River had granted a privilege that was not theirs to grant, Pickering treated as pure nonsense. He denied, in fact, that the United States had ever granted this right to Britain and convincingly demonstrated that the British Government had attained it by the Treaty of Paris of 1763. This treaty had recognized Britain's right to navigate the Mississippi, a right she had never formally relinquished. Moreover, Pickering pointed out that during the negotiations between Godoy and Major Pinckney, the Spaniard had specifically proposed "that Mr. Pinckney on the part of the United States, should enter into a stipulation which would have gone to the exclusion of Great Britain from the navigation of the Mississippi." Pinckney rejected the proposal.[17]

While Pickering was busy demolishing Yrujo's unfounded charges, events in the West seemed to be moving the two nations quickly toward war. For months Andrew Ellicott had been encamped at Natchez awaiting word from Madrid that the Spanish military posts above latitude 31° N. might be evacuated and the boundary line run. With Ellicott at Natchez was a small detachment of American troops under the command of Lieutenant Percy Pope. Ellicott, even less sympathetic with Spanish vagaries than Pickering, came into conflict with both Governor Carondolet and his subordinate (and later replacement) Gayoso de Lemos. Verbal clashes led eventually to an abortive uprising among some of the American inhabitants at Natchez in which Ellicott and Pope were indisputably implicated.

The activities of Ellicott and Pope gave Yrujo still another avenue of attack in his efforts at making a case for Spanish refusal to put the treaty in effect. Yrujo charged that, according to the treaty, the Spanish posts on the Mississippi were to be evacuated only after the boundary line had been drawn. Yet Ellicott had demanded the evacuation of the posts in direct contradiction to the agreement and finally

---

[17] Pickering to Yrujo, May 17, 1797, *A.S.P., F.R.,* I:2, 16–17.

had "hoisted the American flag over territory which would not belong to the United States until after the two nations had jointly made astronomical observations for ascertaining the course of the line." Ellicott had gone so far, Yrujo angrily charged, as to attempt to exert authority over this territory, which for the same reason was still to be considered Spanish. Baron Carondolet had attempted to explain to Ellicott that it was impossible to give up the posts because of the danger of an attack upon upper Louisiana by the British. Ellicott's response to Carondolet's explanation, Yrujo stated, was to incite the population against the Spanish and "to attempt to get possession of the fort of Natchez by surprise."[18] Naturally, Yrujo concluded, his Government was deeply disturbed by these occurrences, and he requested that Ellicott be replaced by a man of sounder political judgment.[19] At last what had been implicit in the situation for some time came out in the open. The Spanish had linked their unsubstantiated charges of British intents to aggression in Louisiana with their refusal to live up to their treaty obligations.

Pickering, his righteous nature and combative spirit now fully engaged, had no intention of replacing Ellicott, even if the surveyor had been somewhat precipitate in his actions. As for the recent assertion that Spain retained her military positions above 31° N. "to guard against an attack by the British from Canada," Pickering was skeptical, and, in a report to Congress that was published in newspapers throughout the United States, he asserted that Yrujo's suspicions had never been supported by "one solitary fact." From all the existing circumstances, Pickering wrote, "I have ever believed the suspicion to be groundless." He further noted that the British Ministry had fully substantiated his view when it "declared that no such expedition had been or is intended by the British Government." It appeared to Pickering that, for whatever reason, Spanish officials in America had decided that "for an indefinite period" they would avoid living up to their treaty obligations. Moreover, Picker-

---

[18] Yrujo to Pickering, June 24, 1797, Department of State, Notes from the Spanish Legation, II; on the same day a long article on the stalemate at Natchez appeared in the opposition press; *Philadelphia Aurora*, June 24, 1797.

[19] Yrujo to Pickering, June 24, 1797, Department of State, Notes from the Spanish Legation, II.

ing flatly asserted that Spanish officers in the Southwest were exercising "an undue influence" over the Indians in that region, preparing them for war with the United States. Spain seemed to be preparing to join France in a clash with the United States. Pickering was obviously warming to his work and, with far more justification than his opponent, had accused the Spanish of bad faith.[20]

It was at this point, just as Pickering was beginning to savor his conflict with Yrujo, that lightning struck in the form of a letter, intercepted by the Department of State, from Senator William Blount of Tennessee to James Carey, an American Indian interpreter working among the Cherokees of the Southwest. The letter seemed to substantiate earlier Spanish charges that the British were planning an attack on Spanish territory. Referring to a conference between a certain Captain John Chisholm, an associate of Blount's, and Robert Liston, which took place during the preceding winter, Blount asserted that "the plan then talked of will be attempted this fall, and if it is attempted, it will be in a much larger way than then talked of, and if the Indians act their part, I have no doubt but it will succeed. . . . A man of Consequence," he wrote, "has gone to England about the business; and if he makes arrangements as he expects, I shall myself have a hand in the business, and probably shall be at the head of the business on the part of the British."[21]

This intercepted letter in an instant revolutionized the entire diplomatic situation, for it now appeared that the British had been planning some sort of foray in the Southwest and that American neutrality would be violated if the plan were put into operation. Spain's earlier fallacious, unsubstantiated, and — one might add — unrelated accusations could not be ignored, and Pickering could no longer refuse them credence. Vexed and puzzled, he sought to give the British Minister every opportunity to explain the letter. He wrote to thank Liston for his recent disavowal of any British intention of attacking upper Louisiana, but inquired whether there were any other plans to attack Spanish territory from United States territory. To preclude

---

[20] Additional Report on the situation in the Southwest, submitted to the President on July 3, 1797, *A.S.P., F.R.*, I:2, 66–67.

[21] *Debates and Proceedings in the Congress of the United States*, 5th Cong., 2d Sess., 2349–50.

any possibility that Liston might attempt to conceal his talks with Chisholm, Pickering added that this unusual question was "not the result of *suspicion*, but of *information* (in which your name is introduced) that some project of the kind has been contemplated, and that the means proposed for carrying it into execution could not but be highly detrimental to the United States." [22] Pickering was desperate, for a lie from Liston would have spelled disaster for both Pickering's Spanish diplomacy and for the tenuous amity with Britain the Secretary had been cultivating.

Liston admitted that during the course of the preceding winter "some persons did actually propose to me a plan for an attack on the Floridas and the other possessions of His Catholic Majesty adjoining to the territories of the United States." Briefly he explained that the plan called for an attack to be launched by Britons, Americans, and some of the Indian tribes of the Southwest. These forces would use American territory as the base from which to launch the attack, and they would be aided in their efforts by a British squadron, which would provide the needed naval support for such an operation. Admitting his receipt of the proposal, Liston stated that he did "not give any encouragement" to the project and that he had two major objections to it. He had little sympathy for any scheme that would violate American neutrality, and he was opposed to the "inhumanity" of using the Indians.[23]

After the disclosure of Blount's letter to Carey, Liston could only be grateful for the fact that he had remained relatively uninvolved in the project and that Grenville had since written to reject Chisholm's proposal. What never would come to light in the investigations that followed was the extreme interest Liston had, at the time, displayed in Chisholm's proposals. The British Minister had been convinced that Louisiana and Florida would soon fall into French hands and, consequently, viewed the project as a feasible

---

[22] Pickering to Liston, July 1, 1797, Department of State, Domestic Letters, X, 72–73; *Philadelphia Aurora*, July 8, 1797; *Gazette of the United States*, July 6, 1797.
[23] Liston to Pickering, July 2, 1797, Department of State, Notes from the British Legation, II; *Philadelphia Aurora*, July 8, 1797; *Gazette of the United States*, July 6, 1797.

means of countering this event. He considered Chisholm "a man of good sense and judgment and of a steady and determined character."[24] While it is true that he did not approve of the use of the Indians in the projected attack, and while he disapproved of a violation of American neutrality, Liston was very friendly to the adventurous frontiersman and extremely interested in his plan.

Early in the affair, in March, 1797, when no news of the British Ministry's reaction to the Chisholm proposals had yet reached Philadelphia, Liston went so far as to provide the anxious Chisholm with the funds for a passage to England, there to plead his case in person. In explaining his actions to Lord Grenville, Liston emphasized that there was a danger that Louisiana might soon fall into French hands and that this should be avoided if at all possible. Of secondary importance — at least to Liston — were unenumerated advantages Britain might acquire from "even a temporary possession" of the area.[25] Impressed by Chisholm, he believed that the entire project might be carried out with practically no cost and no risk.

Liston continued to demonstrate his interest in Chisholm's proposal even after Yrujo had made his first unrelated charge of a projected British attack on Florida. Because of these Spanish accusations, Liston became more cautious and noted that restrictions along the Florida frontier had been tightened. He warned the Ministry against entrusting any important papers to Chisholm, since he might be arrested by American or Spanish officials if he attempted to get into Florida. Nevertheless, he continued to favor the project and suggested that an agent in the guise of a Canadian merchant be sent to Florida as an advance man for the attack.[26]

When the affair came to light and Pickering queried Liston about his part in it, the British Minister sought to disguise as well as he could his own sympathy for the project. Stretching the truth considerably, Liston explained to Pickering that he had been unsympathetic to Chisholm's proposals from the very beginning, but that

---

[24] Liston to Grenville, February 13, 1797, Great Britain, Foreign Office, F.O. 115.
[25] Liston to Grenville, March 16, 1797, Great Britain, Foreign Office, F.O. 115.
[26] Liston to Grenville, May 10, 1797, Great Britain, Foreign Office, F.O. 115.

the importance of the proposals themselves made it impossible for him to reject them on his own authority. Consequently, he explained, he wrote home for instructions. When, by early March, 1797, no reply had been received, Chisholm importuned him for money with which to purchase his passage to London, there to plead personally with the British Government. Liston agreed, only to get Chisholm out of the way.[27] The clincher in Liston's personal defense was a dispatch from Lord Grenville, rejecting Chisholm's proposal. This dispatch Liston supplied to Pickering immediately.[28]

The Secretary of State was willing, indeed anxious, to accept these explanations, since they absolved the British of any complicity in the projected attack upon Spanish Florida and therefore strengthened his position in the debate with Yrujo. He could continue to contend that there had never been any plot by the British to use the Great Lakes as a starting point for an attack upon upper Louisiana. Moreover, it could be clearly demonstrated that, when given the opportunity for an attack upon Florida, they had rejected the scheme.

Pickering was anxious to absolve Liston of any complicity in the plot. He vociferously insisted that the British Minister had cooperated completely with him in revealing the various aspects of the planned attack. The project, he asserted, was not British in its origins but was the product of the fertile minds of some "corrupt Americans." Engaging in more than his usual amount of double thinking, Pickering rationalized both Liston's long silence regarding the plan and the fact that the British envoy had paid Chisholm's passage to London as acts done unwillingly and only in the line of duty.[29]

---

[27] The fact that Liston actually paid Chisholm's passage to England must have come out in subsequent conversations between the British Minister and Pickering, for this information was not included in Liston's reply to Pickering's questions and yet Pickering knew of it.

[28] Grenville to Liston, April 8, 1797, "Instructions to British Ministers to the United States," Bernard Mayo, ed., *American Historical Association Annual Report for 1936*, III, 132.

[29] Pickering to Ellicott, July 28, 1797, Department of State, Domestic Letters, X, 91–95. The Pickering Papers are among the most useful in uncovering material on the Blount Conspiracy. Another valuable source is the *Debates and Proceedings of Congress* for the Fifth Congress, 1797–1799. Frederick Jackson Turner has published some of the key documents in an article entitled "Documents on the Blount Conspiracy, 1795–1797," *American Historical Review*, X,

Pickering hoped that the entire affair might remain a secret, so much so that he went to the extent of arranging for secrecy with Liston.[30] Anxious to encourage Anglo-American amity, he believed that the disclosure of even a vague British interest in such a project as Blount's and Chisholm's could do nothing but damage. Moreover, the credence the entire episode seemed to lend earlier Spanish charges of a projected British attack on Spanish territory would seriously embarrass him in his heated debate with Yrujo.

It was the President who, differing with Pickering, made sure that the entire affair became public. Liston was undoubtedly correct in asserting that Adams feared that the issue might well become public in any case, and that, if it did after he had suppressed it, he would be accused of "throwing a veil over a project calculated to favor a nation towards whom his enemies already accuse him of entertaining a culpable partiality."[31] Adams publicly exposed the incriminating letter, and an investigation followed. Nonetheless, Minister Liston's explanation of his activities was respected, and, on the face of it, the evidence indicated that the British had acted in good faith in rejecting the Blount-Chisholm proposal for the violation of American neutrality.

While Pickering was making every effort to avoid the disruption of Anglo-American relations, Spanish-American relations grew continually worse. During the height of the investigation of Blount's letter, Yrujo chose to renew his rancorous struggle with Pickering and in a long and bitter note attacked the Administration's foreign policy in general and the Secretary of State in particular. He accused the New Englander of practically every indiscretion and unneutral act short of overt belligerency. This unparalleled personal attack aroused Pickering. To David Humphreys, the American Minister in Madrid, he wrote that the possibility that he and Yrujo might be able to reach some diplomatic agreement was virtually out of the question. Yrujo, he remarked, "appears incapable of distinguish-

1905, 574–606. The only biography of Blount, William H. Masterson, *William Blount*, is useful.

[30] Liston to Grenville, July 8, 1797, Great Britain, Foreign Office, F.O. 115.

[31] *Ibid.*; *Gazette of the United States*, July 6, 1797; *Philadelphia Aurora*, July 8, 1797; *New York Timepiece*, July 12, 1797.

ing between the reproach or slander imputed by word and the dishonor which attaches to falsehood, deceit and prevarication."[32]

Once again engaged in violent personal conflict, Pickering was in his element. He took a long month to reply to Yrujo's attack, this in itself a personal insult to the Chevalier. Finally, and almost calmly, he sent a reply that took up each charge leveled at him by the Spaniard. Yrujo had accused him of lying when, in an earlier published report to the President, he had stated that he had been provided with no evidence of the projected British attack on upper Louisiana. Pickering in turn accused Yrujo of prevarication: "There was nothing but your naked suspicion to act upon," and, he asserted in intentionally insulting fashion, "this was not enough." Pickering was angered at Yrujo's complaint that, despite his warnings of imminent attack, American military posts in the Northwest were not alerted or reinforced. "When you made a formal statement of your suspicions," Pickering replied, "without any fact to show that they were founded: when the government of the United States possessed no other information, nor the knowledge of any circumstances indicative of the expedition; and when, it itself, appeared destitute of even the shadow of probability; it was an act of complaisance to assure you that it 'would be anxious to maintain the rights of their neutral situation, and on all occasions adopt and pursue those measures which should appear proper and expedient for that end'. What these measures should be, and when to be taken, the government itself would judge."[33]

In defending himself the Secretary could not resist the opportunity to use his barbed pen to its full effect. Yrujo had deplored Pickering's earlier report to the President on Spanish-American relations as a corrosive, acting on "the bonds of friendship which unite Spain and America."[34] "Friendship," Pickering reminded the fiery Spaniard, "cannot subsist without mutual confidence; and confidence springs from sincerity." The actions of Spain's representatives both in Philadelphia and in Louisiana, Pickering concluded, "have shaken

[32] Pickering to Humphreys, July 18, 1797, Pickering Papers, VI, 439.
[33] Pickering to Yrujo, August 8, 1797, *A.S.P., F.R.*, I:2, 90.
[34] Yrujo to Pickering, July 11, 1797, *A.S.P., F.R.*, I:2, 68.

the confidence of the Government and of the citizens of the United States; and my report to the President only exhibits a summary of those procedings; . . . then and before presented to his view. And I dare venture to say, that every independent American has from the same premises drawn the same conclusions." [35]

By the middle of July, 1797, Spanish-American relations were stalemated in bitterness. In the West, Ellicott and Pope, with their little detachment of troops, stood firm in a defensive posture, awaiting Spain's next move and wondering whether the Spaniards would agree to evacuate the posts and run the boundary line or whether the four hundred Spanish troops at Natchez would try to drive them out and in the process precipitate hostilities. In Philadelphia relations between Yrujo and Pickering had degenerated into personal conflict, with neither giving an inch.

From this point onward, Pickering's diplomacy was actually aided by the fact that he labored under two major misconceptions. By late August, he had erroneously come to believe that Carondolet, Yrujo, and Gayoso were playing a game not sanctioned by the Spanish Government. They were gambling, he believed, on the probability that a war would erupt between the United States and France and that, under such circumstances, their Ministry would regret the consummation of Pinckney's treaty. Carondolet, he believed, was using the mythical threat of a British attack upon Louisiana as an excuse for refusing to run the boundary.[36] Angered by this transparent deceit, Pickering nonetheless believed they would eventually be forced to give in, for at this time he felt that peace with France would quickly be arranged.[37] Throughout the summer and well into the autumn of 1797, therefore, he was content with the *status quo*, believing that orders would soon arrive from Madrid requiring that the treaty be put into effect.[38]

While Pickering, because he believed that Spain would soon comply with her treaty obligations, was content to allow matters to

---

[35] Pickering to Yrujo, August 8, 1797, *A.S.P., F.R.*, I:2, 90.

[36] Pickering to John Adams, August 26, 1797, Pickering Papers, VII, 124.

[37] Pickering, it will be recalled, during the summer of 1797 was convinced that the French would settle peaceably with the United States.

[38] Pickering to Ellicott, August 30, 1797, Pickering Papers, VII, 133.

remain unsettled for the moment, Yrujo was preparing still another massive attack upon the American Government's foreign policy and upon Pickering as well. It was late in November when he surprised the Secretary with another note. Two days later, under the pen name of Verus, he published essentially the same letter in Bache's *Philadelphia Aurora*. Yrujo once again accused Pickering of being a virtual British agent and attacked American foreign policy just as he had on previous occasions. What Yrujo had begun as an effort to create a set of rationalizations for a refusal to put into effect Pinckney's treaty had become a violent personal combat with Pickering. Each man had accused the other of charlatanry, prevarication, and worse, and each man's pride had become a factor in the quarrel. At this stage, then, Yrujo's attack was more a personal effort than an effective statement of the Spanish case.[39]

Pickering, for once calmer than his opponent, replied to the attacks of Yrujo in two ways. First, in conference with President Adams it was decided that, as a result of the published letter of November 23, the American Government would not "hold any further communications with such a minister." Humphreys in Madrid was ordered to make clear to the Spanish Ministry that a change of ministers in Philadelphia, while not demanded, would be very much appreciated.[40] While taking diplomatic action to have Yrujo removed, Pickering also carried on publicly his personal feud with the Spaniard. In a report to Congress, which he made public after Yrujo had published his attack in the *Aurora*, he reviewed Spanish-American relations from the beginning of 1797 and once again summarized the arguments raised by Spanish officials for refusing to put into effect the agreement that had been made in 1795. In his denunciation of Spanish perfidy he charged that pretences "more frivolous, or more unfounded and unwarrantable, were perhaps never urged as reasons to excuse a violation of the faith of treaties."[41]

[39] Verus to Pickering, November 23, 1797, *A.S.P., F.R.*, 1:2, 101; *Philadelphia Aurora*, November 23, 1797.

[40] Pickering to Humphreys, December 7, 1797, Department of State, Diplomatic Instructions, IV, 182–83.

[41] Report to the President on Spanish-American Relations, January 23, 1798, *A.S.P., F.R.*, 1:2, 79.

On January 24, 1798, the day following the presentation of his report to Congress, Pickering asserted in a scorching letter to Yrujo that the actions of Carondolet and Gayoso de Lemos were doing great "dishonor" to His Catholic Majesty and that he was sure that there had been no order from Madrid authorizing any of the actions taken by them in obstructing the implementation of the treaty.[42] Yrujo replied, on the day following, defending the King's officers in the strongest terms and denying that they had either dishonored or done a disservice to the King by their actions. Indeed, he argued, they had merely acted in defense of Spain's subjects "against the conspiracy which was planned in the Territory of the United States and which," he sarcastically continued, "you have not been pleased to believe, because the English minister assured you of the contrary."[43] He concluded this reply with a demand for either an explanation of the charges that Spanish officials had dishonored their King or an apology. In an act of studied contempt, Pickering waited for more than a month before answering Yrujo. When he did reply, it was not to apologize.

Although neither combatant knew it at the moment, the war was over. The danger of an open break with the United States had been too much for Godoy, and late in September, just after learning of the abortive uprising at Natchez in June, he buckled. Rescinding his earlier order, he instructed Gayoso to evacuate the posts at Walnut Hills and Natchez and ordered the boundary line run without further delay.[44] By late February, Pickering had unofficial but unimpeachable reports of the event.[45] It was not until late in April, however, that he tasted the fruits of personal victory. It was at that time that Yrujo, in a curt note, informed him that orders had been received for the final consummation of the Treaty of 1795.[46]

Godoy had been frightened into his decision to live up to his agree-

---

[42] Pickering to Yrujo, January 20, 1798, Department of State, Domestic Letters, X, 333–36.
[43] Yrujo to Pickering, January 24, 1798, Department of State, Notes from the Spanish Legation, II.
[44] Whitaker, *Mississippi Question*, 65–66.
[45] Higginson to Pickering, February 22, 1798, Pickering Papers, XXII, 44.
[46] Yrujo to Pickering, April 24, 1798, Department of State, Notes from the Spanish Legation, II.

ment with the United States. In large measure his decision was a product of the position taken by Timothy Pickering. Righteous in the knowledge that Spanish officials in America sought means for violating the treaty agreement, and blithely unaware that policy was being made by Godoy and not by Carondolet, Pickering stood firm in his demand that Spain live up to her commitments. His refusal to recall Ellicott and Pope after the unsuccessful uprising at Natchez and his determination to keep them in a defensive posture there, despite Spanish protests, worked to maintain the pressure on the Spanish frontier and made clear that the power of the American Government was behind this pressure. It is true that American power was relatively insignificant in 1797. But in this case, with Spain menaced by Britain as well as by her ally France, it did not need to be great to be effective. Spain was in no position to defend herself in the Western Hemisphere. Perhaps it was through fear that an American invasion might sweep through Louisiana, Florida, and down into South America, that Godoy surrendered.

In some diplomatic situations, Timothy Pickering's combative and unrelenting spirit proved detrimental to American interests, but in his confrontation with Spain, these same qualities did much to win the diplomatic victory. The victory itself was of major significance, for, although at the time Pickering did not fully realize its consequences, he had cleared away one great international question by removing the threat of a clash with the Spanish and lessening the danger of Western schism, just in time to prepare for the final confrontation with France.

8

THE XYZ CRISIS

*A*LTHOUGH THE DEPARTMENT OF STATE had received no direct communications from America's envoys in Paris, rumors filtering into the United States in January, 1798, indicated that they had failed to arrange a settlement.[1] There were some, like Oliver Wolcott, Jr., who paid no attention to such rumors. Wolcott was totally dejected and had been so since the envoys were commissioned, for he believed a settlement between France and the United States inevitable. To him, nothing could have been worse. A Franco-American agreement could work only to exacerbate Anglo-American antagonisms. Moreover, a settlement would strengthen the Republican opposition within the United States and commensurately weaken the Federalists. A bit more shrewd than the French themselves, he observed that the Directory was far "too wise and politic to do anything which would rouse and unite the country."[2]

Wolcott's sentiments did not reflect those of the majority of Fed-

---

[1] Cabot to Pickering, January 9, 1798, Pickering Papers (Massachusetts Historical Society), XXII, 8; Higginson to Pickering, January 10, 1798, *ibid.*, 12; *Philadelphia Aurora*, January 17, 1798; *New York Timepiece*, January 24, 1798.

[2] Wolcott to Fredrick Wolcott, February 27, 1798, in Oliver Wolcott, *Memoirs of the Administrations of Washington and Adams*, George Gibbs, ed. II, 13.

eralists. By the latter part of January, President Adams had gone
so far as to seek the Cabinet's advice on future policy, should the
mission fail. Such an occurrence, as he saw it, would leave the United
States little maneuverability and offer her only two unhappy alternatives — war or a general embargo on all trade with France.[3] Although hesitant in approaching his decision, the President preferred
war.

The Secretary of State, although he was aware of the rumors of
failure and was daily growing more skeptical about the possibilities
for the success of the mission, reserved, for the time, his judgment.
Nevertheless, by late February, when still no communications had
been received from the envoys, he had become thoroughly agitated.
"We cannot account for the lack of direct information from them,"
he wrote to William Vans Murray at The Hague, "on any other
principle than their letters are intercepted."[4]

At last, early in March, 1798, the first five dispatches from the
envoys arrived. From these, the American Government learned that
its emissaries had not even been received. Instead, they had been
kept cooling their heels in the salons and antechambers of Paris for
months. While the Directory refused to recognize their presence in
the French capital, France's cynical foreign minister, Talleyrand,
had, through his agents (designated as X, Y, and Z in the dispatches),
sought to extort a bribe from the American envoys as the price for
using his influence with the Directory to gain accreditation for them.
On the few occasions that Talleyrand's agents had informally discussed the terms of a possible settlement, they had spelled out humiliation for the United States. The envoys admitted that there
seemed no hope for the success of their mission.[5]

Besides informing Philadelphia of the hopelessness of their mission, the envoys included in their dispatches news of a new French
maritime decree that was in direct violation of the conditions of

---

[3] Adams to Pickering, January 24, 1798, Pickering Papers, XXII, 19.
[4] Pickering to Murray, February 26, 1798, Pickering Papers, VIII, 161.
[5] Albert J. Beveridge, *The Life of John Marshall*, I, 214–373. This is the best
published account of the mission. Albert Hall Bowman, "The Struggle for
Neutrality: A History of the Diplomatic Relations Between the United States
and France, 1790–1801," is better for French sources. It also puts Talleyrand in
far better perspective.

the Franco-American treaty of commerce of 1778. Under the stipulations of the new edict, any neutral ship found to be carrying British goods would, along with its cargo, be considered a legal prize. At the height of its power, the Directory felt American commerce too valuable an economic and strategic asset to allow the British to avail themselves of it.

The American representatives could hardly have picked a less opportune time than the autumn of 1797 to attempt to re-establish amicable relations with France. The reconstituted Directory, having just successfully overturned constitutional government in France, was not in a talking mood. The armies of France were almost everywhere successful. The Continental allies had been crushed, and England seemed about to be vanquished. An invasion force was being readied in France to bring the war to English soil. If the attack succeeded, terms could be dictated to the United States; if it failed, there would be plenty of time later to talk.[6]

John Quincy Adams, from his observation post in Berlin, was cogent in reporting on the situation. Neither England nor France wished the other to monopolize the American trade. Either side, given the opportunity, would deny to the other this great advantage, and each was no doubt striving to involve the United States as a party in the war. Although he believed the best interests of the United States would be served through noninvolvement in the affairs of Europe, he felt that diplomatic and economic connections, which surely could not be sacrificed, made a continuation of American neutrality next to impossible. Adams saw only one possibility for remaining unentangled — the creation of a third force in the form of a league of armed neutrals devoted to the defense, by force if necessary, of their neutrality.[7]

The news that the envoys had not only failed, but had also been humiliated in Paris, came as no surprise to the young Adams. He was, nevertheless, furious with the French and hoped that firm

---

[6] Bowman, "The Struggle for Neutrality," 341–42.
[7] John Q. Adams to John Adams, January 31, 1798, Adams Papers (Massachusetts Historical Society), Letters Received and Other Loose Papers, January–March, 1798, reel #387.

measures, including the arming of American merchant vessels, would promptly be taken. It seemed obvious to him that the Directory wished to force the United States to fight in defense of its neutrality. Adams did not fear the contest: "The terrible Republic can hurt us little by sea, if we will but resist her, and I am sick, heartily sick, of the servile acquiescence with which we have so long received from her buffetings and indignities, and returned her thanks."[8]

In Philadelphia the President, after having read the dispatches from his unsuccessful representatives, reached the same conclusions as his son. Angered by this new manifestation of French arrogance and annoyed at Talleyrand's demand for a bribe, he believed that war was the only honorable course left to his Government. France's new maritime decree, a virtual declaration of war upon American commerce, left no alternative. On the question of war aims, Adams was specific. By no means ready to join with England in a European war, he hoped to fight a limited naval conflict against France in defense of America's neutrality.[9] At any time the French might have peace by dealing justly with the United States.

If Adams was angered by French arrogance, he was chagrined at the manner in which the American representatives had behaved. He deplored their lack of professionalism. Only Marshall, of the three the most firm in his opposition to informal talks with Talleyrand's agents, comported himself in line with Adams' standards for good diplomatic conduct. "W and X, with all their tittle tattle," remarked the President, "ought to have been not attended to, nor any word said to them, till the envoys were received by the Directory and some one selected with full powers to treat." America's emissaries had completely misplayed their hand. They should have made

---

[8] John Q. Adams to Murray, March 6, 1798, John Q. Adams, *The Writings of John Quincy Adams*, W. E. Ford, ed., II, 265–66.

[9] Page Smith, *John Adams*, II, 954–57. Smith does a fine job of describing the anger of Adams upon receiving the dispatches. He argues that at first Adams hoped for a declaration of war from Congress, but he feared Congress would not give him war without first requiring the dispatches. Since he was not ready to reveal the exact details of the dispatches, Adams decided to recede to a defensive posture and ask only for vigorous measures of defense from Congress.

no refusals nor any commitments without first receiving diplomatic recognition.[10]

Not even the volatile John Adams responded to the news of the envoys' humiliation at the hands of the Directory as did Timothy Pickering. The Secretary of State exploded in indignation. To Stephen Higginson he wrote that nothing would "satisfy the ambitious and rapacious rulers of that nation but universal dominion of the sea as well as of the land with the property of all nations at their disposal, to seize and keep what portion they please." He deplored the Americans' failure to rise earlier to the French challenge. "Judging from our past forbearance the villains think that the *real Americans* will hardly dare appeal to arms against their imaginary *omnipotence*; or if they dare, that their friends here are numerous enough to prevent it."[11] Pickering too was ready for war, but his concept of the objectives of such a war was far different from that held by either Adams.

From the moment that the X Y Z dispatches arrived, Pickering's mind was whirling in anticipation of the conflict to come. It was not, however, to be a war fought alone or merely in defense of America's neutral rights. Rather, Pickering viewed the situation as a superb opportunity to join England as a full-fledged member of the coalition fighting against not only an aggressive France but the ideology of its revolution as well.

Instead of the limited war in defense of American neutrality the President envisaged, Pickering hoped for full-scale conflict. That Pickering had no sympathy with neutralism and that he did not consider its defense a worthy objective in war became quickly apparent as he moved to halt the informal negotiations John Quincy Adams had been carrying on in Berlin for the re-creation of the old

---

[10] Marshall, Pinckney, and Gerry to Adams, October 22, 1797, Dispatch #1, Adams Papers, Letters Received and Other Loose Papers, October–December 1797, reel #386. Adams noted his impressions on the dispatch itself as a marginal note. See also Smith, *John Adams*, II, 953.

[11] Pickering to Higginson, March 6, 1798, Pickering Papers, VIII, 187. This letter contains a complete explanation of the implications of the new French decree upon American commerce. The news of the decree arrived in the envoys' dispatches on the previous day. It was this decree that prompted the envoys to write their "no hope" dispatch.

Armed Neutrality. Instead, he urged Adams to work to convince Europe's neutrals to enter the struggle against France. Certainly, the American example should prove to the neutrals "that those powers who have avoided becoming parties in the present war . . . will finally have no reason to rejoice; they were only reserved for future plunder and oppression." [12]

The humiliating results of the effort to restore amity between the United States and France had led Pickering to the dangerous conclusion that negotiations could never succeed with a power like France. Because Pickering believed the best alternative to be an alliance with England in a full-scale war, he became the emphatic opponent of any plan for a league of neutrals that might hinder the operations of the British on the high seas. Such a league could operate only in favor of the French. In another dispatch to John Quincy Adams, he wrote that "the safety of the portion of the civilized world not yet subjugated by France greatly depends on the barrier opposed to her boundless ambition and rapacity by the Navy of England. If this navy were crushed or subjugated to the power of France, she would instantly become the tyrant of the seas, as she is already of the European continent." [13]

The moment of war having apparently arrived, the Secretary turned to Alexander Hamilton for advice. In the strictest confidence, he briefly but thoroughly summarized the contents of the dispatches from the envoys and then sought the New Yorker's opinion regarding the possibility of an alliance with Britain. The opposition, he noted, believed that a secret alliance had already been negotiated. Unfortunately, they were incorrect. "Not one syllable," Pickering complained, had yet been written to King in London regarding even the possibility of negotiations. Time was running out, and Pickering believed the opportunity should not be allowed to pass. [14]

Hamilton replied at once, urging the importance of strenghtening America's defenses but, although perhaps sympathetic to the idea, disapproving the proposed alliance with Britain. Not two years had

[12] Pickering to J. Q. Adams, March 17, 1798, Pickering Papers, VIII, 206.
[13] Pickering to J. Q. Adams, May 28, 1798, Pickering Papers, VIII, 481.
[14] Pickering to Hamilton, March 25, 1798, Pickering Papers, VIII, 241.

passed since Washington had made his Farewell Address to the nation, an address written in large part by Hamilton that warned against foreign entanglements. Could the Government now repudiate the words of Washington without granting to the Republicans a new and formidable weapon? Hamilton clearly thought not. Moreover, he was convinced that the majority of the American people still held deep within them too much hostility toward Britain to embrace her as an ally. Furthermore, the New Yorker had doubts about the need for an alliance. Britain would be moved by her own interests to grant military aid to the United States, without a treaty. America might have all the advantages of cooperation with Britain without any of the disadvantages that would stem from a formal agreement. In Hamilton's view, a treaty that was not only politically dangerous but militarily unnecessary and that might well become a diplomatic liability at some future time, should not be sought.[15]

To Pickering's dismay, Adams shared Hamilton's views. Opposition was futile. America would not seek a treaty with Britain, but would engage in "small cooperations" from time to time against the mutual enemy. Simultaneously, she would keep herself free to negotiate a peace with France at the most advantageous moment. Ready for a war against France, Adams was nonetheless unwilling to lock the nation into a European conflict in which American interests were not vitally involved.[16]

Characteristically, Pickering could not accept the President's decision. Frustrated and isolated, he still hoped for an alliance, and he made his feelings known where they would be most effective — to the British Minister. "From the tenor of the Secretary of State's conversation," Liston wrote, "I can entertain no doubt that he himself is clearly of opinion that such a concert ought to take place; but he is deterred from speaking frankly, in part on account of the numbers and strength of the party who declaim against every sort of connection with Great Britain, and partly because he has received

---

[15] Hamilton to Pickering, March 27, 1798, Pickering Papers, XXII, 92.
[16] Pickering to King, April 2, 1798, Pickering Papers, VIII, 288.

no instructions on the subject from the President of the United States." [17]

As the crisis with France grew more pronounced, Pickering used his office to further his own policy views. He made every effort to attain a closer understanding with Britain and to cooperate in every possible way with her against the common enemy, France. Grenville, eager for an ally, was naturally cooperative. A series of agreements was reached with Britain in the summer of 1798, which augured well for the Secretary's hopes for an eventual alliance. In June, at Pickering's request, the British Ministry agreed to return twenty-four cannon that had served as coastal defense for Charleston Harbor during the Revolution and that had been taken by the British when they withdrew in 1783. In July, he suggested the exchange of recognition signals between American and British naval vessels. Such an arrangement was quickly agreed upon. [18]

Even on the very touchy issues revolving around the island of Santo Domingo, Pickering and the British were able to cooperate. The Caribbean island had recently been wrested from France by the rebel leader Toussaint L'Ouverture. This man, the "Black Napoleon," was at the time on the verge of completing his already successful rebellion by declaring the island independent of France. He awaited only a guarantee that the United States would agree to trade with his country and supply the provisions and goods the new nation required for survival.

Toussaint's successful rebellion created a dangerous situation both for Great Britain and the United States, and each nation sought to cooperate with the other in dealing with it. As far as the British were concerned, Santo Domingo's independence presaged the end of British colonialism in the West Indies. William Pitt the Younger, then serving as Prime Minister, fully expected that, in time, Britain

---

[17] Liston to Grenville, August 31, 1798, Great Britain, Foreign Office, F.O. 115, United States of America, Correspondence of British Diplomatic Representatives, Selections, 1791–1902, P.R.O.

[18] Bradford Perkins, *The First Rapprochement: England and the United States: 1795–1805*. Perkins views the period as one in which a substantial growth in Anglo-American amity took place. He exaggerates, however, the depth of that feeling, overemphasizing the significance of the cooperative arrangements made at the time.

would be forced to withdraw from her holdings in the area. Nevertheless, both he and Grenville agreed that it was necessary to soften what they considered to be the inevitable collapse of colonialism. Jamaica should be spared the violence of "black rebellion." Pitt and Grenville hoped to quarantine effectively Santo Domingo in order that neither revolutionaries nor revolutionary ideology should traverse the short span of water between Santo Domingo and Jamaica. This separation they hoped to accomplish, in cooperation with the United States, by monopolizing and controlling all commerce with L'Ouverture's stronghold, thus regulating all sea-borne traffic with the island.[19]

Pickering too feared the effect of the revolution in Santo Domingo, particularly as an example to the Negroes of the American South; he too was anxious to quarantine the infected island. Always aware of the commercial implications of foreign policy, however, he was also stimulated by the prospects of a possible monopoly on the trade with Santo Domingo. Indeed, he looked upon it as the only opportunity American merchants might have to be reimbursed in some way for the losses they had suffered at the hands of French privateers and cruisers. Certainly, he looked for no future reparations from France.

The Secretary showed real skill in his management of the entire affair. First, on the Administration's urging, Congress altered the embargo it had placed on trade with French possessions and granted to the President the discretionary power to open trade with any of France's possessions whenever such a territory should guarantee to halt privateering within its jurisdiction. This change in policy gave to the Administration the power to lift the embargo on trade with Santo Domingo if and when L'Ouverture should effectively quash the privateers on the island. Following this action in Congress, after weeks of friendly talks between Pickering, Liston, and the former British Commander in Santo Domingo, General Maitland, an agreement was worked out between the two nations that effectively quarantined the island. It simultaneously granted to the United

---

[19] King to Pickering, January 10, 1799, Rufus King, *Life and Correspondence of Rufus King*, Charles R. King, ed., II, 500.

States a virtual monopoly on the trade in provisions and raw materials with the new Caribbean nation. Once agreement had been reached between the British and the American negotiators, L'Ouverture was presented with the joint proposal, which he could accept or reject.[20]

A generally conciliatory atmosphere did not obscure all the bones of contention between Britain and the United States, but it is evident that both governments did their best to alleviate problems as they arose. For example, impressment, which had only recently subsided as a major issue, remained insignificant, due in large measure to the constant efforts of British officials and the restraint of many naval officers.

Problems arose in other areas, however, which called for action. In that crucial spring of 1798 British privateers and naval vessels increased their aggressions against American shipping in the Caribbean, and the Vice-Admiralty Court at Mole St. Nicholas condemned every American vessel brought before it. At the moment that Pickering planned war with France, it was more than embarrassing for new British injustices to occur, and he warned against them in a vigorous protest to London. Public discontent in the United States was rising at a moment when "conciliatory conduct" on Britain's part was more important than at any other time.[21] In this instance, the British Government acted quickly. The court at Mole St. Nicholas was repudiated by London. Those American merchants who had suffered unjust condemnations were granted recourse in Britain's High Court of Admiralty.[22] As America came closer to war with France, Britain became more conciliatory and cooperative.

In the weeks following the receipt of the envoys' first dispatches the Secretary dedicated himself with great success to strengthening the accord with Britain, and he simultaneously hoped to demolish

[20] Pickering to Edward Stevens, April 20, 1799, Pickering Papers, X, 606–13. For a more complete analysis of the Santo Domingo question, see Rayford W. Logan, *Diplomatic Relations of the United States with Haiti, 1766–1891*; C. C. Tansill, *The United States and Santo Domingo, 1798–1873*.

[21] Pickering to King, April 26, 1798, Pickering Papers, XXXVII, 298; see, for example, *New York Timepiece*, April 25, 1798.

[22] King to Hamilton, June 8, 1798, Papers of Alexander Hamilton (Library of Congress).

a major obstacle on the road to full-scale war with France, Republicanism. Since May, 1797, Republicans had voiced the most vigorous opposition to the Administration's policy. In the House of Representatives they had blocked all but the most meager appropriations for the increase of America's defense establishment. Pickering believed that the publication of the envoys' dispatches would destroy the Republicans.[23] The disclosure of France's arrogant refusal to receive the American envoys could not fail to stir the people. By divulging in exact detail the wretched efforts of Talleyrand to extort a bribe from the envoys and the French demands for a large forced loan from the United States as the price of peace, Pickering hoped to stimulate that national unity and universal support for the Administration for which he yearned.

Throughout the middle weeks of March, 1798, despite Pickering's urgings, the President reluctantly refused to publish the dispatches. The envoys had written that they would make one last effort to negotiate before requesting their passports. Since then, there had been no news of either success or failure of their effort or of the envoys' whereabouts. Consequently, and much to Pickering's unhappiness, the President dallied, awaiting news of his emissaries and hoping that, if their talks had failed, as he supposed, they were safely out of the reach of the Directory. If a published account of the dispatches reached the French before the envoys left the country, they might be placed in real physical danger. The Directory had on more than one occasion violated the person of a foreign minister. Charles Lee, the Attorney General, fully agreed with Adams and warned strongly against publication.[24] Pickering and McHenry on the other hand, ignored the question of the personal safety of the envoys, arguing that precious time was being wasted and that the President should publish the dispatches immediately for the maximum effect upon public opinion.[25]

---

[23] Pickering to Hamilton, March 25, 1798, Pickering Papers, VIII, 241.

[24] Lee to Adams, March 14, 1798, Adams Papers, Letters Received and Other Loose Papers, January to March, 1798, reel #387.

[25] McHenry to Adams, March 14, 1798, Adams Papers, Letters Received and Other Loose Papers, January to March, 1798, reel #387; DeConde, *The Quasi-War*, 68.

Adams had done much soul-searching before deciding not to publicize the dispatches. Like Pickering, he was anxious to disclose them; national unity was his object, and the dispatches seemed to provide the opportunity to achieve it. If he had known that the envoys were safely out of France and on their way home, he would without doubt or hesitation have published their dispatches. In the circumstances, he was sorely pressed by opposite motives and for a time wavered in his decision. He had in his hands the power to cripple and perhaps destroy the Republican faction. "It is a very painful thing to him," Abigail Adams wrote to her sister, "that he cannot communicate to the public dispatches in which they are so much interested, but we have not any assurance that the envoys have left Paris and who can say that in this critical state of things their dispatches ought to be public?"[26]

One thing was clear. News of the receipt of the dispatches and some explanation of their contents would have to be made, for it had been a long nine months since the envoys had sailed for the Continent. This long silence had done the Administration no good. It had even led some among the Republican leadership to assume that the commission had worked out an amicable settlement with the French that, because of its determination to force a war, the Administration was attempting to keep secret.

In a special address to Congress, Adams attempted to straddle, stating that, as a result of dispatches received from the envoys, no hope remained for a peaceful settlement with France. He did not, however, provide Congress with the dispatches. "While I feel a satisfaction in informing you that their exertions for the adjustment of the differences between the two nations have been sincere and unremitted," he told the assembled congressmen, "it is incumbent on me to declare, that I perceive no ground of expectation, that the objects of their mission can be accomplished on terms compatible with the safety the honor or the essential interests of the nation. . . . After a careful review of the whole subject with the aid of all the information I have received I can discern nothing which could have

---

[26] Abigail Adams to Mary Cranch, March 20, 1798, Abigail Adams, *New Letters of Abigail Adams, 1787–1801*, S. Mitchell, ed., 146–47.

ensured, or contributed to success, that has been omitted on my part, and nothing further which can be attempted consistently with maxims for which our country has contended at every hazard and which constitute the basis of our national sovereignty." He concluded by firmly asserting that peace no longer seemed a possibility. He urged Congress to take immediate action to strengthen the national defenses.[27]

Pickering might never have seen the publication of the dispatches had it not been for the aid he received from the Republicans. Jefferson, who referred to the President's message as "insane," plotted a course for Republicans in Congress that played directly into the hands of the Secretary of State. His doubts about Adams' honesty having led him far astray, the Virginian believed that Congress should immediately press the President for the envoys' dispatches, for he believed they would show that there was no cause for the warlike speech the President had delivered. "If Congress are to act on the question of war," he wrote, "they have a right to information." Of course Jefferson believed the dispatches would prove that the President had at least exaggerated the situation and that war was not so inevitable as Adams would like the nation to believe. On another tack, Jefferson hoped to block the move to war by passing "a legislative prohibition to arm vessels" instead of the measure for the arming of merchant vessels Adams had proposed. In this way the Congress would indicate its unwillingness to adopt aggressive measures and quell the movement to war.[28] If the Virginian had no doubt that the American people were still desirous for peace and eager to avoid a war, he did have some doubts about the uncommitted moderate congressmen in the House of Representatives. President Adams' speech had influenced some in this group, and they showed signs of going over to the Federalists.[29]

---

[27] Adams' address to Congress, March 19, 1798, John Adams, *The Works of John Adams*, C. F. Adams, ed., IX, 156–57; Stephen G. Kurtz, *The Presidency of John Adams*, 284–306; Smith, *John Adams*, II, 956–57.

[28] Jefferson to Monroe, March 21, 1798, Monroe Papers (Library of Congress).

[29] This was an important reason in moving the Republicans to challenge the President. Adams' speech, even without the support of the dispatches, had driven a wedge between the Republicans in the House and the moderate

In Congress, following the pattern set by Jefferson, the Republicans immediately took the initiative, introducing two resolutions designed to challenge the Administration on the issue of peace or war. The first of these stated "that under existing circumstances, it is not expedient for the United States to resort to war against the French Republic." The second resolution suggested that "provision ought to be made by law for restricting the arming of merchant vessels, except in cases in which the practice was heretofore permitted." The battle was thus joined and a bitter three-day debate ensued, which, much to the chagrin of the Republicans, the Federalists with the aid of the moderates in Congress won. Moderates in the House may not have been ready for war, but neither were they willing to tie the nation to an inflexible policy at a moment when such action might prove dangerous.[30]

Only momentarily halted, Republicans in Congress determined upon a new and bolder line of attack, and on March 30, they introduced a resolution requesting that the President "communicate to this house the dispatches from the envoys." Virginia's William B. Giles was quick to second the resolution, flatly asserting as he did that he was not satisfied that the President had been sincere in his diplomacy. Particularly suspicious with regard to the instructions the envoys had been given, he demanded that the President present these, as well as the dispatches, to Congress. When Representative John Allen of Connecticut, himself an extreme Federalist, suggested that the President might withhold any parts of the dispatches or instructions which, if made public, might endanger the prospects of "any existing negotiation," Virginia's John Nicholas demurred. The President had declared negotiations at an end. Certainly, in such a critical period, the Congress could not be asked "to act upon less information than that upon which the President himself had acted."[31]

With men like Allen and Robert Goodloe Harper, the extreme

---

unaligned congressmen who had previously formed with the Jeffersonians the ruling coalition in the House.

[30] *Debates and Proceedings in the Congress of the United States*, 5th Congress, 1797–1799, 1353–55.

[31] *Debates and Proceedings*, 5th Congress, 1797–1799, 1358.

Federalist from South Carolina and intimate of Timothy Pickering, agreeing wholeheartedly with their demands, the Republicans should have realized that they were constructing a trap for themselves. Some, such as Albert Gallatin, did, but for the most part, caught in a snare of their own creation, they joined with Federalists in both houses in calling for the dispatches.

Only unwillingly had Adams passed up the opportunity that had earlier presented itself to disclose the documents. The insulting call from Republicans in Congress offered him a second chance, which he was loath to refuse. Moreover, it was far easier to assume the initiative at this time, since Pickering, busy behind the scenes, had, more than a week previously, dispatched special instructions recalling the envoys from Paris.[32] His conscience assuaged and, convinced that the envoys might yet withdraw safely from French territory before the dispatches could reach France, Adams speedily prepared to submit the papers to Congress. In triumphant irony, Abigail Adams wrote to her son John Quincy that the "House yesterday passed a vote of call, for the instructions to and dispatches from our envoys, and today *they will receive them.*"[33] Americans had been too long supine and "regardless of the future" but now, thought the First Lady, the passions of the people would be aroused and the nation would unite in the defense of liberty.

The disclosure of the dispatches to Congress sent Adams' Republican opponents into a ragged withdrawal. Although the Republican leadership, including Jefferson, attempted to minimize the meaning of the envoys' communications, their efforts were of little effect.[34] Moderates in the House of Representatives, who controlled the balance of power and who until recently had been supporting the

---

[32] Pickering to Marshall, Pinckney, and Gerry, March 23, 1798, Department of State, Diplomatic Instructions, IV, 249–52 (National Archives).

[33] Abigail Adams to John Q. Adams, April 4, 1798, Adams Papers, Letters Received and Other Loose Papers, April–May, 1798, reel #388.

[34] The reader may find an example of these efforts in Jefferson's analysis of the dispatches in a letter to Madison dated April 6, 1798, in Thomas Jefferson, *The Writings of Thomas Jefferson*, Paul L. Ford, ed., VII, 26. Here Jefferson seeks to reduce the implications of the dispatches to mere French animosity over Adams' speech of May, 1797, and argues that all that stands in the way of a peaceful arrangement with the Directory is an apology for the uncomplimentary remarks leveled against France by the President. See also Nathan Schachner, *Thomas Jefferson*, 2 vols. (New York, 1951), II, 599–609.

Republicans in their opposition to costly measures of defense, now moved over into the Federalist camp. Despondently Jefferson wrote to his son-in-law Thomas Mann Randolph that the publication of the dispatches had carried the moderates — "waverers" as he referred to them — into a working coalition with the Federalists. He believed Republican power in the House had been broken.[35]

Almost immediately Jefferson's fears came to fruition as Federalists joined by moderates passed, over Republican objections, a bill providing for the publication and distribution of ten thousand copies of the instructions to the envoys as well as of their dispatches home. Secretary Pickering could not have been more delighted. Once the printing was completed, he hurried the pamphlets into circulation. Selecting trustworthy Federalists in all sections of the nation, he sent them bundles of the pamphlets with careful instructions to be sure that back-country and rural folk, the backbone of Republican support, were given every opportunity to read or at least hear about the infamous X Y Z Affair.[36]

The immediate and violent public reaction to the disclosures dealt a shattering blow to the Republicans. During the spring and summer, addresses of devotion and loyalty to the Government poured into Philadelphia until, to the casual observer, it seemed that a tidal wave of ever-widening proportions threatened to wash Republicanism from the country. Even Jefferson was forced to admit that the democratic movement had been momentarily halted by the recent disclosures and that outright opposition to the Administration at this juncture would be foolish. Convinced, however, that tempers would cool and the fever of the moment would pass, if given time, he advised his colleagues to await the reversal of public opinion. To John Taylor of Caroline he wrote: "A little patience and we shall see the reign of witches pass over, their spells dissolved, and the people recovering their true sight, restoring their government to its true principles."[37]

---

[35] Jefferson to T. M. Randolph, April 19, 1798, Papers of Thomas Jefferson (Library of Congress).

[36] Pickering to Carrington, August 8, 1798, Pickering Papers, IX, 168; August 10, 1798, 179.

[37] Jefferson to Taylor, June 1, 1798, in Jefferson, *Writings*, VII, 265.

Jefferson's convictions were founded upon the shrewd observation that the "great mass of the people" were not behind the movement toward war. Nor did they seem to be taking a part in the public show of hostility toward France. Jefferson rather observantly judged that the anti-Republican, anti-French outburst was coming primarily from coastal trading towns. He might have added that Federalist-officered militia units were providing more than their share of addresses of support for the President. Jefferson was convinced, and justly so, that the fervent show of public indignation was the product of a numerical minority and that the only real danger lay in the possibility that the majority might allow itself to be led to war without registering its opposition to such a course. This he believed unlikely for, as war with France became a more definite possibility and taxes were increased to pay for the military expenditures that would inevitably follow, the people, their economic interests involved, would rouse themselves to oppose the Administration's policy.[38]

While Jefferson prepared to ride out the storm and await the voice of the majority, the closest supporter of the Administration was convinced that at last the majority of the people had spoken. "The effect of the communications which has been made in compliance with the request of the House of Representatives has made the blind to see and the deaf to hear. . . . It has been like an electrical shock," exulted Abigail Adams. She added that "the *emissaries of France remain unchanged*. But real Americans who have been deceived, and betray'd by falsehood, and deception; are the mass of the lower class of the people. They are unityng & united, and I would fain hope that the hyden monster of jacobinism is smashed never to rise with such mischevious effects again."[39]

Among Federalists there was a marked difference of opinion as to the depth and significance of the public outcry that had been stimulated by the recent disclosures. Pessimistic observers noted that, while a semblance of unity had been created and while the American

---

[38] Jefferson to Madison, April 26, 1798, Jefferson, *Writings*, VII, 246.
[39] Abigail Adams to John Q. Adams, April 21, 1798, Adams Papers, Letters Received and Other Loose Papers, April to May, 1798, reel #388.

people had been convinced of the importance of defending themselves against French aggression, they were not as yet willing to
unite in an aggressive policy. For instance, the chance that the Administration would get the overwhelming popular support necessary,
if it should request a declaration of war from Congress, was negligible. Many among the extreme Federalists were convinced, despite
all the public fervor being shown, that the nation would not support
a war. Oliver Wolcott, Jr., for example, was actually depressed when
the envoys' dispatches were published, for he believed that open
conflict between Federalists and Republicans could no longer be
avoided. Unless the Congress declared war upon France, a circumstance Wolcott believed unlikely even given the impetus of the furor
over the X Y Z Affair, he felt that Jacobinism would eventually
triumph in the United States.[40] The Massachusetts Federalist Joseph Hopkinson, visiting in New York at the time of the disclosure
of the dispatches, was also disturbed by what he observed. He believed that most of the people in that large and important state
were almost totally uninterested in the crisis with France and certainly not eager for war. Indeed, he wrote, "French sentiment," far
from being dead in New York, was more virulent and more important than the nationalist anti-French feeling that had been generated by recent events.[41] Fisher Ames, too, was concerned about
what he considered to be the inadequate force of warlike sentiment.
He viewed the strong public display against France as only transi-
tory, and he warned that Americans loved peace too much to maintain their anti-French ardor for long.[42]

Either because he was less observant than his friends or more
moved by his own desires for a full-scale war with France, Pickering was extremely pleased by the popular reaction. He believed that
the majority of the American people would support war. Even Republicans in Congress, he thought, had been chastened. Since the

[40] Wolcott to Hamilton, April 5, 1798, in Wolcott, *Administrations of Washington and Adams*, II, 49.
[41] Hopkinson to Wolcott, May 17, 1798, Wolcott, *Administrations of Washington and Adams*, II, 49–50.
[42] Ames to Pickering, June 4, 1798, Fisher Ames, *The Works of Fisher Ames*,
Seth Ames, ed., II, 227.

publication of the dispatches, he noted that they had made little effort to oppose the Administration's policy. The Secretary believed that many former "French devotees" had learned their lesson and either had, or soon would, return to the support of their own Government. In the not too distant future, Pickering predicted, Americans would rise against the "insults and injuries" they had suffered at the hands of "the most corrupt government upon Earth."[43]

The closer public opinion seemed to move toward a consensus with his own views, the more Pickering's usually limited faith in the people increased. As addresses of support poured into Philadelphia, his spirits rose accordingly. "I never despaired of the commonwealth; and I have now no doubt of the requisite union and spirit of our citizens." The people of the United States would defend themselves "against all the open or insidious attempts of France" to destroy American independence.[44] At last, Pickering believed, the unity he had long desired was being created.

In that glorious April of 1798, only Adams' commitment to a limited war in defense of neutral rights troubled the Secretary, but even the President gave Pickering some cause to be encouraged for the future. At the very least, Pickering realized, the President was sympathetic to the idea of a declaration of war and was doing all he could to feed the flames of national indignation. That, after all, was the most important factor. Once at war with France, an alliance with England might more easily be achieved.

Adams, who believed humiliation to be the only alternative to conflict, was determined to whip up sentiment for war among the people.[45] The earliest manifestation of this attitude was his decision

---

[43] Pickering to Washington, April 14, 1798, Pickering Papers, XXXVII, 294.
[44] Pickering to Humphreys, April 19, 1798, Pickering Papers, VIII, 356.
[45] Adams admitted that at this time he was determined to lead the nation into war and, further, stated that this required a good deal of work on his part apparently because public opinion was not ready for aggressive action. See Letter III of his "Letters to the Boston Patriot," in John Adams, *The Works of John Adams*, C. F. Adams, ed., VIII, 247–49. Although Adams adds that he was simultaneously "determined . . . to listen to every proposal and embrace the first opportunity to restore peace whenever it could be done consistent with the honour and interests of the country," it remains clear that he set out to stimulate a war fever in the United States. Moreover, in the summer of 1798, Adams' anger was such that it is not likely that he actually did want peace

to set aside May 9, 1798, as a day of humiliation, fasting, and prayer for the nation, an act designed to dramatize the national emergency and to stimulate a patriotic spirit. When Adams received an anonymous letter warning that, on the day he had set aside for fasting and prayer, the Jacobins planned to burn Philadelphia and massacre many of the people, he was startled but probably incredulous. "Look to that grandest of all grand villains, that traitor to his country — that infernal scoundrel Jefferson," the letter warned, "he has too much hand in the conspiracy." [46] That Adams actually believed the Republicans, with Jefferson at their head, planned such an outrage is questionable. Nevertheless, the day of fasting and prayer was one of wild activity in Philadelphia, as Adams called out the militia to guard his home as well as the city against the threatened attack. The attack, of course, never materialized. But the tolling of the city's bells in constant alarm, the flashing of bayonets, and the hurried hoofbeats of cavalry horses served another purpose; they stimulated in the minds of Americans an awareness of the dangers all about them and increased their willingness to accept the idea of war.

In other ways as well, Adams sought to encourage the growth of national fervor. Consistently, throughout the spring and summer of 1798, in his replies to the addresses of loyalty and devotion that poured in upon him, Adams attempted to stimulate America's determination to fight rather than submit to humiliation at the hands of France. "When immense sums of money are demanded as the price of negotiation," he wrote in answer to the memorials of the towns of Plymouth and Kingston in Massachusetts, "a compliance would not only compromise our neutrality: but debase our minds, corrupt our souls, and make our own government, in a few years as profligate as theirs. It would be the beginning of an habit in the minds of our government and people of submission to insolence, injustice and disgrace. It would lay the foundation for employing our own money and cor-

---

except on terms that would completely humiliate the French. It is far more likely at this time that Adams was determined upon a war and that he did not cool down to the point where he actually wanted a peaceful settlement until the autumn of 1798.

[46] Anonymous to Adams, April 18, 1798, Adams Papers, Letters Received and Other Loose Papers, April to May, 1798, reel #388.

rupting our own elections. This very money would be employed in hiring venal writers and printers of scandal against virtue and panogyrick upon vice. It would. . . . But I must forbear."[47] In a reply to a similar address from Vermont, Adams suggested that, in refusing to negotiate with America's chosen envoys, the Directory was actually attempting to dictate not only American policy, but the very composition of the American government as well. Adams warned that, if the French were allowed to deal with the United States in so contemptuous a fashion, the people of America might as well surrender their independence to France. "Rather than this," he continued, "I say with you, let us have war."[48] Again, in reply to an address from the people of Harrison County, Virginia, he struck upon the theme of conflict and emphasized that, at this stage in Franco-American relations, while the prospect was "alarming," a war with France would be both "just" and necessary. He applauded the growth of unity that appeared "to prevail generally throughout our land."[49] To the inhabitants of Danvers, Massachusetts, he wrote: ". . . the injuries committed against us, have been the most provoked, the most wanton, and the most capricious, and abominable, adding the most premeditated insults to the most intollerable injuries. The treatment of our government and its ambassadors surpasses all example, and can never be forgiven, without reparation."[50]

The President's emotional outpourings aroused a mixed reaction among Federalists. Pickering, of course, approved; he hoped that the President would finally ask for a declaration of war. Robert Troup, an important New York Federalist, also lauded Adams. He wrote to his friend Rufus King that "no man that has figured in our theater, will go down to posterity with greater luster than John Adams —

---

[47] Adams to the towns of Plymouth and Kingston, June 8, 1798, Adams Papers, Letters Received and Other Loose Papers, June, 1798, reel #389.

[48] Adams to "the officers and soldiers of the Cavalry, Artillery, and Infantry, and other inhabitants of Burlington and its Vicinity in the County of Chittenden and the State of Vermont," August 16, 1798, Adams Papers, Letters Received and Other Loose Papers, July to August, 1798, reel #390.

[49] Adams to the "citizens of Harrison County, Va.," August 16, 1798, Adams Papers, Letters Received and Other Loose Papers, July to August, 1798, reel #390.

[50] Adams to "the inhabitants of the town of Danvers, Mass.," August 15, 1798, Adams Papers, Letterbook, October 17, 1797, to July 8, 1799, reel #119.

I will not even except *George Washington.*"[51] Alexander Hamilton, however, was more cautious. He feared that the President's vigorous public statements might work to exacerbate once again political divisions within the country that, he believed, were only uneasily and temporarily healed.[52]

Gratified by the President's activities, Pickering was further encouraged by legislative action directed against the French. Privateers were being commissioned and released from their ports to prey on French shipping, while American naval vessels were authorized to fire upon French warships; the Regular Army had been increased by several regiments; the treaties of 1778 with France had been abrogated; the Congress had even gone so far as to enact the Alien and Sedition laws.

The passage of the Alien and Sedition laws was greeted with particular enthusiasm by the Secretary of State, who had for some time urged such legislation. Incapable of distinguishing between treason and legitimate political opposition, he had long ago decided that the Republicans were in reality simply agents of the French attempting to divide the nation from within. Switzerland, Holland, and various Italian states had all been the victims of such men as these. The Alien and Sedition Acts, however, provided the American Government with weapons to fight both alien and native subversives, while simultaneously bringing the force of law to bear upon the fundamental problem of creating national unity.

The Alien Act never really fulfilled Pickering's expectations. This failure was partially due to the reluctance of President Adams to enforce it in a broad and sweeping fashion. Pickering, who was charged with administering the law, hoped to use it to deport French consular officers resident in the United States, an action Adams at the time considered too extreme.[53] The Secretary was also hamstrung by the President's refusal to sign blank warrants for the arrest of dangerous aliens. Adams would not delegate his authority.

Despite the limitations placed upon him by the President, the Secretary of State pressed his efforts at enforcing the law. The re-

---

[51] Robert Troup to Rufus King, July 10, 1798, in King, *Life and Correspondence*, II, 363.
[52] Hamilton to Wolcott, June 5, 1798, Hamilton Papers.
[53] Pickering to Adams, October 11, 1798, Pickering Papers, IX, 453–54.

sults proved negligible. Not one alien was deported under the Alien Act. Paradoxically enough, it was the zeal of the Secretary that accounted for this strange fact. One known alien was eminently well qualified for deportation, and Pickering secured the President's permission to test the law upon him. This person was the French general Victor Collot, who had for some time been traveling in the United States. Collot, whom he could easily have apprehended, Pickering merely kept under surveillance, hoping that he would lead the Government's investigators to additional suspects. The Secretary was disappointed, and Collot remained within the United States until after Pickering had left office and the Alien Act had expired.[54]

The enforcement of the Sedition Act was also placed in the hands of the Secretary, and the results proved at once more pleasing and fruitful to him. Here, the President gave Pickering free rein to interpret the law in broad fashion. Under the direction of the aggressive New Englander, the Government brought "at least seventeen indictments" against Republican newspapers throughout the country.[55] By the summer of 1800, during the heat of the presidential campaign, the Republican press had been, if not muzzled, then at least haltered.[56]

Despite the encouraging signs of the summer, Pickering grew more agitated as the time passed. Week after week of precious time went by while the Congress moved to provide for national defense but remained unwilling to vote a declaration of war. Although Pickering would never have admitted it, in refusing to declare war Congress was probably reflecting the general sentiments of the people at large. Fisher Ames saw its inaction in this light and, in a letter to the Secretary of State, observed that "ripe as the citizens are for self-defense, they reluct at offence; they would yield much, far too much, for peace; and this hope would delude them, if proud France would condescend to hold it out."[57]

Like Pickering and Ames, Stephen Higginson, by this time violent for war, was deeply distressed over Congress' failure to declare

---

[54] James M. Smith, *Freedom's Fetters: The Alien and Sedition Laws and American Civil Liberties,* 175–76.

[55] Smith, *Freedom's Fetters,* 185–86.

[56] Smith, *Freedom's Fetters,* 186–87.

[57] Ames to Pickering, July 10, 1798, Pickering Papers, XXII, 278.

it and was further aroused by the lack of warlike verve among the people. In June, he wrote to Pickering to urge the importance of a war, but he sorrowfully noted that New Englanders in general were not yet aroused enough to support one. To his chagrin, the people of the South seemed far more excited. Some "new event," he feared, would be needed to stimulate New England to war. This was a most serious matter; a backward movement at this time, he believed would be very dangerous. Higginson feared peace far more than war. While at peace, the nation was exposed to the dangers of internal subversion.[58]

In his letter to Pickering, Ames partially disagreed with the Boston merchant. Although sharing Higginson's desire for war, Dedham's first consul realized that the people were not ready for an outright declaration of war, and he cautioned against one. An unpopular war would be worse than no war at all. Yet war was essential, and if the people would not support a declared war, they might nevertheless be moved to support an undeclared war. Consequently, Ames urged Pickering to "wage war and call it self-defense, forbear to call it war." The people hoped for peace, but in peace Ames saw the same dangers as did Higginson. The only alternative was to deceive the people, moving step by step into conflict with France.[59]

The problem, of course, was that Congress and not Pickering held the power to declare war. When Congress ended its deliberations without having taken such action, those "high" or extreme Federalists who supported war were deeply pessimistic. Higginson in his distress wrote Pickering that "nothing but an open war can save us, and the more inveterate and deadly it shall be the better will be our chance of security in the future."[60] But war had not been declared, and the Boston merchant was deep in gloom. The arming of American merchant vessels and the loosing of America's infant navy upon French privateers and cruisers did not go far enough. The people seemed opposed to war, and Congress would not declare it. George Cabot, too, deplored the failure of the Congress in this matter:

---

[58] Higginson to Pickering, June 9, 1798, Pickering Papers, XXVI, 202.

[59] Ames to Pickering, July 10, 1798, Pickering Papers, XXVI, 278.

[60] Higginson to Wolcott, July 11, 1798, Wolcott, *The Administrations of Washington and Adams*, II, 71.

It is impossible to make the people feel or see distinctly that
we have much more to fear from peace than war: That peace
cannot be real, and only leaves open a door by which the
enemy enters; and that war would shut him out; that the
French are wolves in sheeps clothing, entreating to be received
as friends, that they may be enabled to destroy and devour.
But war open and declared would not only deprive our exter-
nal enemy of his best hopes, but would also extinguish the
hopes of internal foes. The rights and duties of every citizen
in a state of war would be known and regarded.[61]

Unlike more pessimistic Federalists, Pickering believed that Congress had failed to act in line with the desire of the people. Fisher
Ames, the Secretary of State believed, was in error. The nation was
ready, indeed anxious, for war with France. He wrote to Rufus
King, castigating the Congress for its blindness and prophesying
that in the coming elections those who had opposed war would be
defeated. "The prevailing sentiments of the country," he wrote, "are
undoubtedly expressed correctly in the general spirit of the addresses
to the President of the United States, which you have seen and will
see in the newspapers." [62] Unwilling to adopt the pessimism of
others, the Secretary believed that the December session of Congress
would rectify the situation and that public opinion — that is, the
opinion demonstrated by the numerous addresses of loyalty and devotion sent daily to the President — would not allow the nation to
remain for long at peace.

That summer of 1798, although in some ways gratifying, must
have been a wearying period for Pickering. He could discuss with
his Federalist friends the wisdom of war with France, but he realized that nothing he could do would change the situation. The
Secretary was learning by bitter experience that a Cabinet member's
life could be deeply frustrating. He might assert that he was an independent member of the Government, but there was a truth more
telling than this assertion: He was powerless.

---

[61] Cabot to Wolcott, October 6, 1798, George Cabot, *The Life and Letters of
George Cabot*, Henry Cabot Lodge, ed., 168–70.
[62] Pickering to King, August 29, 1798, Department of State, Diplomatic
Instructions, IV, 343–47.

9

PICKERING ADAMS, AND THE ARMY

DURING THAT SUMMER OF 1798, differences between Pickering and Adams over war aims led to considerable bitterness and open conflict within the Administration. The immediate question was the extent to which the United States required a trained standing army to face the conflict brewing with France. Far more than being a military matter, however, the size and condition of the army had the broadest political implications for the future of Adams' Administration. These factors offer the keys to understanding the important diplomatic decisions that John Adams later made and that led to a negotiated settlement to Franco-American differences.

Although it has already been noted, it is worth reiterating that Adams hoped that the war would be limited to a naval conflict in defense of American neutrality. It was to be a war fought at sea, with America using her infant navy and a band of privateers to sweep the French from the Caribbean and give minimal protection to America's far-flung commerce. Most importantly, the war was to be brought to a close as soon as the Directory was willing to restore amicable relations on honorable terms.

Since he saw no need for large-scale military operations on land, Adams did not approve of the idea of a large standing army. Too often in the past, standing armies had been instruments of revolution and new tyranny. Perhaps, too, Adams was concerned with the political implications of his Administration's becoming involved in the establishment of a large army. Such a force would unquestionably necessitate a tax increase at a time when taxes had already been significantly increased to pay for the augmentation of the Navy and for coastal defense. He was well aware, from his own revolutionary experience, of the political dangers that an increase of taxes held for his Administration.

Pickering opposed the President and sympathized with his friends in Congress who were pressing for the establishment of a large standing army. Hopeful for an eventual alliance with England and a full-scale war against France, the Secretary viewed a regular standing army of at least fifty thousand men as essential. There can be no doubt that Pickering's feelings on the question of the Army stemmed in part from his exaggerated respect for French military potential in North America. For some time he had harbored the fear that the French would take Louisiana and Florida from Spain. With New Orleans as a base of operations, it would be relatively simple for France to detach the West from the Union, incite slave rebellion in the South, or launch a full-scale attack upon the United States. Pickering may have wondered how Republicans in the United States would react to such an attack. Might they not aid the invaders? Although there is no direct evidence to support this suggestion, it is not an entirely groundless supposition, considering Pickering's characteristic tendency to exaggerate the danger from French ambitions in the New World. In any case, a large standing army seemed vital to the Secretary of State.

Although Adams opposed the measure, "high" Federalists in Congress proposed the establishment of a standing army of fifty thousand men. This augmentation of the military was to be paid for by a substantial increase in taxation. Moderates in the Congress, eager for defense at low cost, whittled away at the proposal until a compromise, which increased the Regular Army by several regiments and authorized the establishment of a provisional army of ten thousand men, was reached. The provisional force would be called into service at the discretion of the President.[1]

Pickering was disgusted with this half measure. Did Congress believe that armies sprang into being overnight? When, he wondered, would the President decide that America was endangered — when the French were at the doorstep? As far as he was concerned, the invasion of England or even the military occupation of the Batavian Republic by France, an act that would serve to concentrate British naval power in the Channel and would leave the Atlantic open to a French fleet, endangered the United States. Aware that time is required to recruit and train armies and that militia are unmanageable and ineffective, Pickering feared for the future.[2]

Adams was disturbed by the fact that extreme Federalists in Congress, supported by the Secretary of State and others in the Cabinet, had opposed him on this issue, but he was not completely dissatisfied with the result of their actions. The provisional army would cost nothing, since Adams believed it would never be called into service. On the other hand, he found politically useful the patronage afforded him in the form of commissions to be filled in the provisional army. The establishment of the provisional army gave the President the opportunity to play a little politics.[3]

Simultaneously, the congressional augmentation of the Army gave Adams another opportunity to emphasize the seriousness of the situation vis à vis France. The appointment of Washington as Commander-in-chief could serve an important function in fostering national unity. Never really believing that the old Commander would ever have to take the field, Adams unofficially offered him the post, explaining that "we must have your name, if you will in any case, permit us to use it — there will be more efficacy in it than in many an army."[4]

---

[1] *Debates and Proceedings in the Congress of the United States*, 5th Congress, May 11, 1798, II, 1700.

[2] Pickering to Hamilton, June 9, 1798, Pickering Papers (Massachusetts Historical Society), VIII, 536.

[3] Stephen G. Kurtz, *The Presidency of John Adams*, 247.

[4] Adams to Washington, June 22, 1798, Adams Papers (Massachusetts Historical Society), Letterbook, January 18, 1797, to February 22, 1799, reel #117.

Washington, who was as convinced as Adams that the French would never attack the United States, agreed to accept command, upon two conditions; the aging patriot was loath to surrender the quiet of Mount Vernon for the harassment of public life and military command except under extreme circumstances. He stipulated that he would take command of the Army only if and when the French actually threatened an invasion. Second, in the unlikely event of a French attack, Washington was especially interested in having staff officers of his own choosing. Consequently, he made his acceptance of the commission as Commander-in-chief contingent upon the President's agreement that he might "have such characters associated with" him as would "render the turmoil of war and the burthen of the command" as light as the nature of it "would admit." [5] Even before Washington's reply had reached him, Adams had, with the Senate's consent, appointed the old warrior Commander-in-chief of the Army. The name of Washington was thus brought to bear in support of the Administration. This is as far as John Adams wanted the matter to go.

Timothy Pickering, however, was determined that the Army, whatever its size, should be more than a myth. A strong standing army was fundamental to his whole concept of foreign policy. Without an army to defend the government against attacks from both without and within, the nation might be overwhelmed. Pickering found in Alexander Hamilton an ally in his plans to vitalize the Regular Army and to bring the provisional army into service. The New Yorker's caution regarding possible conflict with France evaporated as his old military ambitions were rekindled.

Earlier, in the spring of 1798 Hamilton had discovered that the strained diplomatic situation between the United States and France promised a dramatic opportunity for military operations in the Western Hemisphere. Hamilton's friend and America's Minister to England Rufus King had been approached by the South American adventurer Francisco de Miranda, then in London attempting to involve the British Government in the revolutionary movement in

---

[5] Washington to Adams, July 4, 1798, Adams Papers, Letters Received and Other Loose Papers, July–August, 1798, reel #390.

Latin America.[6] The United States also would be interested in such an undertaking and, thought Miranda, would probably wish a part in the venture if only to have some voice in the future of the continent to the south. King, although interested, remained noncommittal, because he was as yet unaware of the results of the negotiations then going on in Paris. If a settlement with the French should emerge, the United States would, of course, be in no position to aid in an attack upon the colonial holdings of France's ally Spain.

By the end of February, 1798, Miranda had, to an extent, succeeded in his efforts in England, having convinced the British Government of the practicality of his scheme. King informed Pickering that the Pitt Ministry had decided that, so long as Spain remained independent of France and capable of holding on to her colonies, the British would make no effort to overturn the Spanish colonial empire. But, if she should prove unable to retain her independence, and if France should threaten to take over in the colonies in Latin America, Great Britain then would be forced to act, in order to keep Latin America from falling into the hands of France.[7]

By the spring of 1798, the issue, at least as far as Rufus King was concerned, seemed clearly drawn. He saw little chance for the efforts of Marshall, Pinckney, and Gerry to succeed. France, he believed, would rely upon internal subversion rather than upon negotiation to settle her disputes with the United States. Moreover, Latin America would be revolutionized by France as soon as the invasion of Continental Spain — an event he considered imminent — was completed. As a result, King became an ardent advocate of the Miranda scheme, which he considered a means of thwarting the imperial aims of the French. "The French system once established in South America and the West Indies," he warned, "we shall be in perpetual risk: on the other hand the independence of South America on wise principles, will put an end to the old colony and commercial system, and with obvious combinations presents wealth and security to the

---

[6] William S. Robertson, "Francisco De Miranda and the Revolutionizing of Spanish America," *American Historical Association Annual Report, 1907*, 32; Robert Ernst, *Rufus King*, 264–68.

[7] King to Pickering, February 26, 1798, Rufus King, *Life and Correspondence of Rufus King*, Charles R. King, ed., II, 284.

United States, and a new balance among nations." In the summer of 1798, after news of America's diplomatic failure in Paris had reached him, King wrote to Hamilton, urging a policy of aggressive military action in cooperation with Great Britain in Latin America. "The destiny of the New World," he wrote, "is in our hands. We have a right and it is our duty to deliberate and act not as secondaries but as principals."[8]

Hamilton was intrigued by Miranda's scheme and impressed by the fact that there was an excellent chance of British cooperation in the project.[9] He realized that, although Washington had been given the command of the Army, the old General was to be more or less a figurehead and whoever was second to Washington would, to all intents and purposes, have effective control of the Army. "Second-in-command" was the position Hamilton wanted.

Hamilton had a staunch ally in Timothy Pickering. Although the two men had previously disagreed on many vital issues, Pickering held Hamilton in the highest regard and believed that his organizing genius was essential if the Army were to become an effective fighting force. Working through the Cabinet, Hamilton at first made a direct approach for his appointment. Pickering, in this case acting as the New Yorker's willing agent, suggested to the President that Hamilton was the best qualified man for the position of major general and second-in-command to Washington. At first, Adams ignored his fellow New Englander's suggestion, but when Pickering persisted, Adams, whose venomous hatred for Hamilton was well known, summarily rebuffed the idea.[10]

Then, Pickering's fiercely independent spirit came into play. The President, he believed, was acting from his own irrational dislike of Hamilton and was therefore incapable of accurately assessing the true qualities of the man. Having failed in his direct approach, the

---

[8] King to Pinckney, Marshall, and Gerry, April 2, 1798, King, *Life and Correspondence*, II, 301; King to Hamilton, July 7, 1798, *ibid.*, 361; King to Hamilton, July 31, 1798, *ibid.*, 375.

[9] Hamilton to King, August 22, 1798, Papers of Alexander Hamilton (Library of Congress).

[10] Pickering to Washington, July 6, 1798, Pickering Papers, IX, 7.

Secretary therefore sought other means of forcing Adams into a position from which he could not refuse to appoint Hamilton.

The key to Pickering's hopes lay with Washington. Together with Hamilton and McHenry he worked to convince the old General that Hamilton was the popular choice for second-in-command and that he, Washington, ought to insist upon Hamilton's appointment. The task was made easy by the fact that Washington, who had always relied upon Hamilton as an adviser, had already decided that Hamilton should occupy some important position in the Army. Washington's prestige, the conspirators realized, was so tremendous that his desires could not be rejected, even by the doughty John Adams. They knew too that the former President, who had as yet only informally agreed to serve, had already made clear that he wished the right to personal appointment of his staff officers. If he requested Hamilton as his second-in-command, Adams could not refuse without causing a political tempest.

While McHenry went in person to Mount Vernon to deliver Washington's official commission to him and to discuss other matters pertaining to the Army (among which was undoubtedly Hamilton's appointment), Pickering wrote to the former Chief Executive, urging him to use his influence with the President to have Hamilton appointed second-in-command. "From conversations I and others have had with the President," he wrote, "there appears to be a disinclination to place Col. Hamilton in what we think is his proper station and that alone in which we suppose he will serve — the *second* to *you* and the *Chief* in *your absence*." Playing upon what he knew to be Washington's own sentiments, he remarked: "In any war and especially in such a war as now impends, a commander-in-chief ought to know and have confidence in the officers most essential to insure success in his measures." Assured that Washington had the greatest faith in Hamilton, Pickering suggested that "in this case it may be equally important that you should intimate your opinion to the President." [11] As he had done in times past, Pickering was living up to his own views of the duties and obligations of

---

[11] Pickering to Washington, July 6, 1798, Pickering Papers, IX, 7.

a Cabinet officer. The President was obviously being "wrongheaded" again, and it was the Secretary of State's duty, indeed his patriotic obligation, to make sure that Adams' narrow prejudice against Hamilton should not obstruct the national interest. In this way the self-righteous Secretary rationalized this conspiracy in opposition to his chief.

Pickering and McHenry were successful in convincing Washington of the importance of Alexander Hamilton to the Army. On July 12, 1798, McHenry wrote the President from Mount Vernon, informing him that General Washington had formally accepted his commission, on the condition that he would not be called into service until it became apparent that military action was imminent. He went on to state that Washington was in the process of drawing up a list of staff officers for the Army, that he believed these men "best qualified for his confidential officers," and that he probably would refuse to serve if the appointments were not made as he requested. Two days later Washington forwarded his own formal letter accepting the appointment as Commander-in-chief of the Army. He included a list of the general officers he expected to be appointed. Heading the list of three major generals was the name of Alexander Hamilton, followed by those of General Charles C. Pinckney and General Henry Knox.[12] Adams, who had previously entertained no intention of appointing Hamilton to any important military position, had been outmaneuvered. He was forced to appoint him Major General and Inspector General of the Army. Moreover, as far as Washington, Pickering, McHenry, and Hamilton were concerned, the order in which the names of the major generals appeared on the list established their relative ranks. Hamilton, they all believed, would be second-in-command. Whether Adams would accept this interpretation, however, remained to be seen.

Not content with once humbling the President, Pickering almost immediately added a personal insult. Colonel William Stephens Smith was John Adams' son-in-law and, from all descriptions, little

---

[12] McHenry to Adams, July 12, 1798, Adams Papers, Letters Received and Other Loose Papers, July–August, 1798, reel #390; Washington to Adams, July 22, 1798, Papers of George Washington (Library of Congress).

more than a dilettante who was an active source of irritation to the President.[13] Smith's one attainment was as a soldier, and during the crisis of 1798 Washington chose him to serve as brigadier general and suggested him as one of three possibilities for appointment as The Adjutant General.[14] Adams was glad to nominate his son-in-law for these important military positions.

Pickering was aghast when he learned of Smith's imminent appointment and objected vigorously. Not long before, Smith had been involved in a major land speculation that had failed, and Smith's financial ruin was accompanied by more than a hint of illegal land sales on his part. As Pickering explained it, Smith could not be considered a man of character. Certainly he did not merit an appointment as a general officer in the Army.

Although Pickering nowhere mentions it, there may have been another reason for his opposing Smith's appointment. The Colonel had been identified — whether accurately or not is of no consequence — with Republican political leaders, and Pickering may have believed this charge. If he did, he would certainly have been disturbed at the thought of a Republican in one of the most important positions in an army designed in part to fight republicanism.

Pickering made no effort to convince Adams of the mistake he was making in nominating Smith to responsibility in the Army. He saw no purpose in it, since the President was determined to seek confirmation for the appointment immediately. Instead, Pickering went to the Senate, where he lobbied vigorously against Smith. "I spoke to so many, and with such little reserve," he wrote of the episode to John Jay, "that I thought it not improbable that my interference would eventually be known to the President: but I chose to hazard his displeasure rather than the approbation of that nomination."[15]

The Senate, impressed by Pickering's lobbying, delayed for one day their action on the appointment of general officers. In the interim, a delegation of Federalist senators called upon Adams, urging

---

[13] Page Smith, *John Adams*, II, 978–79.
[14] Washington to Adams, July 4, 1798, George Washington, *Writings of George Washington*, J. C. Fitzpatrick, ed., XXXIV, 312–15.
[15] Pickering to Jay, July 20, 1798, Pickering Papers, IX, 70.

him to withdraw Smith's name. When the President inquired for the senators' grounds for making such a request, he was told that Smith's character was in question and that his politics were "anti-Federal."[16] Adams of course refused to withdraw the nomination, and on the following day the Senate rejected it. The President never forgot this insult or the role his Secretary of State had played in it.[17]

Pickering, together with his cohorts in the Cabinet, had successfully conspired to force the President to appoint Hamilton a major general in the Army. The President, however, had no intention of calling the New Yorker or the other general officers into active service. Adams was content to allow Hamilton to languish, a general, as it were, in the "inactive reserve." The President, it was obvious, still held some high cards in his hand.

Hamilton almost immediately began to seek means of overcoming this obstacle to forming an army and exerted every possible pressure to force the President to call him into active service. The business at hand — the organization and training of the army that he hoped to lead down upon Spanish America — seemed of the most pressing importance. Hamilton's anxiety was all the greater for the realization that the Secretary of War, James McHenry, was completely incompetent and, should the organization of the Army be left in his hands, failure and confusion could be the only results.[18] Knowing that personal appeals to the President would do no good, Hamilton worked through Pickering, McHenry, and Wolcott. Within a week, all three had written to urge the President to call up the three major generals in order that they might aid in the organization of the Army.[19]

As Adams observed the anxiety the members of the Cabinet were displaying in their efforts to place Hamilton on active service, he thought he saw an opportunity to deny Hamilton the rank of second-

---

[16] Smith, *John Adams*, II, 979.
[17] Abigail Adams to Thomas Boylston Adams, July 20, 1798, Adams Papers, Letters Received and Other Loose Papers, July–August, 1798, reel #390.
[18] Hamilton to Washington, August 1, 1798, Hamilton Papers.
[19] McHenry to Adams, August 4, 1798; Pickering to Adams, August 8, 1798; Wolcott to Adams, August 13, 1798, Adams Papers, Letters Received and Other Loose Papers, July–August, 1798, reel #390.

in-command of the Army. The idea of Hamilton in this powerful position bothered Adams, for the spectre of the diminutive Caesar from New York at the head of even a small but efficiently organized army made him tremble for the Republic. The instrument by which Adams sought to deprive Hamilton of his place behind Washington now presented itself. General Henry Knox, who had far outranked Hamilton during the Revolution, threatened to decline to serve in the new army unless he were made second-in-command and ranked as first major general.[20] Since all three major generals had been appointed and their commissions signed on the same day, the only factors that gave Hamilton precedence over Knox were Washington's listing his name before those of the other two appointees and the Senate's ratifying their appointments in that order.

Adams took the side of Knox, arguing that Washington had not determined the relative rank of the major generals by placing Hamilton first on the list. Admitting that he had agreed that Washington might have a free hand in the choice of his staff officers, Adams denied that this agreement had given the General the right to dictate their relative ranks. The three major generals had all been officially appointed on the same day and consequently were all at least equal in rank. On the basis of precedent and law, Adams contended, Knox and Pinckney, both of whom had outranked Hamilton during the Revolution, should outrank him now.

Adams hoped to play Hamilton's desire to be on active service against his urge to be second only to Washington. "Calling any other general officers into service at present," he wrote to McHenry,

> will be attended with difficulty, unless the rank were settled. In my opinion, as the matter now stands, General Knox, is legally entitled to rank next to General Washington, and no other arrangement will give satisfaction. If General Washington is of this opinion and will consent to it you may call him into actual service as soon as you please. The consequence of this will be that Pinckney must rank before Hamilton. If it shall be consented that the rank shall be Knox, Pinckney and Hamilton, you may call the latter too into

---

[20] Knox to McHenry, August 5, 1798, Adams Papers, Letters Received and Other Loose Papers, July–August, 1798, reel #390.

immediate service, when you please, any other plan will
occasion long delay and much confusion, . . .[21]

The President was proposing a compromise. If Hamilton were as
anxious as Adams thought to get into the military limelight, he
would settle for the rank of third major general. If he refused, the
President, who saw little need for an army in any case, was prepared to delay indefinitely the assignments of the major generals to
active duty. In a letter to McHenry, late in August, 1798, Adams
reaffirmed his determination that Knox would have to be second-in-
command and that Hamilton should rank below both of the other
major generals. In concluding his letter to McHenry, he angrily
accused him and other members of his Cabinet of having conspired
against him in the matter, asserting: "There has been too much
intrigue in this business both with General Washington and with
me. If I shall ultimately be the dupe of it, I am much mistaken in
myself."[22]

At this point Hamilton again sought the active intervention of
Washington. If the old General should demand that he be made
second-in-command, Hamilton knew that Adams could not resist.
Moreover, Hamilton realized this would be a simple matter, since
Washington himself believed that the relative rank of the major
generals had been established by the order in which they had appeared on the list earlier sent to the President. Knowing full well
that Washington wanted him, but too clever to plead his own case,
Hamilton played the game in gentlemanly fashion, writing to Washington only of his embarrassment. He felt committed to his own
pretensions and did not see how he could gracefully give way; yet,
he concluded, he could not allow Washington to be embarrassed
by such a situation. He placed the matter entirely in Washington's
hands; he would serve in any position the former President thought
would be "for the general good."[23]

While Hamilton on the surface appeared willing to allow Knox

---

[21] Adams to McHenry, August 14, 1798, Adams Papers, Letterbook, January 18, 1797, to February 22, 1799, reel #117.
[22] Adams to McHenry, August 29, 1798, Hamilton Papers.
[23] Hamilton to Washington, August 20, 1798, Hamilton Papers.

precedence over himself, his coconspirator Pickering, with the full knowledge of the New Yorker, wrote to urge Washington to intervene in Hamilton's behalf.[24] Frankly asserting that only the President had any predisposition to place Knox ahead of Hamilton, he said that Adams was supported in his position by no other men of sound judgment. Lashing out at Adams, he wrote, "altho' I respect the President for many great and excellent qualities, I cannot respect his errors, his prejudices or his passions. And I have been plain and explicit, that you might be fully appraised of the mischiefs which your opinion and influence alone can avert."[25] Less than two weeks later, Pickering sent another letter to Washington, openly stating that the President's decision to place Knox first and Hamilton third on the list of major generals was a product of the President's personal animus and hatred for Hamilton.[26]

Pickering's efforts brought quick results. Washington exploded in wrath at what he considered Adams' bad faith. In a letter to McHenry that was quickly brought to Adams' attention, Washington wrote in part: "I can perceive pretty clearly, that the matter is, or very soon will be brought to the alternative of submitting to the President, forgetfulness of what I considered a compact or condition of acceptance of the appointment, with which he was pleased to honour me, or to return him my commission."[27] Any thought that Washington was not threatening to resign if Hamilton were not made his second-in-command was quickly erased by a letter from Washington direct to Adams. In it he stated categorically that it had been his assumption that he could decide upon the relative rank of his staff officers. Washington made clear to Adams that, if Hamilton was not made second-in-command, he, Washington, would return his commission.[28]

---

[24] Pickering to Hamilton, August 21, 1798, Hamilton Papers. This letter makes it apparent that the letters of Hamilton and Pickering were written cooperatively.

[25] Pickering to Washington, September 1, 1798, Hamilton Papers.

[26] Pickering to Washington, September 13, 1798, Pickering Papers, IX, 309.

[27] Washington to McHenry, September 16, 1798, Papers of George Washington.

[28] Washington to Adams, September 16, 1798, Adams Papers, Letters Received and Other Loose Papers, September–October, 1798, reel #391.

Earlier, the President had written to Wolcott:

> If I should consent to the appointment of Hamilton as sec-
> ond in rank, I should consider it as the most responsible action
> of my whole life and the most difficult to justify. Hamilton
> is not a native of the United States, but a foreigner, and I be-
> lieve has not resided longer, at least not much longer in
> North America than Albert Gallatin. His rank in the late
> army was comparatively low. His merits with a party are the
> merits of John Calvin.
>
>> Some think on Calvin heavens own spirit fell,
>> While others deem him instrument of hell.
>
> His talents I respect; his character . . . I leave. . . .[29]

Not long after dispatching this letter, the President was forced by
the threat of a political break with Washington to surrender on
this point, to recognize Hamilton as second-in-command, and to
bring him into active service. At this juncture, Abigail Adams wrote
to her husband: "Serious people are mortified: and every Uriah must
tremble for his Bathsheba."[30]

Adams' surrender marked a great tactical victory for Timothy
Pickering. The zealous New Englander had conspired methodically,
industriously, and successfully against the President. Pickering's success, however, was achieved only at great cost. It caused Adams,
stung in that October by the humiliating political defeat he had
suffered, to reconsider his own ardor for war. Still menaced from
without by France, the nation now seemed threatened from within,
not only by the Republicans, but perhaps more seriously by the possibly autocratic designs of Alexander Hamilton. The President found
himself faced with a dilemma. He hoped to avoid the dangers posed
by both political extremes. One way in which this might be achieved
was by reaching a peaceful diplomatic arrangement with France,
which would at once steal the thunder on the left while ending the
need for, and justifying the abolition of, the Army.

The conflict over the organization of the Army serves to high-

---

[29] Adams to Wolcott, September 24, 1798, Adams Papers, Letterbook,
January 18, 1797, to February 22, 1799, reel #117.

[30] Abigail Adams to John Adams, January 12, 1799, Adams Papers, Letters
Received and Other Loose Papers, January–March, 1799, reel #393.

light the conflicting views of the President and his Secretary of State. To Pickering the Army was a fundamental necessity; to Adams it was a dangerous extravagance. The significance of their conflict reached far deeper, however. It marked a turning point in the relations between the two men. In the autumn of 1798, Adams turned resolutely toward the establishment of peace and Pickering's influence and importance in the Cabinet diminished noticeably.

10

TURNABOUT

$\mathcal{T}$HE IRONIC RESULT of Pickering's efforts at encouraging the organization of a strong army and placing Alexander Hamilton at its head was to give President Adams serious doubts about the wisdom of a war with France. By that autumn of 1798, the President was far more receptive to the possibility of renewed negotiations with France than he otherwise might have been. Unhappily for the Secretary of State, it was at this precise moment that Adams learned of indications that the French had reconsidered their earlier unfriendly attitude and were willing to negotiate. The bearer of this news was Elbridge Gerry, who, arriving at Quincy early in October, 1798, brought with him assurances from Talleyrand that France was prepared to negotiate in good faith and that a settlement of the differences between the nations could be arranged on American terms. Gerry himself assured the President that Talleyrand and the Directory were this time sincere in their desire to negotiate.[1]

The impact of Gerry's words was lessened by the fact that, when he arrived in the United States in that autumn, he had lost much of the trust the President had earlier placed in him. Months before,

---

[1] Page Smith, *John Adams*, II, 984.

in June, Philadelphia had learned that Gerry had done the unthinkable and had divided the commission by refusing to leave France with his fellow envoys. Since Adams had warned Gerry specifically on this point, he was doubly angry with his friend. He was, moreover, astonished when he discovered that Gerry had not decided of his own volition to stay, but had been bullied into remaining by Talleyrand's threats that his departure would be considered by the Directory a declaration of war.

Although Gerry did all that he could to convince the President that France's desire for peace was sincere, Adams remained skeptical. The Directory had not as yet proved itself trustworthy. Adams believed that there was an excellent chance that Gerry, in his own anxiety for peace, had been deceived by the adroit Talleyrand. Perhaps Talleyrand was again attempting, by holding out the promise of peace, to exacerbate America's internal political divisions. Deeds, Adams thought, and not words, would have to express France's intentions. Despite his own skepticism, the President made one concession. His bellicose addresses to the people diminished noticeably at just this time. His decision in this matter was significant, for he thus indicated a receptiveness to further peaceable advances from France.

Even Adams' hesitant interest in Gerry's report seemed dangerous to Pickering. Since June, when he had first learned of Gerry's apostasy at Paris, Pickering had been furious with the erratic envoy. At first the Secretary had believed that Gerry would assume total responsibility for the mission and negotiate a new treaty with France.[2] Even after a letter from Gerry assured him that he had no intention of entering into official negotiations with the French, Pickering's fury continued unabated. Gerry's decision to remain in Paris after Marshall and Pinckney had left, struck a devastating blow to Pickering's hopes for war. Gerry's presence in Paris gave life to the hope among many for peace, challenged the growth of unity and fervor

---

[2] Pickering to King, June 12, 1798, Pickering Papers (Massachusetts Historical Society), XI, 259-60. A delighted opposition press gave considerable comment on Gerry's decision to remain in France. See *Philadelphia Aurora*, June 4, 6, 1798.

for war at home, and proved a wellspring of revived political factionalism.

As early as June, it was apparent to Pickering that Gerry's decision to remain in Paris and to continue in unofficial conversations with Talleyrand served as a check upon Adams' bellicosity. With Congress in a defensive mood and seemingly unwilling to vote a declaration of war, leadership could come from only one source. The President would have to ask Congress for a declaration of war. Certainly, during the spring and summer of 1798, Adams was willing, but he was hamstrung so long as Gerry, his personal friend and official representative, continued his talks in Paris. Under such circumstances Adams could do no more than he was doing, that is, encourage national unity and the growth of sentiment for war at home, while waiting for Gerry to get out of France. In Pickering's view, the errant envoy seemed a major obstacle on the road to war. The longer he remained in Paris, the greater would be the tendency among Americans to factionalize. If Gerry had returned with the other two envoys, there could have been no significant opposition to war.

At first Pickering was merely angry with Gerry and, late in June, sent him a peremptory and hostile letter of recall. As the weeks dragged on, however, Pickering's fury mounted. By the middle of August, he had become desperate, for matters were not moving as smoothly as he had believed they would. The Congress had of course, by this time, adjourned without declaring war, and the President could not act alone. Under such circumstances, the significance of Gerry's talks in Paris became magnified in Pickering's mind. Believing Gerry deep in diplomatic conversations with Talleyrand, he feared that he would return with French promises for a peaceful settlement and that the President might yet decide to negotiate. The thought so disturbed Pickering that he wrote to Adams, then in Quincy, urging him to discount any French promises Gerry might bring with him upon his return.[3] When, in mid-September, he received news that Gerry had been seen in Paris as late as June 26, Pickering became beside himself with anger. He envisoned the

---

[3] Pickering to Adams, August 18, 1798, Pickering Papers, XXXVII, 319–20.

timorous Gerry, browbeaten and bullied, awaiting the "ultimatum of the French government! ! !" What a "contemptible animal" Gerry was.[4]

Gradually Pickering came to believe that Gerry had actually connived with Talleyrand to disrupt the peaceful efforts of his two colleagues in Paris. When he read some passages in the journal that John Marshall had kept during his stay in the French capital, indicating that Gerry had been involved in private and secret conversations with Talleyrand, Pickering was exultant. Again, as in the case of Edmund Randolph, Providence had seemingly provided the Secretary of State with a weapon with which to discredit an adversary. All the evidence he had, of course, was that Gerry had held some conversations with Talleyrand in private, but this was enough for his purposes. From this slight evidence he constructed in his own mind a tale of treason. "Yes," he wrote to Marshall, "I have no doubt that he communicated to Talleyrand the train of your and General Pinckney's thoughts and determinations and thus betrayed the commission."[5] Convinced of Gerry's disloyalty, Pickering proceeded to cloak himself in that really frightening aura of self-righteousness he usually assumed before entering the arena of public debate. By the time Gerry finally returned, in October, Pickering had set the stage for conflict.

Gerry, who realized that he would be under vigorous attack from extreme Federalists, had prepared a defense of his diplomacy before he arrived in the United States. He wrote to Pickering, recalling to the Secretary's mind that at the moment he had made his decision to remain in Paris after the other envoys' departure, France seemed to be sweeping all of Europe before her and was at the time preparing for an invasion of England. If French victories had continued, their power would have been so overwhelming as to threaten the United States with national extinction. On the other hand, if their progress toward total victory faltered, they would have been more amenable to peace. In either case, war could only have been detri-

---

[4] Pickering to Goodhue, August 25, 1798, Pickering Papers, IX, 222; Pickering to Goodhue, September 11, 1798, IX, 302.

[5] Pickering to Marshall, October 19, 1798, Pickering Papers, IX, 486.

mental to American interests. Consequently, Gerry contended, rather than leave at a crucial moment and risk precipitating an open break, he had remained in Paris — but only to await orders from Philadelphia. While he waited, through the long weeks between early April and mid-May, Talleyrand had attempted to persuade him to begin formal negotiations, but he had steadfastly refused. Nevertheless, Gerry admitted, he had entered into informal talks with Talleyrand regarding the outlines of a possible treaty and was impressed by what he believed to be the sincerity and willingness to negotiate that Talleyrand displayed during these talks. When orders from Philadelphia finally arrived in May, recalling him, he immediately requested his passports, only to be ignored by the Foreign Minister, who seemed intent upon arriving at a tentative agreement immediately. Only late in July did he finally get his passports. Without any further hesitation he then departed for the United States.

In Gerry's view, the arrival of the published version of the X Y Z dispatches in Paris had considerably altered the diplomatic situation there. He went so far as to suggest that had the Administration not decided to publish them, he and Talleyrand might well have been able to arrive at a formula for a treaty that would easily have been negotiated later. Before the arrival of the dispatches, Gerry wrote, "the minister appeared to me sincere and anxious to obtain a reconciliation. . . . Indeed his views in general, as far as I could then ascertain them were liberal in regard to a treaty. . . . I had a full expectation that, by the middle of June at farthest, we should have agreed on a plan of a treaty; and that a French minister would have been sent to America for completing it. I was likewise informed of the candidate. But after the arrival of the dispatches, although the minister, in the name of the Executive Directory, declared . . . their pacific intentions, he himself grew more aloof." Despite this change in the atmosphere, Gerry believed that when he left France late in July there was every indication that the French Government retained its friendly dispositions toward the United States and that the French wanted peace.[6]

---

[6] Gerry to Pickering, October 1, 1798, *American State Papers, Foreign Relations*, I:2, 209.

No explanations, however rational or adroit, could have pacified the Secretary of State. Gerry's, on the other hand, could not have been better calculated to arouse Pickering's indignation. The envoy's decision to remain in Paris had perhaps blocked a declaration of war by France. Moreover, he had returned with promises of peace. Determined to precipitate conflict, Pickering publicly denounced Gerry's role in Paris. In a widely circulated letter to the freeholders of Prince Edward County, Virginia, he characterized Gerry as at best the weak and puerile pawn of the wily Talleyrand and indirectly suggested that Gerry might even have willingly abetted French aims while in Paris.[7]

Gerry was thunderstruck at Pickering's blatant misrepresentation of his diplomacy. Shortly after his return to the United States, he sent a long letter in defense of his actions to Adams, asking that this too be published by the Administration.[8] Adams, who saw nothing wrong in giving equal opportunity for Gerry to present his case, sent the letter to Pickering, asking him to "have it inserted in a public print. It will satisfy him," wrote the President, "and do no harm to anyone." Pickering was flabbergasted. He firmly refused to publish the letter unless he could add his own comments, and he warned that with this presentation of Gerry's diplomacy he would display "not his pusillanimity, weakness and meanness alone — but his *duplicity* and *treachery*."[9] The smell of combat was in the air. Pickering wrote to his friend, Senator Benjamin Goodhue of Massachusetts, that soon "a paper war" between himself and Gerry would begin.[10]

Adams had other ideas on the subject. In that autumn of 1798, the tendency toward national unity was stronger than it had been since his first address to Congress, in May, 1797. He feared that a

---

[7] Pickering to the freeholders of Prince Edward County, Virginia, September 29, 1798, Octavius Pickering and Charles W. Upham, *The Life of Timothy Pickering*, III, 471–78.

[8] Gerry to Adams, October 20, 1798, Papers of Elbridge Gerry (Library of Congress).

[9] Pickering to Adams, November 5, 1798, Adams Papers (Massachusetts Historical Society), Letters Received and Other Loose Papers, November–December, 1798, reel #392.

[10] Pickering to Goodhue, November 3, 1798, Pickering Papers, IX, 553.

pamphlet war between Gerry and Pickering would renew violent political conflict throughout the country at a time when the diplomatic situation showed signs of resolution. Renewed dissension at home might spawn more problems with France. Consequently, Adams returned Gerry's unpublished letter, asking that he delay its publication and promising that his forthcoming Presidential message to the opening session of Congress would rectify matters.[11] Gerry agreed, and for the moment the impending duel of pamphleteers was postponed.

Gerry's return to the United States proved catastrophic for Pickering's hopes. The returned envoy soon became the focus of a new peace movement in which Adams, albeit cautiously, participated. George Cabot was crestfallen at this turn of affairs and wrote to the Secretary of State that Gerry's return with the promise of peace had renewed "the clamours of the factions and the hopes of the credulous."[12] He was, of course, correct. Gerry had given republicanism much-needed reassurance and had sent a fog of "creeping Gerryism" rolling across the American political landscape. From this time on, a growing popular sentiment for peace made matters increasingly difficult for the "war faction" in general and for Timothy Pickering in particular.

Even the French seemed determined to thwart Pickering. The President had required some concrete sign that France was sincere about the desirability of new talks, and Talleyrand was working toward achieving the same objective. Even before Gerry had left France, the Foreign Minister was using every device at his disposal to convince the Directory to alter its hostile policy or at least to end some of its worst excesses. The culmination of this effort was a report on Franco-American affairs that Victor du Pont, son of Pierre Samuel du Pont de Nemours, wrote for Talleyrand. Du Pont, who had only recently returned from America, produced a scathing attack upon French policy. French privateers in the West Indies, he reported, were no better than pirates. Their excesses "have been beyond limit

[11] Adams to Gerry, November 5, 1798, Gerry Papers.

[12] Cabot to Pickering, November 7, 1798, George Cabot, *Life and Letters of George Cabot*, Henry Cabot Lodge, ed., 179–81.

and also contrary to the principles of justice as well as sane policy." This judgment he founded upon a conversation he had held with Jefferson in which the Virginian had bemoaned the Directory's policy and suggested that French hostility was defeating the chances of the Republican faction in the United States. The course of wisdom, Du Pont believed, would be to adopt a policy of conciliation that would strengthen American republicanism.[13] On July 27, Talleyrand submitted Du Pont's report, together with his own conciliatory recommendations to the Directory. France's governing body responded with a rigid ruling on privateering in the West Indies designed to force the privateers to work within the laws of nations. Unwilling to repeal any of the maritime decrees that had so aggravated Franco-American relations, the Directory nevertheless made a beginning at demonstrating through action that it would no longer sanction, even by indifference, the illegal acts of privateers flying the French flag.

Pickering's hopes for war were being further eroded by Talleyrand's successful efforts at reopening lines of communication with the United States. Citizen Louis Pichon, former Secretary of Legation in Philadelphia and at the time Secretary of Legation at The Hague, had specific instructions to make peace feelers in the direction of the American Minister there, William Vans Murray. Talleyrand's choice was a fortunate one, for Murray had open communications not only with Pickering in the Department of State but with the President as well. Pichon's situation was difficult. French policy had long been designed to deepen political divisions within the United States and had been transparent to all from the outset. In that feverish summer of 1798, he experienced great difficulty in convincing even a moderate "Adams Federalist" such as Murray of his sincerity.

At first Murray, who was completely incredulous toward Pichon's overtures, believed that the French sought to use him to stimulate once again American hopes for peace, hopes that would once more di

---

[13] Cited in E. W. Lyon, "The Directory and the United States," *American Historical Review*, XLIII, 43 (April, 1938), 529.

vide the nation.[14] He was determined not to be a second Elbridge Gerry. After several informal conversations with Pichon, however, Murray changed his views. Although retaining his opinion that the French were deeply hostile to the United States, he felt that they had somehow become convinced that a war held no advantages and some serious disadvantages for them. He reported to the President that they sensed the need for a change of policy in order to avoid war.[15]

When Pichon openly admitted to Murray late in August that he had been sent to The Hague specifically to arrange a settlement with the United States, Murray, still cautious, encouraged him. He reminded Pichon that before any more American ministers would be sent to negotiate, "assurances" would have to be made that they would be given "treatment worthy of the ministers of a great, free & independent nation."[16] Murray played the game carefully, virtually quoting the stipulations laid down by Adams himself for the resumption of negotiations. Nonetheless, Murray wrote the Secretary of State a few days later that he expected to receive from the French the assurances the President had earlier demanded as precursors to further negotiations.

In all of America's diplomatic affairs during the age of sail, delay in the communication of news from Europe played a major role. In this situation, the uncertainties of wind and water again entered the negotiations. Although dispatches from Murray containing his changed attitude toward the French reached Adams before the opening of the December session of Congress, a letter from Talleyrand with assurances that future negotiations would prove amicable and successful did not arrive in the United States until the second week in January of 1799. This delay, in effect, meant that during the autumn and early winter of 1798, the President was guided only by his own desire for peace, whatever consolation he could glean from Murray's impressions, and the assurances Talleyrand had sent with Elbridge Gerry.[17]

---

[14] Murray to Adams, July 17, 1798, Adams Papers, Letters Received and Other Loose Papers, July–August, 1798, reel #390.

[15] Murray to Pickering, September 8, 1798, Pickering Papers, XXIII, 125.

[16] Murray to Pickering, September 1, 1798, Pickering Papers, XXIII, 99.

[17] He placed absolutely no faith in the words of George Logan, prominent

Adams' dilemma, simply stated, was this: On the one hand, extreme Federalists had made war with France undesirable; on the other, there was no guarantee that the French peace feelers were to be regarded as serious. Adams, like Murray, feared the French were holding out the promise of peace in order to enliven political divisions within the United States and to counteract the movement toward national unity that had followed the disclosures of the X Y Z dispatches.

As the December, 1798, session of Congress approached, it became imperative for Adams to resolve his dilemma and decide upon a policy. The "high" Federalists were urgent for war. The downcast Republicans were pleading for peace. Adams finally decided to take the middle ground. He rejected the idea of asking Congress for a declaration of war, but he simultaneously continued to emphasize the need for vigorous new defensive measures. Much to Pickering's disappointment, Adams' speech at the opening of Congress left ajar the gate to future negotiations and even invited them. Adams noted that "harmony between us and France may be restored at her option." Of course, he continued, France would have to initiate such a move, for America could not demean herself further by sending "another minister, without more determinate assurances that he would be received. . . . It must, therefore, be left to France, if she is indeed desirous of accommodation, to take the requisite steps."[18] None of this meant that Adams was committed to another negotiation; he was determined to be anything but precipitate. Nevertheless, if further assurances of French sincerity were received, and if her actions, especially on the seas, indicated that her words had some meaning, the President would negotiate.

The reaction of the "war faction" to the President's opening address to Congress was predictable. Stephen Higginson, who had expected Adams to demand a declaration of war, wrote to Pickering of his disappointment. He feared that the President had "com-

---

Pennsylvania Republican leader who had gone to France on his own initiative and after conversations with French officials had returned to testify to French sincerity in searching for a peaceful arrangement.

[18] Adams to Congress, December 8, 1798, *Debates and Proceedings in the Congress of the United States*, 5th Congress, III, 2420–24.

mitted himself too far respecting his desire for peace, and the terms on which he would negotiate." He and his friends believed that the French would seize the opportunity presented by Adams and make the necessary assurances. Adams would then be trapped into new talks from which he could not extricate himself without incurring widespread unpopularity. Pickering provided Higginson with his only hope that war might yet prove the outcome of the Administration's policy. The Secretary of State was urged to guard against the "mistakes" Adams might make and to continue in his efforts at guiding the nation away from negotiation and toward war.[19]

Pickering was disgusted with the President's speech and had little hope for future developments along lines he considered desirable. Dejectedly he sent a copy of the recent Presidential address to Murray at The Hague. "It is a subject of regret," he wrote in the letter that accompanied it, "that he held out the most distant idea of sending another minister to France." Nor was his depression any the less for the knowledge that he could do nothing to influence the course of future events. Some, like Higginson, believed that Pickering was in a position to thwart the President's policy, but Pickering himself knew better. In a letter to George Cabot he explained that, despite his high office, he was virtually powerless and that Adams had listened to none of his advisers in the Cabinet when drafting his recent speech. "We were anxious," he wrote, "that it [the speech] should have a different form — we wished it to be peremptory not to send another ambassador to France . . . and we were unanimously of that opinion." Pickering's only remaining hope was that the Directory would be too proud to make the assurances required. This was a thin reed upon which to lean, and Pickering realized it. The Directory, he thought, would stop at nothing to prevent open war. Yet only in war was there safety for America. Even a completely favorable treaty would provide no security. Indeed, the more satisfactory the treaty, the more likely that at some future and more convenient time the French would "find a pretext" for breaking it.[20]

---

[19] Higginson to Pickering, January 1, 1799, Pickering Papers, XXIV, 1.
[20] Pickering to Murray, December 11, 1798, Pickering Papers, X, 39–40; Pickering to Cabot, February 2, 1799, *ibid.*, 317.

Perhaps Pickering's greatest failure as a politician was his refusal to consider the importance of public opinion as a factor in the policy-making function of the Government. He believed that, once elected, governmental officers should be free from the influence of the untutored public and should be able to make decisions based upon what they, as "experts," believed to be in the best interests of the nation. Despite considerable evidence to the contrary, Pickering insisted upon maintaining the view that the United States was a representative republic that was in no way a democracy. Blinded by this gross failure in his political insight, he refused to accept the fact that Adams' policy, which carried both the olive branch and the sword, was not only wise but politically expedient as well.

Unlike Pickering, Adams, who had some concern for public sentiment, was aware that it had been swinging against the Administration. The shift was a result of the increase in taxes required to support America's growing military and naval force. Any doubt of this change in public opinion was erased on the President's journey between Quincy and Philadelphia, prior to the December session of Congress. Adams' nephew and private secretary William S. Shaw wrote at the time to Abigail Adams, who had remained in Quincy, that "all the way as we rode through Massachusetts, . . . great prejudices had been made against the land tax." At one stopping place, Marlborough, the minister of a local congregation had told Adams and his young secretary "that a number of his parishioners had told him that they voted for Mr. Varnum [a Republican] for no other reason than as he was a great opposer to the land tax." In Shaw's view, if Elbridge Gerry, the symbol of peace with France and consequently of reduced taxation, "had consented to have stood as a candidate [for Governor], he would have had a very great majority." [21]

Despite the political wisdom of the act, Adams' decision to leave the door open for further negotiation sent Pickering and the rest of the "high" Federalist faction into a panic. They sought a means of circumventing the President and his policy. Earlier, Adams had not

---

[21] William S. Shaw to Abigail Adams, November 25, 1798, Adams Papers, Letters Received and Other Loose Papers, November–December, 1798, reel #392.

wished the establishment of an army, but Congress had founded one. He had not wanted Alexander Hamilton in virtual control of the Army, yet there he was. This time the "war faction" hoped Congress might declare war without the President's sanction. Desperately, they called for a caucus of Federalist and moderate congressmen at which they hoped to gain the support of the moderates for a declaration of war.[22] This time, however, they had gone too far. The moderates did not provide enough support, and the caucus failed to recommend war. As a result, in that crucial December session of the Fifth Congress, the "war faction" abstained from any effort at forcing upon Adams a declaration of war.

Scarcely a month following Adams' fateful opening address to the December session, William Vans Murray's dispatches of September and October arrived. In one message addressed directly to the President, Murray enclosed a letter from Talleyrand to Pichon, which was actually intended for Adams. It contained, at least in rough outline, the assurances the President had earlier required as a *sine qua non* to future negotiations. Murray was relatively unimpressed, believing that in this letter Talleyrand had not fully complied with the President's earlier demands. The letter was not addressed directly to Adams, nor was it a public letter. Nevertheless, Murray handed it on for the Chief Executive's perusal.[23] Like Murray, John Quincy Adams, who had learned of the contents of Talleyrand's letter through his friend at The Hague, was equally unimpressed. While he felt that Murray should continue his talks with Pichon, he did not believe that the moment was yet right for the dispatch of a new minister to France. If the French were sincere, a little more time spent in testing them would mean nothing; if they were not, a little more time would expose their duplicity.[24]

Despite the doubts of others, the President, moved far more than either his son or Murray by his more intimate knowledge of the politi-

---

[22] Thomas Jefferson, *The Complete Anas of Thomas Jefferson*, F. B. Sawvel, ed., 153.

[23] Murray to Adams, October 7, 1798, Adams Papers, Letters Received and Other Loose Papers, September–October, 1798, reel #391.

[24] John Q. Adams to Murray, October 20, 1798, John Q. Adams, *The Writings of John Quincy Adams*, W. C. Ford, ed., II, 374–77.

cal situation within the United States, decided that the French had substantively met his requirements and that a new negotiation with France might begin. Undoubtedly, he too had his doubts about the sincerity of the French, and he went forward with trepidation. But Adams had almost no alternative. Aside from the political considerations that must have weighed heavily with him, his decision was made virtually inevitable by the fact that, by mid-January of 1799, it was apparent that Congress would not declare war against France. Finally, and perhaps no less tellingly, Adams had come to view the possibility of another negotiation with less fear, as a result of his recent loss of the struggle over the relative ranks of the major generals.

11

INTO OPEN OPPOSITION

$\mathcal{O}$N THE MONTHS FOLLOWING THE OPENING OF CONGRESS in December, Pickering made a serious and prolonged effort to halt the movement in the direction of a negotiated settlement with France. But the forces moving the nation toward peace were too powerful to be diverted. Some of these have already been discussed. One of the most serious factors remaining to be considered was the deterioration of that quasi-Anglo-American amity Pickering had worked so hard to develop. Predictably, it was Britain's activities upon the high seas that caused the greatest difficulty. In December, 1798, the same month in which Adams began the alteration of his earlier belligerent attitude toward France, an encounter of a politically explosive nature occurred between American and British vessels of war. The American sloop-of-war *Baltimore*, convoying a number of American merchantmen in the Caribbean, was stopped by a British squadron of far superior force. Captain Loring, in command of H.M.S. *Carnatic*, searched the *Baltimore*, impressed five of the unresisting ship's complement, and seized three of the American merchantmen, ostensibly for carrying contraband.[1]

---

[1] L. Trezevent and W. Timmons to G. C. Morton, November 18, 1798,

When, within the month, news of the event reached the United States, it sent not only Adams and Pickering, but the general public as well, into a rage. Never before had any nation, even Britain, claimed the right to impress seamen from on board a United States Navy vessel of war. So enraged was Adams upon learning that Captain Phillips of the *Baltimore* had submitted to this disgrace without resistance, that he stripped the officer of his command and discharged him from the service. He also immediately dispatched orders to all American naval commanders, informing them that any repetition of these tactics by British vessels was to be resisted to the last extremity. Pickering, who was as upset by the stupidity the British commander had demonstrated as by the event itself, wrote a letter to Rufus King, excoriating the British and warning that "the right of searching and stripping public vessels of war of their hands, if it exists at all must be reciprocal, and it need not be asked whether a British naval commander would submit to it: neither will ours."[2] This time the British had gone too far, even for Timothy Pickering. When, only a few days following the arrival of news of the incident between the *Carnatic* and the *Baltimore*, Bache's *Aurora* carried a story detailing an unprovoked British assault upon an American merchantman, Pickering fired off another dispatch to King, urging a further protest. "The injury done to that vessel by the Frigate *Latona* and Captain Southern," he wrote, "is so outrageous and inhuman, as to dishonor the king's service."[3] While he continued to believe the British essentially friendly, he grew uneasy for the future.

The *Carnatic*'s seizure of three of the merchant vessels being convoyed by the *Baltimore* accentuated another growing problem, the increasing number of American merchant vessels being taken by British cruisers. For some time, British commanders had been interpreting Article XVIII of the Jay Treaty (which defined con-

---

American State Papers, Foreign Relations, I:2, 203–4; *Philadelphia Aurora*, January 10, 1799.

[2] Pickering to King, January 8, 1799, Department of State, Diplomatic Instructions, V, 49–52.

[3] Pickering to King, January 12, 1799, Pickering Papers (Massachusetts Historical Society), X, 185.

traband of war) in a ludicrous fashion in order to seize American ships making the voyage from the eastern seaboard to New Orleans. Such things as four-penny nails, painters' oils, linseed oil, and cheap cotton cloth were considered "wrought iron," "naval stores," and "sail cloth" by British commanders eager for prize money.[4]

Before the spring of 1799 was far advanced, relations between the British and United States governments had worsened. British spoliations, particularly in the Gulf of Mexico, increased dramatically. By May, Pickering was deep in gloom. The "political mischiefs" of British attacks on American shipping were "as much to be lamented as their direct injury to our merchants." Only the "common enemy," France, profited from the continuation of these attacks. Pickering strove to convince Liston of the truth of this.[5]

Despite his efforts, the depredations continued and at an increasing rate. By the late summer it seemed to Pickering as though the desperate years of 1793 and 1794 were repeating themselves. Even the British courts of admiralty acted more rapaciously than previously. At Bahama, for instance, if any portion of a cargo was judged by the court to be contraband, the entire ship and cargo were condemned. Unfriendly France had done no worse.[6] As the year 1799 went on, what troubled Pickering most was that it was becoming increasingly difficult to distinguish the friend, England, from the enemy, France.

Pickering feared the effect of renewed British depredations upon public opinion and wrote imploringly to King, asking if it were not "possible to introduce a more just, liberal and politic system of conduct towards the United States?"[7] Especially disturbing to the Secretary was the fact that to British cruisers unarmed merchantmen from the United States seemed more attractive as quarries than French or Spanish naval vessels.[8] Pickering's protests, however, went unanswered while British seizures mounted. Vainly he urged King

---

[4] Pickering to King, December 15, 1798, Pickering Papers, XXXVII, 372.
[5] Pickering to Liston, May 7, 1799, Pickering Papers, XXXVII, 414.
[6] Pickering to Edward Stevens, September 5, 1799, Pickering Papers, XII, 10; Pickering to King, October 2, 1799, *ibid.*, 136.
[7] Pickering to King, December 15, 1798, Pickering Papers, XXXVII, 372.
[8] Pickering to King, May 22, 1799, Department of State, Diplomatic Instructions, V, 219–20.

in London to press the British Ministry for some agreement on the meaning of Article XVIII of the Jay Treaty while continually warning, but with seemingly little effect, that the British would do well to alter their policy for both political and commercial reasons.[9]

The deterioration of Anglo-American relations made more important in Adams' view the United States' avoidance of conflict with the other major European power, France. The President, therefore, reinforced the trend toward peace, and in early 1799 he decided to publish the diplomatic correspondence between France's Foreign Minister Talleyrand and Elbridge Gerry. These were the notes the two men had exchanged during the time Gerry had remained alone in Paris. The President also decided to publish, along with these letters, the long explanation of his actions that Gerry had written upon his return to the United States, in which the former envoy attested to the sincerity with which the French were seeking a peaceful arrangement. The correspondence was an astonishing performance, considering the treatment the three envoys had received between September of 1797 and the following March. It clearly showed the French literally begging Gerry to open negotiations and virtually promising that such talks would result in a treaty that would be favorable to the United States.[10] The publication of these letters, Adams knew, could not fail to stimulate the growing public desire for peace with France.

Pickering, already deeply troubled by his inability to keep the English in line, was totally taken aback by this new evidence of Adams' quixotic temperament. For nearly a month he refused to turn the Talleyrand-Gerry correspondence over to the President. On three separate occasions, Adams politely requested the correspondence and finally received it only when he sent his personal secretary to Pickering with an unmistakable demand for the papers.[11] Pickering had, in one sense at least, been wasting no time. He had

---

[9] Pickering to King, May 8, 1799, Pickering Papers, XI, 57.

[10] Gerry to Pickering, October 1, 1798, *A.S.P., F.R.,* I:2, 231.

[11] Memorandum from Elbridge Gerry upon a conversation between himself and President Adams, discussing Pickering's attitude toward the publication of the Gerry-Talleyrand correspondence. March 26, 1799, Papers of Elbridge Gerry (Library of Congress).

been preparing a special "report" on the correspondence that, he hoped, would be published with it. No less than Adams, he realized that the publication of the correspondence might well end all hope of a war with the French. Gerry's credibility had to be destroyed, and Pickering's "report" was designed to accomplish this task.[12]

When Pickering informed Adams that he had prepared a report on the Talleyrand-Gerry correspondence and that he wished it published, Adams was naturally reluctant. He replied that neither he nor the Congress needed such a report.[13] Pickering persevered, personally challenging the President. Adams later recalled that confrontation with Pickering and his own amazement at the report which he considered a

> most violent false and calumnious philippic against Gerry.
> I read it with amazement. I scarcely thought that prejudice
> and party rage could go so far. I told him it would not do: It
> was very injurious and totally unfounded. I took my pen and
> obliterated the whole passage as I thought but after all I in-
> advertently let some different expressions pass which ought
> to have been erased. Pickering reddened with rage or grief
> as if he had been bereaved of a darling child. He even went
> so far as to beg that I would spare it and let it go to Congress
> but I was inexorable.[14]

Pickering, appalled at the enormity of the abridgment Adams had demanded, engaged the President for the better part of the night in violent argument. Returning on the following day, he again demanded that the President reinsert the attack upon Gerry that he had previously erased. Again he was refused.[15] As Pickering's report finally went to Congress, it was far from the virulent attack it had originally been. Almost all of the derogatory references to Elbridge Gerry had been expunged. Although the report was thus de-

---

[12] "Report of the Secretary of State on French Affairs in Relation to the United States," (unabridged), January 16, 1799, Pickering Papers, X, 188. See also Pickering to Adams, January 18, 1799, *ibid.*, 245.

[13] Gerry's memorandum to himself, March 26, 1799, Gerry Papers.

[14] Adams to William Cunningham, March 20, 1809, Adams Papers (Massachusetts Historical Society), Letterbook, March 7, 1797, to June 20, 1797; March 23, 1801, to November 26, 1812, reel #118.

[15] Gerry's memorandum to himself, March 26, 1799, Gerry Papers.

nied some of Pickering's violent personal touch, it nonetheless stated the "high" Federalist position with some clarity. The French, Pickering argued, had forced a division among the envoys in order to keep up the hopes of peace within the United States and, consequently, to divide the American people. Next, they had sought to force Gerry into negotiating a treaty, the terms of which, Pickering argued, the Government of the United States would not have been able to accept. This treaty, they had calculated, would lead to further division within the United States and would give them new hope for the success of their subversive tactics in fomenting democratic revolution. Having failed in their efforts to seduce Gerry into negotiating an unsatisfactory treaty, Pickering argued, they were now attempting, once again through Gerry, to stimulate divisions within the United States.[16]

The report failed to achieve Pickering's major purpose, which was to destroy Gerry's credibility. For this he naturally blamed the President. In a succession of wild letters to his Federalist friends, the Secretary vented his spleen against the President, while expressing his fears that Gerry's views would be generally accepted. "In my report I had noticed (in as gentle terms as possible) Mr. Gerry's conduct as wrong in principle, and in many particulars very reprehensible: but these (contrary to my wishes) were omitted." Many people, he believed, would "read and respect his [Gerry's] opinion without examining and discovering that it is without foundation." The same fears were expressed more fully in a letter to John Jay: "As much . . . as Mr. Gerry deserves chastisement, I would not have introduced a single word of reproach or censure, had I not conceived it expedient to destroy or lessen the weight of his opinions, which many readers, without information, would adopt, groundless & absurd as they are."[17]

Pickering's animosity toward the President soon reached new strengths when Adams, acting without any prior consultation with his Cabinet, nominated William Vans Murray as America's new

---

[16] "Report of the Secretary of State on French Affairs in Relation to the United States," (abridged), January 16, 1799, *A.S.P., F.R.,* I:2, 321.

[17] Pickering to Washington, February 2, 1799, Pickering Papers, X, 134; Pickering to Jay, February 1, 1799, *ibid.,* 309.

Minister Plenipotentiary to the French Republic. Adams, in this case convinced that members of his Cabinet would oppose the nomination, simply ignored them. This tactic bitterly antagonized the Secretary of State. He could argue, cajole, and question, but all of his efforts generally had little influence upon the President's decisions. In the final analysis, Adams was his own Secretary of State and expected little save compliance of the man from Essex County.

Angry at the President's refusal to consult with him and fearful that Adams' action would destroy the remaining hopes for a conflict with France, Pickering eased his frustrations by sending another spate of angry letters to friends and sympathizers, denying any part in Murray's nomination. Righteous in the assurance that his own views were correct and that Adams had made a serious mistake, he wrote confidentially to Rufus King, announcing that all were "thunderstruck by the President's nomination" and assuring him that no one knew "that the President had any such intention." To George Cabot he wrote, begging that his fellow Essexman "believe that it is the sole act of the President. Not one officer about him," Pickering related, "had any knowledge of his design."[18]

Even as Pickering deplored Murray's nomination, he tacitly admitted that it was relatively popular and that opposition to it would fail. Even the conservative Senate, he realized, could not be trusted to reject the nomination because the moderates, "timid and feeble federalists," as Pickering viewed them, would not support his position. They would join with the Republicans in the President's support. Still, there remained a chance that the evils of the situation might be ameliorated. The Senate committee to consider the nomination, a committee that was, incidentally, composed of five ardent Federalists, planned with Pickering's knowledge and approbation to reject Murray. "The committee," Pickering reported to Cabot, "will study to invent some change by which the measure may be rendered less mischievous." On another subject, however, Pickering was less hopeful. Adams had this time gone too far. "The President's character," Pickering wrote, could "never be retrieved." He could

---

[18] Pickering to King, February 19, 1799, Pickering Papers, X, 391–94; Pickering to Cabot, February 21, 1799, *ibid.*, 401.

never regain "the confidence of the Federalists."[19] Certainly in the upcoming elections, no "right thinking men" would support the President.

It was an austere group of Federalist senators that called upon Adams a few days after he had nominated Murray. They began their conference by urging the President to withdraw the nomination, but without success. The President was inflexible.[20] Later, it was suggested that the negotiations with France be placed in the hands of a commission of three instead of being left to Murray alone. When Adams learned, on the eve of the vote in the Senate, that the Federalists would oppose the nomination of Murray but would support the proposed commission, he decided to accept the compromise measure. Despite America's recent unhappy experience with "commission diplomacy," Adams withdrew the nomination of Murray as Minister Plenipotentiary to France and, instead, appointed him, along with Oliver Ellsworth of Massachusetts and Governor William R. Davie of North Carolina, to a commission to negotiate with the French. Moreover, in what must have been an effort to pacify the extreme Federalists, he stated that neither of the two commissioners still within the United States would sail for France until such time as the American Government was assured by the Directory that they, like Murray, would be received with due courtesy and that representatives would be appointed to negotiate with them.[21]

There is little doubt that Adams was to some degree concerned about the political future when he made these concessions. Anxious to win re-election in 1800, he realized that he had weakened his position by antagonizing extreme Federalists with his decision to negotiate. He even pretended to despair of being re-elected as a result of his decision. To his wife he wrote that rivalries had "been irritated to madness" and that Federalists had "merited the sedition law." The new nominations were the cause of this division in the party, yet there had been no alternative. His decision, he believed,

[19] Pickering to Cabot, February 21, 1799, Pickering Papers, X, 401.
[20] Pickering to Murray, July 10, 1799, Pickering Papers, XI, 407–11.
[21] Adams' speech to Congress, February 25, 1799, *A.S.P., F.R.*, I:2, 240.

had been "unavoidable."[22] It was politically expedient, then, to concede something to "high" Federalists in order to regain their support.

Although politics undoubtedly had something to do with Adams' decision to temporize on the move for peace, diplomatic considerations also played a large role. Adams was by no means convinced of French sincerity even after the assurances conveyed by Gerry and Murray. At the moment, the French might believe a peaceful arrangement best for their own interests, but the President had no doubt that the hostility which had moved them to intefere in America's internal political affairs was a continuing factor. He was certainly not averse to testing French sincerity further. If they really wished peace, then they would quickly send the further assurances he demanded before dispatching Murray's colleagues. Since Adams was sure that actual war would come only if France wanted it, a few months more or less could matter little, especially since the West Indies had been virtually cleared of privateers and French seizures of American ships had been reduced drastically. With the initiative on the seas having fallen to the United States, Adams had no aversion to taking time in order fully to explore the intentions of the French.

The President's decision to test French sincerity led him not only to give in to the "high" Federalist senators in their demands for a commission of three negotiators, but it also convinced him that, once negotiations actually began, America should seek complete justice and not simply a compromise arrangement. Talleyrand had promised peace on American terms, and Adams was determined to hold him to his promise. Would the Directory accept a set of terms drawn up in large measure by Timothy Pickering, Oliver Wolcott, Jr., and James McHenry? Adams determined to find out, and he allowed the Cabinet a free hand in drawing up the instructions for the envoys.

Pickering was momentarily ecstatic. Adams, he believed, had given him the opportunity to block a successful negotiation by pricing peace too high. In a private letter to King, he described the terms

---

[22] John to Abigail Adams, February 22, 1799, Adams Papers, Letters Received and Other Loose Papers, January–March, 1799, reel #393.

the Cabinet had agreed upon, asserting that, while they were just, he was sure that France would never agree to them. This tactic, he wrote, with a deep sense of relief, "has placed us all much at our ease." Pickering's hopes that the French would not accept the terms, however, did not last. His pessimism once again taking hold, he soon came to believe that they would agree even to the terms he had helped draw up, if it served their purposes to do so. No time, he later suggested, "could be *favorable* to treat with a nation or government which is *utterly destitute of faith* and such is France." Pointing out that many of the then currently revolutionized nations of Europe, including Naples, Switzerland, Sardinia, Geneva, and Genoa, had made treaties with France, only to be ultimately overwhelmed, he contended that "war would have saved them: by *treaties* they have been undone!" Pickering believed that, even if France allowed the United States to draw up a treaty on her own terms, there would be no security in it.[23]

The fact is that by the summer of 1799 Pickering had shut his mind to the idea that a settlement with France could be accomplished without eventually precipitating a war with England. The history of the preceding eighteen months seemed to demonstrate the truth of his view. Until the latter part of 1798 Anglo-American relations had been, if not amicable, then at least tolerable. But then, as Adams reversed the thrust of American policy, the British Ministry turned cold, and American commerce began to suffer severely from the ravages of Britain's cruisers. Worst of all, the British seemed at the time to be in a position to administer a sound thrashing to an ungrateful America, for during that summer of 1799 the allied powers appeared on the verge of a conclusive victory in Europe.

Pickering's distress was mirrored in the minds of other extreme Federalists who, after the nomination of Murray, believed the future very grim. George Cabot wrote:

> Indignation, grief & disgust in a rotatory succession are the only sentiments excited by the nomination of Mr. Murray in the breasts of well informed decided Federalists, . . . The

[23] Pickering to King, March 12, 1799, Pickering Papers, X, 476; Pickering to Arthur Campbell, June 14, 1799, *ibid.*, XI, 234.

weak and feeble think any road to peace is good. . . . They
will not listen to the painful proofs that a safe peace, which
they truly desire, is rendered less attainable by this new evidence of our weakness, this new encouragement to French
artifice while the temporizers, trimmers, & Federal hypocrits
with Jacobin hearts rejoice.[24]

Fisher Ames went even further, asserting that no negotiation under
any conditions could be defensible. Since peace with France, the
goal of negotiations, was in his view a positive evil, all means to
that end he considered equally evil. Referring to Adams, he added:
"No one respects more sincerely the talents and virtues of our chief,
but few know better than I do the singularities that too frequently
discredit his prudence."[25]

While the "high" Federalists disapproved, criticism of the President was not general. The Republicans, of course, were ecstatic, but
more importantly, among moderate Federalists, the President's decision to make another effort at negotiation was greeted with approval. The Adams family, of course, supported the President. Abigail
Adams went so far as to call Murray's nomination "a masterstroke of
policy." More significantly, Henry Knox too believed that Adams
had acted wisely. He even suggested that the opposition to Adams'
policy came from less than 1 per cent of the total population. Perhaps most heartening of all was the support the President received
from John Marshall, who had served on the first commission to
France. His Francophobia tempered by distance and time, the Virginian gave the President his wholehearted support.[26]

Adams was not the sort of man to depend upon popular approval
for his actions. Still, it must have been heartening to know that
there were many who supported his position. His recent confrontation with Federalists in the Senate had not been comforting. His
losing effort against Hamilton over the issue of that gentleman's
relative rank in the Army still rankled. Especially galling to him

---

[24] Cabot to Pickering, March 7, 1799, Pickering Papers, XXIV, 140.
[25] Ames to Pickering, March 12, 1799, Pickering Papers, XXIV, 171.
[26] Abigail Adams to John Adams, February 27, 1799; Knox to Adams,
March 5, 1799; Lee to Adams, March 14, 1799, Adams Papers, Letters Received
and Other Loose Papers, January–March, 1799, reel #393.

was the presence of Timothy Pickering in the Cabinet. Again and again he and the Secretary had clashed over all varieties of issues, some of major importance. By the spring of 1799, the Secretary's vehemence had become so strong, his self-righteousness so objectionable, that Adams allowed himself the rare luxury of a written complaint. To the Attorney General, Charles Lee, he wrote that, if it had accomplished nothing else, Murray's nomination had at least served one purpose: "To me it has laid open characters. Some of these," he wrote, referring directly to Pickering, "will do well to study a little more maturely the spirit of their stations. But vanity has no limits; arrogance shall be made to feel a curb. If any one entertains the idea, that, because I am President by three votes only, I am in the power of a party, they shall find that I am no more so than the Constitution forces upon me." Threatening to resign and allow Jefferson to succeed him, he warned that "if combinations of Senators, generals, and Heads of department shall be formed such as I cannot resist, and measures are demanded of me that I cannot adopt, my remidy is plain and certain. I will try my own strength at resistance first, however." [27] In his vehemence and obstructionism, Timothy Pickering had at last gone too far even for the long-suffering Adams. He had spoken and written too widely and too strongly against the President. From this time onward the rift between the two men was unbridgeable; a reorganization of the Cabinet became inevitable.

The following months were a time of waiting. While a desultory naval war continued between France and the United States, Adams' demand for further assurances from the French made its perilous way across the Atlantic. In Quincy with his frail wife, the President was content with the stalemate and convinced that French sincerity was undergoing a necessary and effective test. If the assurances did come, the self-abasement the French Government had undergone in order to make them would surely indicate that they were sincerely interested in a negotiation. If France refused to cooperate, America would be saved the indignity of further embarrassment at

---

[27] Adams to Lee, March 29, 1799, Adams Papers, Letterbook, October 17, 1797–July 8, 1799, reel #119.

the hands of French diplomatists. In Philadelphia Pickering had no doubts, so convinced was he that the French would inevitably make the assurances.[28]

It was August, 1799, when news finally arrived that the French had fully satisfied the President's requirements. Adams immediately ordered Pickering to draw up a final draft of the instructions that had previously been agreed upon and to inform the two envoys to make ready to depart for France with all haste. Although he had long expected this disastrous news, the Secretary of State was nevertheless crestfallen when it arrived. His gloom was deepened by news that arrived from Europe, indicating that the vaunted Republic would not survive to see the new century. At a moment when the Allies seemed victorious and the United States should have been striving to ingratiate herself with France's enemies, the President had determined to carry out his own headstrong policy, to settle peacefully with France, and to risk the ire of the Allies. The real course of wisdom, thought Pickering, was war, not peace. That course would have been followed were it not for the obstinacy of the President who, in Pickering's eyes, stood as a monument to the dangers a nation faced when its leader was too vain and headstrong to accept the advice of the "best men" of the country.[29]

Since the contents of the instructions to be drafted had been agreed upon before he left the capital, Adams saw no reason to journey to Philadelphia. He wrote to the Secretary of State to this effect and asked only that the instructions be sent to him in Quincy for perusal before they were given to the envoys.[30] Pickering, since he did not at all sympathize with the policy being carried out, delayed.

---

[28] Years later, the President stated that he had gone home to Quincy in March and had awaited there for weeks on end a copy of the instructions to the ministers that he, together with the Cabinet, had agreed upon before his departure from the capital. He further testified that Pickering knowingly stalled the drawing up of the finished copy of the instructions and consequently was responsible for the long delay between March, when it was decided to send a new mission, and November, when it sailed. Actually, Pickering was not responsible for all of this long delay. Adams had decided to await further assurances, and these did not arrive until the first week in August of 1799.

[29] Pickering to Higginson, September 12, 1799, Pickering Papers, XII, 45.

[30] Adams to Pickering, August 6, 1799, Adams Papers, Letterbook, July 10, 1799–March 2, 1801, reel #120.

Anxiously awaiting further news of the war in Europe, he spent more than a month drawing up a set of instructions that should have been completed in less than a week. His remaining hope for thwarting Adams was that news of Allied victory might reach the United States before the envoys set out for France.

During the second week in September, just as the Secretary was reluctantly finishing his draft of the instructions, news arrived that once again raised his hopes for a suspension of the mission. Another revolution had occurred in France; the Directory had been overturned. The men who had given the assurances Adams had required as a *sine qua non* for negotiation no longer occupied the seats of power in France. The question now before the Administration was whether or not the new French Government would honor the promises of the old and would negotiate with America's emissaries. Pickering desperately hoped that the President might be convinced to use this crisis as a justification for the suspension of the mission. He believed that the French had not experienced their last internal upheaval and that the next one might well be a counterrevolution that would restore the monarchy in France. Pickering was, of course, most disturbed by what seemed to him to be the very distinct possibility that the Allies would soon win the war. In such a situation, Pickering believed it foolhardy to negotiate a settlement with the French. The victorious Allies would undoubtedly turn on the United States for an act they would regard as treacherous and would destroy America's commerce and possibly threaten her existence as a nation. So overwrought did Pickering become at these prospects, so angry was he at Adams' single-mindedness and obstinacy, that he wrote to Stephen Higginson of his fervent hopes that, if the "President remains firm in his decision to negotiate, the envoys themselves will devise a suspension. What a figure they would make to arrive in Europe, envoys to the Directory, and find a monarch on the throne." [31]

Angry and desperate because he believed the President remained determined to send the mission even under these new circumstances, Pickering acted quickly to round up support in the Cabinet for a

---

[31] Pickering to Higginson, September 12, 1799, Pickering Papers, XII, 45.

proposal to suspend the mission. Although neither Charles Lee nor Secretary of the Navy Benjamin Stoddart believed that the situation in Europe required a suspension of the mission, Pickering wrote to the President, falsely indicating that the changes within France had led the Cabinet to believe that the mission should be suspended, at least until the situation had been clarified.[32] Not content with his own efforts at dissuading the President, Pickering urged George Cabot to suggest to Oliver Ellsworth that he use his influence with the President to urge the suspension of the mission. He knew that the Chief Justice fully supported his views and that he was no more eager than Pickering himself to see the mission proceed.[33]

Pickering had little hope, however, that the President would agree to suspend the mission. Adams had seldom in the recent past accepted the advice of the Cabinet, and Pickering was sure that he was so angry over the recent opposition he had encountered from the "war faction" and was so personally vain and inflexible, that he would not now accept the advice offered him. Frustrated by his impotence, Pickering wrote to Higginson, lashing out at Adams:

> How long must a man live to be known? How long may a man be conspicuous in public affairs, and yet to almost all his fellow citizens remain unknown? If a public man be a villain, he will ere long be detected, punished or dismissed: but if, with upright views, he is an opinionist — inordinately vain — what mischief may he not do? Of all possible qualities in a public man, on whose decision great affairs depend, vanity I have thought the most dangerous.[34]

Although Adams did not regard the Allies as near victory as did Pickering, he believed that, in the unsettled situation which faced him, it would be wise to await further news of political developments from inside France. He therefore wrote to affirm Pickering's judgment and to order a temporary suspension of the mission. The Secretary's surprise at reading the President's orders can only be imagined. For more than two months Adams had remained in his self-

---

[32] Pickering to Adams, September 11, 1799, Adams Papers, Letters Received and Other Loose Papers, 1799, reel #396.
[33] Pickering to Cabot, September 13, 1799, Pickering Papers, XII, 47.
[34] Pickering to Higginson, September 12, 1799, Pickering Papers, XII, 45.

imposed seclusion in Quincy. Several times he had been urged to come to the capital for consultation. Even Pickering had earlier believed the President's presence was desirable. The President, however, anxious over his wife's delicate health, steadfastly refused to leave her side. The instructions for the envoys having already been drawn up, he saw no need for his presence in Trenton.[35] Only when he received a letter from the Secretary of the Navy, Stoddart, indicating that political conspiracy was brewing, did the President decide to go to Trenton. Stoddart warned, in part, that Adams' absence from the capital at so crucial a moment would be used against him by political opponents. He wrote "artful designing men might make such use of your absence from the seat of government, when things so important to restore peace with one country, and to preserve it with another, were transacting, as to make your next election less honorable than it would otherwise be."[36] Adams ought to be on the scene. Perhaps it was this last warning or perhaps it was the cumulative effect of numerous other warnings that moved the President to action. In any case, his emotions surging within him, the President and his secretary traveled to Trenton without delay. Again, he had apparently discovered that part of his Cabinet were conspiring against him. Moved by anger to precipitate action, he served notice on Pickering, even before he arrived, that the commissioners should be no longer delayed. He expected them to sail before the end of the month.[37]

On October 10, 1799, Adams arrived in Trenton. Almost as though it were timed to his arrival, political news of major importance arrived from Philadelphia, news that redoubled the President's determination to end the dispute with France. The returns from the

[35] Adams to Pickering, September 14, 1799, Adams Papers, Letterbook, July 10, 1799–March 2, 1801, reel #120.

[36] Stoddart to Adams, September 13, 1799, Adams Papers, Letters Received and Other Loose Papers, August–December, 1799, reel #396.

[37] Adams to Pickering, September 21, 1799, Adams Papers, Letterbook, July 10, 1799 March 2, 1801, reel #120. There can be little doubt that the warning from Stoddart set Adams moving. Not ten days before this urgent letter to Pickering, the President had written to say that he would not come to Trenton and that, furthermore, he agreed with the Secretary in his view that suspension of the mission might well be in order.

gubernatorial election in Pennsylvania, only recently rocked by Fries's Rebellion, indicated that the Republicans had won a major victory there. Hundreds of former Federalists had apparently changed their votes in protest against high taxation and the plans for the Army.

His determination increased by the news from Pennsylvania, Adams confronted his Cabinet. Many years later he recalled that the Cabinet members had been aroused "to a perfect enthusiasm & delusion." The French monarchy, with Louis XVIII, they believed, would soon be restored through the combined efforts of Austria and Russia. After listening politely "with the utmost coolness and candor," he answered their arguments with his own, and he ordered the envoys to embark as soon as possible.

What undoubtedly piqued Adams beyond all else was that, when he arrived in Trenton, he discovered Alexander Hamilton there before him. Instinctively he suspected that conspiracy was afoot. Although Adams made it clear that he did not wish to hear any of Hamilton's opinions, the New Yorker forced his views upon the President. "The English nation," he told Adams, "had the most perfect confidence in Mr. Pitt, and Mr. Pitt was determined to restore the House of Bourbon. The two Imperial courts were also determined to restore the Bourbons, their armies were triumphant, Louis 18th would be in glory at Versailles before my ministers could arrive there." [38] This, the very argument Pickering and Wolcott had used in the Cabinet's meeting, had absolutely no influence upon the President. Indeed, coming from Hamilton, it probably worked to the disadvantage of the "war party." Angered by the arrogant pretensions of the New Yorker, Adams redoubled his determination to send the new mission to France.

On November 1, 1799, the American envoys, Governor William Davie and Oliver Ellsworth, set sail aboard the U. S. frigate *United States* to join their colleague William Vans Murray in Paris. There they would negotiate a new treaty to settle peaceably the Franco-American dispute. The crucial decision had been made. John Adams

---

[38] Adams to William Cunningham, November 11, 1808, Adams Papers, Letterbook, March 7, 1797–June 20, 1797; March 23, 1801–November 26, 1812, reel #118.

had chosen peace and had adopted a course both wise and popular — popular, that is, except among the extreme Federalists, where disapproval of the President's decision was unmixed. Some, like Fisher Ames, sought to assign deep political motives to the President's actions. Squire Ames pretended to believe that Adams, by dispatching a peace commission, was appealing to the multitude and to the Jacobins within America. "He may calculate that this will procure and secure popularity, not only with the multitude but with the pretended American Party, as I have heard he terms those who are not of the French or British parties; all which parties he supposes to exist distinctly." Adams, Ames believed, had done the popular thing but not the right thing. Peace with France could only mean war with England and the destruction "of nearly our whole commercial capital in one short season."[39]

Fisher Ames had been upset over the President's decision; Secretary Pickering was rabid. Bitterly he wrote to Senator William Bingham of Pennsylvania, informing him that the "great question has been finally determined as it originated by the *President alone.* This I shall on every occasion make known because I am not ambitious to obtain any portion of the honour to be derived from so inauspicious a measure." Even the Secretary of State admitted, albeit unhappily, that the second mission was immensely popular. "*Once,* I would have relied on the good sense of the people for a remedy of the mischiefs assailing us; but my opinion of that good sense is vastly abated: a large proportion seem more readily to embrace falsehood than truth."[40]

Nor was the issue simply a diplomatic one in so far as Pickering was concerned. It had enormous political implications. Certainly, after what the President had done, good men could not support him in the imminent presidential elections. As a result, the Federalists would be disastrously divided and Jefferson would triumph. As far as Pickering was concerned, the President had only one honorable alternative if he wished to save the political situation: to

---

[39] Ames to Pickering, November 23, 1799, Fisher Ames, *The Works of Fisher Ames*, Seth Ames, ed., II, 270–71.
[40] Pickering to Washington, October 24, 1799, Pickering Papers, XII, 270.

retire at the end of his term. Federalists would then be able to unite on his successor and possibly "save the country from ruin." [41]

From this point onward, Timothy Pickering proved constitutionally incapable of suppressing his anger with Adams. He wrote voluminous letters to almost all of his acquaintances, deriding the President. He spoke openly and vituperatively against Adams. He spoke so bluntly and publicly, in fact, that Adams soon became aware of his utterances. Although there is no record of Adams' own sentiments regarding this constant public outpouring of condemnation by his own Secretary of State, Abigail Adams had something to say about it. "There is a man in the cabinet," she wrote to her sister, Mary Cranch,

> whose manners are forbidding, whose temper is sour and whose resentments are implacable, who nevertheless would like to dictate every measure. He has to deal with *one*, who knows full well their respective departments — and who chooses to feel quite independent and to act so too, but for this he is abused. But I am mistaken if this dictator does not get himself ensnared in his own tail. He would not now remain in office, if the President possessed such kind of resentments as I hear from various quarters, he permits himself to utter. From this fountain have flowed all the unpopularity of the mission to France, which some of the Federalists have been so deluded as to swallow large draughts of.[42]

The bitterness that divided Adams and Pickering grew in intensity as it became apparent that the Secretary of State would not support the President for re-election. Quite openly, Pickering admitted in his correspondence that he no longer considered Adams a "federalist" and that he believed a substitute for the President necessary. His own choice for the position was Oliver Ellsworth. The feud between the two men became common knowledge, and the President's hostility toward his Secretary of State, not surprisingly, became a source of complaint among friends of Pickering. One of them wrote to Rufus King in London, asserting that "the firm and active supporters of

---

[41] Pickering to Cabot, October 22, 1799, Pickering Papers, XII, 260.
[42] Abigail Adams to Mary Cranch, December 11, 1799, Abigail Adams, *New Letters of Abigail Adams, 1787–1801*, S. Mitchell, ed., 219–22.

anti-Jacobin politics are no longer trusted or countenanced by the President. On the contrary he thinks or affects to think them, his enemies, and in their description are included Pickering, Wolcott, and McHenry." [43]

Despite the hostility between the President and the Secretary, Adams did not remove Pickering from office. Pickering, of course, would not resign. Perhaps the President was restrained by the difficulty of replacing the Secretary. Filling Cabinet positions had, after all, been a problem that haunted Washington during his second Administration. Of more likely import, however, were political considerations. His own testimony notwithstanding, it seems indisputable that Adams wanted to win the election in 1800. To win he had to maintain at least a semblance of party unity. This was doubly difficult, since the coalition was literally bubbling with conspiracy. Yet, there is a vast difference between internal discontent or conspiracy within a political coalition and outright civil war. Adams apparently recognized this difference. He also realized that to dismiss Pickering, Wolcott, or McHenry might set off the internal conflict he hoped to avoid. Internecine warfare among Federalists would mean victory for Jefferson.

If it is true that political considerations moved Adams to restrain himself, why then did he choose to dismiss Pickering and McHenry in the second week of May, 1800, long before the election in November? The answer seems to be that, as Adams saw it, the election had already been lost. New York had been crucial to Adams' hopes for re-election. Early in May, news arrived in Philadelphia that the Republicans had won the legislative elections in that state and that its electoral votes would, as a result, go to Jefferson. Less than a week following the receipt of this disastrous political news, Adams addressed a curt note to Pickering, asking for his resignation. Pickering, however, refused to resign. He replied to Adams by sarcastically stating that he intended to stay on until March of 1801, when he expected the whole Administration to be turned out. Adams' response was another short note, this time removing Pickering from

---

[43] Cabot to King, January 20, 1800, Papers of Rufus King (New York State Historical Society), XLII.

office.[44] Upon receiving Adams' letter, Pickering made no direct response. Symbolically, he worked on in the Department's office until the end of the day, left that evening, and entered into open opposition to the President.

Timothy Pickering, at the time, provided many explanations for his dismissal. He believed that his opposition to the appointment of William S. Smith as brigadier general had a good deal to do with Adams' action. He also believed that Adams could not forgive him for his work in support of Alexander Hamilton's appointment as second-in-command of the Army. He even pretended to believe that he had been removed from office as part of a deal between Adams and Jefferson whereby Adams would get the Vice-Presidency un-. der the Virginian in 1800![45] While the first two factors do have some relevance, the answer really lies deeply imbedded within Pickering's personality. The New Englander was a self-righteous, over-zealous bureaucrat, with the highest opinion of himself and the lowest of his chief. John Adams put it well when he wrote: "There is a proverbial saying in our county of Essex, the hive of the swarm, that a Pickering could never be happy in heaven, because he must there find and acknowledge a superior."[46] Partially too, the answer lies in the man's conception of his duties as Secretary of State. On crucial questions of policy he was constantly in opposition to the President, and he never conceived it his obligation to carry out the policies of the President. When argument failed to move Adams, Pickering stooped to conspiracy. Harmony within the Administration was never anything more than a myth, and cooperation never an ideal of the Secretary of State.

---

[44] Adams to Pickering, May 10, 1800, Pickering Papers, XIII, 499; Adams to Pickering, May 12, 1800, *ibid.*, 501.

[45] Pickering to Timothy Williams, May 19, 1800, Pickering Papers, XIII, 514.

[46] Adams to Stoddart, November 16, 1811, Adams Papers, Letterbook, March 7, 1797–June 20, 1797; March 23, 1801–November 26, 1812, reel #118.

Columbia University in the City of New York

Date_____

To_____

From_____

12

CONCLUSION

$\mathcal{D}$URING THE WARS OF THE FRENCH REVOLUTION Timothy Pickering attempted to structure American foreign policy along lines compatible with his personal convictions. A concern for the well-being of New England's commerce, an antipathy for the principles of the French Revolution, and a sympathy for that bastion of conservative constitutionalism, Great Britain, led him, by the middle of 1798, to the ultimate absurdity of believing that there could be no safety for the United States so long as she remained at peace with France. Yet, when he left the Department of State in May, 1800, circumstances had reduced his foreign policy to wreckage. Anglo-American relations had soured, and peace with France was in the making.

To Pickering, an Anglo-American alliance in the war against France had seemed essential to the nation's well-being. Shackled by an ideological antipathy for the French Revolution, he came to believe by mid-1798 that the Directory would accept nothing short of social revolution in the United States; war with France was, therefore, in the national interest. No treaty arrangement with France would protect the United States, for it would only be violated later, at some moment propitious to the French.

When Pickering eschewed his ideological concerns and attempted a definition of national interest in more mundane economic terms, he came again to the conclusion that war with France and alliance with England were both imperative. Defining the national interest primarily in terms of commerce, he was haunted by fears of a crisis with England and consequent commercial disaster. An alliance against France would not only place the United States in active opposition to the French Revolution, but it would also afford the best possible security against British harassment of American shipping.

What Pickering was calling for was a reversal of the principle of nonentanglement, a retreat from neutrality. It is this position that brought him into open conflict with John Adams. The President, a more experienced diplomatist than Pickering, operated upon assumptions very different from those of his Secretary of State. He rejected as practically irrelevant the ideological differences between France and America and correctly assumed that, if peace were in the mutual interest of both powers, it could be arranged through negotiation. He was not seeking ultimate security, but merely a routine arrangement between powers that would last as long as it was in the interest of both powers to preserve it.

Basically, Adams differed dramatically with Pickering in his conception of national interest. The protection of commerce was important, but the preservation of American independence was far more imperative. Adams understood that those small states who became unavoidably entangled in Europe's power struggle were almost inevitably reduced to the status of satellites. He would not forego the opportunity, provided to the United States largely by her geographical location, to remain neutral. Even at that moment, when war with France seemed unavoidable, Adams had no interest in an alliance with Britain. America would fight, if necessary, to defend her neutrality, but she would not be trapped into a dangerous and unnecessary involvement as a subordinate to Great Britain, a power Adams trusted little more than he did France.

Given their essentially divergent assumptions, it was almost inevitable that a rift should have developed between Pickering and

Adams. When the factor of personal animosity was added to the tension, the split became unbridgeable. Two proud and self-righteous men, each convinced of his own rectitude and of the other's vanity and blind intransigence, could not coexist indefinitely within the same official family.

BIBLIOGRAPHY

Manuscript Sources

Columbia University Library
    Papers of Alexander Hamilton
Essex Institute
    Papers of Timothy Pickering
Library of Congress, Manuscript Division
    Papers of Elbridge Gerry
    Papers of Alexander Hamilton
    Papers of Thomas Jefferson
    Papers of James McHenry
    Papers of John Marshall
    Papers of James Monroe (microfilm edition available at Sacramento State College)
    Papers of William Vans Murray
    Papers of Timothy Pickering
    Papers of the Pinckney Family
    Papers of George Washington (microfilm edition available at Sacramento State College)
Library of Congress, Foreign Archives
    Great Britain, Foreign Office, F. O. 5, United States of America, Series II, General Correspondence, Selections (photostats available at Library of Congress)
    Great Britain, Foreign Office, F. O. 115, United States of America,

Correspondence of British Diplomatic Representatives, Selections, 1791–1902, P.R.O., (microfilm available at Library of Congress)
Massachusetts Historical Society
Papers of John Adams (microfilm edition available at University of California, Berkeley)
Papers of Elbridge Gerry
Papers of Thomas Jefferson
Papers of Henry Knox
Papers of Timothy Pickering
National Archives (microfilm editions of these papers are available at the University of California, Berkeley)
Department of State, Diplomatic Dispatches, Great Britain
Department of State, Diplomatic Dispatches, France
Department of State, Diplomatic Dispatches, Spain
Department of State, Diplomatic Instructions
Department of State, Domestic Letters
Department of State, Miscellaneous Letters
Department of State, Notes from Foreign Legations, Great Britain
Department of State, Notes From Foreign Legations, France
Department of State, Notes from Foreign Legations, Spain
The New-York Historical Society
Papers of Rufus King
New York Public Library
Papers of James Monroe
Papers of Timothy Pickering
The Pierpont Morgan Library
Papers of Elbridge Gerry
Papers of William Vans Murray

NEWSPAPERS

(Microfilm editions of these papers are available at the University of California, Berkeley.)
Gazette of the United States and Daily Evening Advertiser, Philadelphia
New York Timepiece and Literary Companion
Philadelphia Aurora and General Advertiser
Philadelphia Minerva

OFFICIAL DOCUMENTS

American State Papers, Foreign Relations. Washington, Gales and Seaton, 1832
Debates and Proceedings in the Congress of the United States. Washington, Gales and Seaton, 1834–1856. 42 vols.
Mayo, Bernard, ed., "Instructions to the British Ministers to the United States, 1791–1812." *American Historical Association Annual Re-*

port for 1936, III. Washington, United States Government Printing Office, 1941. 3 vols.

Miller, Hunter, ed., *Treaties and Other International Acts of the United States*. Washington, United States Government Printing Office, 1931–1948. 8 vols.

Turner, F. J., ed., "Correspondence of the French Ministers to the United States, 1791–1797." *American Historical Association Annual Report for 1903*, II. Washington, United States Government Printing Office, 1904. 3 vols.

LETTERS, DIARIES, MEMOIRS

Adams, Abigail, *New Letters of Abigail Adams, 1787–1801*, S. Mitchell, ed. Boston, Houghton Mifflin Company, 1947.

Adams, John, *Correspondence Between the Honorable John Adams Late President of the United States and, the Late William Cunningham Esq.* Boston, E. M. Cunningham, 1823.

———, *The Diary and Autobiography of John Adams*, Lyman Butterfield, ed. Cambridge, Harvard University Press, 1961. 4 vols.

———, *The Warren-Adams Letters*, W. C. Ford, ed. Boston, Massachusetts Historical Society, *Collections*, 1917–1925. 2 vols.

———, *The Works of John Adams*, C. F. Adams, ed. Boston, Little, Brown and Company, 1850–1856. 10 vols.

Adams, John Q., *The Memoirs of John Quincy Adams*, C. F. Adams, ed. Philadelphia, J. B. Lippincott Company, 1874–1877.

———, *The Writings of John Quincy Adams*, W. C. Ford, ed. New York, The Macmillan Company, 1913–1917. 7 vols.

Ames, Fisher, *The Works of Fisher Ames*, Seth Ames, ed. Boston, Little, Brown and Company, 1854. 2 vols.

Ames, Nathaniel, *Jacobin and Junto; or Early American Politics as viewed in the Diary of Dr. Nathaniel Ames, 1758–1822*, Charles Warren, ed. Cambridge, Harvard University Press, 1931.

Bayard, James A., "Papers of James A. Bayard, 1796–1815," Elizabeth Donnan, ed. *American Historical Association Annual Report for 1913*. Washington, United States Government Printing Office, 1914.

Bowdoin and Temple Papers, Part II, *Collections*, Series 7, VI. Boston, Massachusetts Historical Society, 1907.

Bond, Phineas, "Letters of Phineas Bond," J. F. Jameson, ed. *American Historical Association Annual Report, 1896–1897*. Washington, United States Government Printing Office, 1898.

Cabot, George, *The Life and Letters of George Cabot*, Henry Cabot Lodge, ed. Boston, Little, Brown and Company, 1877.

Cobbett, William, *Letters from William Cobbett to Edward Thornton,*

1797–1800, G. D. H. Cole, ed. London, Oxford University Press, 1937.

Gerry, Elbridge, *Some Letters of Elbridge Gerry*, W. C. Ford, ed. Brooklyn, Historical Printing Club, 1896.

Hamilton, Alexander, *The Works of Alexander Hamilton*, John C. Hamilton, ed. New York, J. F. Trow, 1850–1851. 7 vols.

——, *The Works of Alexander Hamilton*, Henry Cabot Lodge, ed. New York, G. P. Putnam's Sons, 1885–1886. 8 vols.

Higginson, Stephen, "Letters of Stephen Higginson, 1783–1804." *American Historical Association Annual Report for 1897*, J. F. Jameson, ed. Washington, United States Government Printing Office, 1898.

Jay, John, *Correspondence and Public Papers of John Jay*, H. P. Johnston, ed. New York, G. P. Putnam's Sons, 1890–1893. 4 vols.

Jefferson, Thomas, *The Complete Anas of Thomas Jefferson*, F. B. Sawvel, ed. New York, Round Table Press, 1903.

——, *Writings*, A. A. Lipscomb, ed. Washington, D. C., Jefferson Memorial Association, 1904–1905. 20 vols.

——, *The Writings of Thomas Jefferson*, Paul L. Ford, ed. New York, G. P. Putnam's Sons, 1892–1899. 10 vols.

King, Rufus, *Life and Correspondence of Rufus King*, Charles R. King, ed. New York, G. P. Putnam's Sons, 1895–1899. 6 vols.

McHenry, James, *Life and Correspondence of James McHenry, Secretary of War Under Washington and Adams*, B. C. Steiner, ed. Cleveland, Burrows Bros., 1907.

Madison, James, *Writings of James Madison*, G. Hunt, ed. New York, G. P. Putnam's Sons, 1900–1910. 9 vols.

Monroe, James, *Writings of James Monroe*, S. M. Hamilton, ed. New York, G. P. Putnam's Sons, 1898–1903. 7 vols.

Murray, William Vans, "Letters of William Vans Murray to John Q. Adams, 1797–1803." *American Historical Association Annual Report for 1912*, W. C. Ford, ed. Washington, United States Government Printing Office, 1914.

Pickering, Timothy, *A Review of Correspondence Between John Adams and William Cunningham, 1803–1812*. Salem, Cushing & Appleton, 1824.

Rush, Benjamin, *The Letters of Benjamin Rush*, L. Butterfield, ed. Princeton, Princeton University Press, 1951. 2 vols.

Washington, George, *Writings of George Washington*, J. C. Fitzpatrick, ed. Washington, United States Government Printing Office, 1931–1944. 39 vols.

Wolcott, Oliver, *Memoirs of the Administrations of Washington and John Adams, Edited from the Papers of Oliver Wolcott*, George Gibbs, ed. New York, W. Van Norden, 1846. 2 vols.

Wyndham, William, Lord Grenville, *Report on the Manuscripts of J. B. Fortescue, Esq., Preserved at Dropmore*, W. Fitzpatrick, ed. London, Eyre & Spottiswoode, 1892–1897. 10 vols.

BOOKS AND ARTICLES

Adams, E. D., *The Influence of Grenville on Pitt's Foreign Policy, 1787–1798*. Washington, Carnegie Institution, 1904.

Adams, Henry, *The Life of Albert Gallatin*. New York, Peter Smith, 1943.

Allen, Gardner W., *Our Naval War with France*. Boston, Houghton Mifflin Company, 1909.

Austin, James T., *The Life of Elbridge Gerry*. Boston, Wills & Lilly, 1829. 2 vols.

Bemis, Samuel Flagg, *Jay's Treaty: A Study in Commerce and Diplomacy*. New Haven, Yale University Press, 1962.

——, *John Quincy Adams and the Foundations of American Foreign Policy*. New York, Alfred A. Knopf, Inc., 1949.

——, *Pinckney's Treaty: A Study of America's Advantage from Europe's Distresses, 1783–1800*. New Haven, Yale University Press, 1960.

Beveridge, Albert J., *The Life of John Marshall*. Boston, Houghton Mifflin Company, 1916–1919. 4 vols.

Bond, Beverley W., *The Monroe Mission to France, 1794–1796*. Baltimore, The Johns Hopkins Press, 1907.

Brant, Irving, "Edmund Randolph, Not Guilty!" *William and Mary Quarterly*, 3d Series, VII (April, 1950), 179–98.

Burt, A. L., *The United States, Great Britain and British North America, 1783–1812*. New Haven, Yale University Press, 1940.

Charles, Joseph, *The Origins of the American Party System*. New York, Harper & Row, Publishers, 1961.

Chinard, Gilbert, *Honest John Adams*. Boston, Little, Brown and Company, 1933.

Clauder, Anna C., *American Commerce as Affected by the Wars of the French Revolution and Napoleon, 1793–1810*. Philadelphia, University of Pennsylvania Press, 1912.

Cresson, W. P., *James Monroe*. Chapel Hill, The University of North Carolina Press, 1946.

Cunningham, N. E., Jr., *The Jeffersonian Republicans*. Chapel Hill, The University of North Carolina Press, 1957.

Darling, A. B., *Our Rising Empire, 1763–1803*. New Haven, Yale University Press, 1940.

Dauer, Manning J., *The Adams Federalists*. Baltimore, The Johns Hopkins Press, 1953.

DeConde, Alexander, *Entangling Alliance, Politics and Diplomacy Under George Washington.* Durham, North Carolina, Duke University Press, 1958.

———, *The Quasi-War.* New York, Charles Scribner's Sons, 1966.

Drake, Francis S., *Life and Correspondence of Henry Knox.* Boston, S. G. Drake, 1873.

Ernst, Robert, *Rufus King.* Chapel Hill, The University of North Carolina Press, 1968.

Freeman, D. S., J. A. Carroll, and M. W. Ashworth, *George Washington.* New York, Charles Scribner's Sons, 1948–1957. 7 vols.

Gilbert, Felix, *The Beginnings of American Foreign Policy.* New York, Harper & Row, Publishers, 1965.

Hazen, Charles D., *Contemporary American Opinion of the French Revolution.* Baltimore, The Johns Hopkins Press, 1897.

Hutchins, J. G. B., *American Maritime Industries and Public Policy, 1789–1914.* Cambridge, Harvard University Press, 1941.

Hunt, Galliard, *The Department of State of the United States.* New Haven, Yale University Press, 1914.

Hyneman, Charles S., *The First American Neutrality: A Study of the American Understanding of Neutral Obligations During the Years 1792–1815.* Urbana, The University of Illinois Press, 1934.

James, J. A., "French Opinion as a factor in Preventing War Between France and the United States, 1795–1800." *American Historical Review,* 30 (1924), 44–55.

Johnson, Allen, and Dumas Malone, eds., *Dictionary of American Biography.* New York, Charles Scribner's Sons, 1928–1944, 22 vols.

Kurtz, Stephen G., *The Presidency of John Adams.* New York, Frederick A. Praeger, Inc., 1961.

Logan, Rayford W., *Diplomatic Relations of the United States with Haiti, 1776–1891.* Chapel Hill, The University of North Carolina Press, 1941.

Lyon, E. W., "The Directory and the United States." *American Historical Review,* 43 (1938), 514–32.

———, *Louisiana in French Diplomacy, 1759–1804.* Norman, University of Oklahoma Press, 1934.

Masterson, W. H., *William Blount.* Baton Rouge, Louisiana State University Press, 1954.

McMaster, John B., *A History of the People of the United States.* New York, Appleton-Century, 1885. 6 vols.

Miller, John C., *Alexander Hamilton and the Growth of the New Nation.* New York, Harper & Row, Publishers, 1959.

Mitchell, Broadus, *Alexander Hamilton;* Vol. II, *The National Adventure.* New York, The Macmillan Company, 1961. 2 vols.

Moore, John B., *History and Digest of the International Arbitrations To Which the United States Has Been a Party.* Washington, United States Government Printing Office, 1898. 6 vols.

Morison, Samuel E., "Dupont, Talleyrand, and the French Spoliations." *Massachusetts Historical Society Proceedings,* 49 (1915–1916).

——, "Elbridge Gerry, Gentleman Diplomat." *New England Quarterly,* 2 (1929), 3–33.

——, *The Life and Letters of Harrison Gray Otis, Federalist, 1765–1848.* Boston, Houghton Mifflin Company, 1913. 2 vols.

——, *Maritime History of Massachusetts.* Boston, Houghton Mifflin Company, 1941.

Nettles, Curtis P., *The Emergence of a National Economy, 1776–1815.* New York, Holt, Rinehart & Winston, Inc., 1962.

Perkins, Bradford, *The First Rapprochement: England and the United States: 1795–1805.* Philadelphia, University of Pennsylvania Press, 1955.

Phillips, James D., *Salem in the Eighteenth Century.* Boston, Houghton Mifflin Company, 1937.

Pickering, Octavius, and Charles W. Upham, *The Life of Timothy Pickering.* Boston, Little, Brown and Company, 1867–1873. 4 vols.

Robertson, William S., "Francisco De Miranda and the Revolutionizing of Spanish America." *American Historical Association Annual Report for 1907.* Washington, United States Government Printing Office, 1908.

Schachner, Nathan, *Alexander Hamilton.* New York, Appleton-Century-Crofts, 1946.

Seybert, Adam, *Statistical Annals of the United States.* Philadelphia, William Fry, 1818.

Smith, James M., *Freedom's Fetters: The Alien and Sedition Laws and American Civil Liberties.* Ithaca, New York, Cornell University Press, 1956.

Smith, Page, *John Adams.* Garden City, N. Y., Doubleday & Company, Inc., 1962. 2 vols.

Smith, W. B., and A. H. Cole, *Fluctuations in American Business, 1790–1860.* Cambridge, Harvard University Press, 1935.

Tansill, Charles C., *The United States and Santo Domingo, 1798–1873.* Baltimore, The Johns Hopkins Press, 1938.

Tolles, Frederick, *George Logan of Philadelphia.* New York, Oxford University Press, 1934.

Tourtellot, Arthur B., *Lexington and Concord.* New York, W. W. Norton & Company, Inc., 1963.

Whitaker, Arthur P., *The Mississippi Question, 1795–1803: A Study in Trade, Politics and Diplomacy.* New York, Appleton-Century-Crofts, 1934.

White, Leonard D., *The Federalists: A Study in Administrative History.* New York, The Macmillan Company, 1948.

Zimmerman, James F., *Impressment of American Seamen.* New York, Columbia University Press, 1925.

Doctoral Dissertations

Bowman, Albert Hall, "The Struggle for Neutrality: A History of the Diplomatic Relations Between the United States and France, 1790–1801." Columbia University, 1954.

Phillips, Edward Hake, "The Public Career of Timothy Pickering, Federalist, 1745–1802." Harvard University, 1950.

INDEX

Act for Relief and Protection of American Seamen, 46, 77–81

Adams, Abigail: on XYZ Affair, 151, 154, 156; on Hamilton, 170, on second mission to France, 204; on Timothy Pickering, 212; mentioned, 191

Adams, John: Cabinet relations, viii–ix, 1, 90–94, 104–5, 107–8, 111, 141, 177, 200, 205, 211, 214; foreign policy views, viii, 91; on Timothy Pickering, Sr., 2; conspiracy against, in 1796, 59–60; assumption of office as President, 89; on Hamilton, 92; reliance on J. Q. Adams, 94; and Jefferson, 95 96, 106–9; relations with France, 95–96, 106–7, 115, 141, 158–62, 189–93; addresses to Congress, 107–8, 151–52, 189; and Elbridge Gerry, 92–93, 109, 110–11, 180–81, 185–86; and requests for Yrujo's recall, 137; views on XYZ Affair, 143–44, 150–54; opposition to British alliance, 146; and enforcement of Alien Act, 161; and enforcement of Sedition Law, 162; and the Army, 165–67, 178–79; appointment of Washington as military commander by,

167; and appointment of William S. Smith, 172–74; and publication of Gerry-Talleyrand correspondence, 197 98; nomination of Murray by, 200; nomination of William R. Davie by, 201; nomination of Oliver Ellsworth by, 201; denounce ment of, by Pickering, 200–201; and suspension of the mission to France, 208; and dispatch of envoys to France, 209–10; denouncement of, by Ames, 211; mentioned, vii, viii, 64, 124, 174, 182, 204, 214, 216

Adams, John Quincy: key adviser to John Adams, 94; on French politics, 114; fears of French power, 114; and despair of peace with France, 117–18; on noninvolvement in European affairs, 142–43; and Armed Neutrality, 144–45; mentioned, 34, 74, 100, 101, 145, 154, 192

Adet, Pierre: and the case of *Le Cassius*, 41–45; on impressment, 46–47; protest against the Jay Treaty by, 49–50; interference in U.S. election by, 49–50, 58–69; mentioned, 41, 126